The
Heidegger
Dictionary

BLOOMSBURY PHILOSOPHY DICTIONARIES

The Bloomsbury Philosophy Dictionaries offer clear and accessible guides to the work of some of the more challenging thinkers in the history of philosophy. A-Z entries provide clear definitions of key terminology, synopses of key works, and details of each thinker's major themes, ideas, and philosophical influences. The Dictionaries are the ideal resource for anyone reading or studying these key philosophers.

The Derrida Dictionary, Simon Morgan Wortham
The Gadamer Dictionary, Chris Lawn and Niall Keane
The Hegel Dictionary, Glenn Alexander Magee
The Husserl Dictionary, Dermot Moran and Joseph Cohen
The Marx Dictionary, Ian Fraser and Lawrence Wilde
The Sartre Dictionary, Gary Cox

Forthcoming in the series:

The Deleuze and Guattari Dictionary, Eugene B. Young with Gary Genosko and Janell Watson
The Kant Dictionary, Lucas Thorpe
The Merleau-Ponty Dictionary, Donald A. Landes
The Nietzsche Dictionary, Douglas Burnham
The Wittgenstein Dictionary, Edmund Dain

BLOOMSBURY PHILOSOPHY DICTIONARIES

The Heidegger Dictionary

DANIEL O. DAHLSTROM

B L O O M S B U R Y

LONDON • NEW DELHI • NEW YORK • SYDNEY

Bloomsbury Academic

An imprint of Bloomsbury Publishing Plc

50 Bedford Square
London
WC1B 3DP
UK

175 Fifth Avenue
New York
NY 10010
USA

www.bloomsbury.com

First published 2013

British Library Cataloguing-in-Publication Data
A catalogue record for this book is available from the British Library.

ISBN: HB: 978–1–8470–6513–1
PB: 978–1–8470–6514–8

Library of Congress Cataloging-in-Publication Data
Dahlstrom, Daniel O.
Heidegger dictionary / Daniel O. Dahlstrom.– First [edition].
pages cm– (Bloomsbury philosophy dictionaries)
Summary: "A concise and accessible dictionary of the key terms used in
Heidegger's philosophy, his major works and philosophical influences"– Provided
by publisher.
Includes bibliographical references and index.
ISBN 978–1–84706–513–1 (hardback)– ISBN 978–1–84706–514–8 (paperback)–
ISBN 978–1–4411–7102–3 (epub) 1. Heidegger, Martin, 1889–1976–Dictionaries.
I. Title.

B3279.H49D23 2013
193–dc23

2012021337

Typeset by Fakenham Prepress Solutions, Fakenham, Norfolk NR21 8NN
Printed and bound in India

To Max

CONTENTS

FOREWORD

Dictionaries, Heidegger observes, contain mere lexical items or terms (*Wörter*), not words (*Worte*), and the very tradition of dictionaries goes back to a specific way of thinking whose limitations he labors to expose (38: 17, 21, 23). "For a dictionary can neither grasp nor contain the word by which terms come to words" (12: 181). Another judgment is less harsh: "A 'dictionary' can give hints for the understanding of words but it is never an unqualified and binding authority from the outset" (53: 75). He goes on to say that the appeal to a dictionary always remains merely an appeal to an interpretation of a language. The following dictionary aims to provide hints for understanding Heidegger's words, not merely his terms, with the sure recognition that it is anything but a binding interpretation of them. Nonetheless, just as Heidegger was an avid user of dictionaries (51: 88), students of his writings hopefully may find this Dictionary a useful introduction and aid to interpreting his work. The aim of the Dictionary is to provide an introduction to what Heidegger is saying, given the central words on which he relies. Since Heidegger's thinking emerges from critical encounters with thinkers and poets, this introduction also discusses the work of several philosophers and bards significantly involved in those encounters. Given its introductory aim, the present effort is even more an abridgment of the language in question than a standard dictionary would be, and, as such, it will no doubt omit glosses of several key terms and figures. While every effort has been made to keep such omissions to a minimum, they are not only inevitable but inherent in an introductory work, particularly given constraints of page-length and competence. Following glosses of key terms and figures in the first part, the Dictionary's second part contains summaries of the first sixty-six volumes of Heidegger's published writings, lectures, and posthumous works in the Complete Edition. Future researchers will undoubtedly be able to supplement the present work with treatments of words omitted in the first part and passed-over or unedited volumes in the second part.

Heidegger's developing use of terminology presents challenges of its own. While some terms (e.g. "disposition," "existenziell," "conscience," "transcendence," "metontology") have a limited shelf-life, others (e.g. "Dasein," "freedom," "mood") remain in force throughout his career while taking on different meanings. With no claim to exhaustiveness, the Dictionary attempts to identify some of the more significant shifts in Heidegger's terminology. There are other excellent dictionaries of Heidegger's works available, one by Michael Inwood, another by Alfred Denker and Frank Schalow, that I highly recommend. Consultation of these works can make up for many a term not treated or not treated adequately in the present volume.

I wish to express my thanks to Rachel Eisenhauer of Bloomsbury Publishing and Kim Storry at Fakenham Prepress for their expertise and co-operativeness. I am grateful to Ian Dunkle, Nolan Little, Mary Catherine McDonald and Josh McDonald for their careful reading of various drafts and for their many helpful suggestions. Thanks, too, to Claudius Strube, Robert Scharff, Andrew Mitchell, Richard Polt, and my colleagues, Walter Hopp and Manfred Kuehn, and all the members of the Heidegger Circle over the years for providing a constant source of illumination.

This work would not have been possible without the love, encouragement, and support I receive from my wife, Eugenie, and my son, Max.

Method of citation

All numbers followed by a colon and other numbers in parentheses refer to the respective volume of the Complete Edition (*Gesamtausgabe*) of Heidegger's works, followed by the page numbers after the colon. For example,

'(5: 177)'

refers to

> Martin Heidegger, *Holzwege*, Gesamtausgabe Band 5, herausgegeben von Friedrich-Wilhelm von Hermann (Frankfurt am Main: Klostermann, 2003), S. 177.

Within entries, reference to a volume of the Complete Edition is made by using the standard abbreviation 'GA,' followed by the volume number; e.g. 'GA 5' refers to the volume cited above. When no reference is given immediately following a quoted passage, the next parenthetical reference in the respective paragraph contains the reference. Since most English translations include the respective page numbers of the original German edition, it would be redundant to cite the pagination of those translations. However, the most up-to-date English translations of the volumes of the Complete Edition or texts contained in them (if translated from a source other than the Complete Edition) are cited with the list of volumes of the Complete Edition and brief summaries of their contents in Part Two.

'SZ,' followed by numbers, in parentheses refers to the pages of the most widely used edition of *Sein und Zeit*; for example,

'(SZ 75)'

refers to

> Martin Heidegger, *Sein und Zeit* (Tübingen: Niemeyer, 1972), S. 75.

No corresponding English pagination needs to be given for SZ since the page numbers of this edition (issued in multiple years) are indicated in the margins of both standard English translations of this work as *Being and Time*. When my translation of a term from SZ differs from one of these translations, I indicate their translation by citing an abbreviation for the translation, followed by a colon and their translation. 'MR' refers to the John Macquarrie and Edward Robinson translation (San Francisco: Harper, 1962), and 'S' refers to the Joan Stambaugh translation, with a foreword by Dennis Schmidt (Albany, NY: SUNY Press, 2011).

Introduction

"Komm! ins Offene, Freund!"

HÖLDERLIN, *DER GANG AUFS LAND*

Heidegger is a thinker, and, as far as his personal and public life is concerned, one is tempted to say no more than he said of Aristotle: "As for his personality, our only interest is that he was born at a certain time, that he worked, and that he died" (18: 5). Yet this dissociation of thinking and life will not do, especially for someone who so strongly ties how we exist to our self-understanding and, indeed, in a way that underscores practice no less than theory. Nor will it do for someone who so fervently tries to retrieve the all-but-lost nearness of things and who implicates the history of Western philosophy in present-day nihilism—the mindless and unimpeded pursuit of power in a world dominated by markets and powers of production, a rapacious technology, and the calculating, computerized representation of everything. Of course, there are other good reasons for not pretending to divorce Heidegger's thought from his life, notably the traumatic effect of the Great War on his generation, his infamous embrace of National Socialism in 1933, and his refusal, after the war, to make any further apologies for that involvement or its consequences.

Born on September 26, 1889 in the small town of Meßkirch, in an area long known as "Catholic country," Martin Heidegger attends public high schools in Constance and Freiburg from 1903 to 1909. Residing at a seminary in Constance, Heidegger is close to its rector, Conrad Gröber, who is an active figure in conservative Catholic politics, and Heidegger's first publications (1910–12) bemoan modernity and individualism while championing the

Church's "eternal treasure-trove of truth" (16: 7). In 1907 Gröber gives Heidegger a copy of Franz Brentano's 1862 dissertation 'On the Manifold Meaning of Being According to Aristotle', a work whose "question of what is simple in the manifold of being" provided a constant stimulus, as Heidegger later acknowledges, to his 1927 masterpiece, *Being and Time*.

After ill health impedes study for the priesthood, Heidegger studies mathematics, physics, and chemistry, before turning to philosophy, mainly with Heinrich Rickert, at the University of Freiburg. In his 1914 dissertation on "The Doctrine of Judgment in Psychologism," he follows Husserl in arguing that the logical character of judgment lies outside the purview of a psychological study. In 1916 Heidegger completes a qualifying monograph on Duns Scotus' doctrine of categories and meaning, bringing to a close his studies in a Catholic philosophy department. During this time Heidegger marries one of his students, the Protestant Elfriede Petri, and poor health interrupts military service until the final months of the war when he serves as an army weatherman. On home-leaves in Freiburg, he seeks out Husserl, Rickert's replacement, and the two phenomenologists become frequent interlocutors for the next decade.

In 1919, Heidegger writes his friend Engelbert Krebs that "epistemological insights" regarding the theory of historical knowledge "have made the *system* of Catholicism problematic and unacceptable to me—but not Christianity and metaphysics, that, however, in a new sense." With these prescient lines, Heidegger formally signals his break with Catholicism. In addition to the riskiness of such a move career-wise at the time, the decision is particularly revealing for its commitment to metaphysics, albeit "in a new sense." Traditional metaphysics attempts to answer the question: "What are beings?" This leading question of metaphysics is, as Heidegger was fond of emphasizing, really a question of meta-physics, i.e. if not an afterthought to, at least an extension of physics. It attempts to answer this question by determining the fundamental way of being (beingness, *Seiendheit*) and/or the supreme being (*Seiendeste*). For example, for Aristotle, to be is—with one exception—to be a unified structure of actualized and unactualized movements, dependent upon (i.e. caused, by virtue of attraction to) an unmoved, fully actual mover (the singular exception). Contemporary physicalism is the metaphysical view that to be is to be a slice of a space–time energy-field, perhaps caused by the Big Bang. Traditional metaphysics of this variety leaves out the fundamental question that first has to be answered, namely, "What is being? What is the sense of being?" The notion of "sense" here is fundamentally phenomenological, the way in which something is experienced (just as the sense of tree allows me to experience something as a tree). Hence, Heidegger's turn to this new sense of metaphysics is phenomenological, entailing analysis of the experience of being and the sense that makes that possible.

This new approach to metaphysics begins to take shape in the early Freiburg lectures (1919–23) via a radical reformation of Husserlian phenomenology, thanks to investigations of history and religious experience, shaped by readings of St. Paul, Augustine, Luther, Kierkegaard, Schleiermacher, and Dilthey. A hermeneutics of the historicity and facticity of the pre-theoretical experience of living the faith takes the place of Husserl's theory-driven, detached observations of consciousness. Here being is experienced neither as some object set over against a subject nor as something issuing from subjective consciousness. Since Heidegger's phenomenology is hermeneutical, it makes no pretension of being presuppositionless. In Marburg, where he lectures from 1923 to 1928, Heidegger takes pains to spell out the reasons for breaking with Husserl's phenomenology.

These early years in both Freiburg and Marburg are marked by an intensive engagement with Aristotle's texts. Indeed, SZ emerges from an attempt to elaborate categories for a planned Aristotle commentary. SZ's aim is to reawaken the forgotten, supposedly transforming question of the *sense* of being through analysis of the particular being—*Da-sein* or, equivalently, *Existenz*—who has an understanding of being. A fundamental ontology, providing the basis of any other ontology (study of being), was to be the fruit of this analysis of existence. The analysis concludes that time, appropriately construed, is what makes sense of Dasein and, thereby, any understanding of being.

Heidegger planned a second part, aimed at dismantling the history of ontology's myopic equation of being with presence. Yet he aborted the project because the metaphysical language he was employing distorted what he was endeavoring to say (9: 328f). Indeed, while he conceived SZ as an attempt to raise a transforming question that metaphysics traditionally failed to pose, he came to realize that his reliance upon the language of metaphysics led readers of SZ to a basic misunderstanding of it. Exemplifying this reliance is the talk of "conditions of the possibility" and time as the "transcendental [constantly present] horizon" of the understanding of being (SZ 41). The tendency of contemporaries to take SZ's existential analysis to be a version of existentialism, a phenomenological existentialism with Dasein in the role of a transcendental subject, also betrays a fundamental misunderstanding of the text. Nonetheless, though adamant that his philosophy is in no way existentialism with its centering in subjectivity, Heidegger comes to recognize how his language and approach abetted this interpretation. "The being-here [Da-sein] in SZ still stands in the appearance of the 'anthropological' and 'subjectivistic' and 'individualistic' and so forth; and yet the opposite of all that was in my sights" (65: 295). Hence, from the mid–1930s he distances his contributions to philosophy from all metaphysics and from anything ontological or transcendental, including the vestiges of a transcendental subject. The center of gravity gradually shifts from "being and time" to "being and history," i.e. from the temporality of Dasein to the historical relation between Dasein and being, understood as their mutual appropriation and groundless ground. Heidegger commandeers the term *Ereignis* (ordinarily signifying "event") for this ground. From the early 1930s until the end of the war he elaborates this theme through critical studies of the history of philosophy, issuing in highly original and controversial readings of Anaximander, Heraclitus and Parmenides, Plato and Aristotle, Kant and Hegel, Schelling and Nietzsche.

In 1933 Heidegger is elected Rector of the University of Freiburg and becomes a member of the National Socialist party. As Rector, he is outspoken and enthusiastic in his support for the National Socialist regime. What sort of partisan of National Socialism was Heidegger? How closely did his views coincide with official party rhetoric and policy? Was he an anti-Semite? To what extent is his philosophy implicated in his support of National Socialism? There are numerous scholars more qualified than I am to address these fraught questions, and I refer readers to such experts.[1] However, a few points may be made. Heidegger was undoubtedly swept up in the events surrounding the rise of National Socialism, particularly in the first six months of 1933. In mid-December 1932 he writes Rudolf Bultmann that, despite seeing much that is positive in the party, he "is not and never will be a member." However, his tone is vastly different by the end of March 1933, not long after the "Enabling Act" (*Ermächtigungsgesetz*) that eliminated the legislative role of parliament (*Reichstag*), giving Hitler complete governing authority. In a letter to Elizabeth Blochmann on March 31, he writes:

> Present events have for me—precisely because much remains obscure and unmastered—an unusual, gathering force. The willing intensifies as does the sureness of acting in the service of a great mission and helping out in the construction of a world, with a grounding in the people [*völklich*]. For a long time the shallowness and shadowiness of a mere "culture" and the unreality of so-called "values" have sunk to nothingness and left me seeking the new basis [*Boden*] in Dasein. We will only find it and at the same time the calling of Germany in the history of the West if we expose ourselves to being itself in a new manner and appropriation. (16: 71)

These lines betray not only how naively Heidegger looked upon events that proved so ominous, but also how effortlessly he embraced them with the terms of his philosophical project. At the same time Heidegger continues to work with and encourage many Jewish students, though he was not above playing an anti-Semitic card with authorities when convenient.

Heidegger may have never surrendered his belief in "the inner truth and greatness" of a socialist movement grounded somehow in the German *Volk*, retaining the phrase in the 1953 edition of *Introduction to Metaphysics* and refusing after the war, as noted above, to make further apologies for his earlier "mistakes." Nevertheless, he becomes disaffected with the regime and its policies, resigning in 1934 after one year as rector. According to posthumous publications and students' reports, he is also increasingly critical of the regime and what it stands for from 1934 through the end of the war. For example, while frequently unsparing in his criticism of Americanism and Bolshevism, by 1940 he writes that "the danger is not 'Bolshevism' but *we ourselves* since we supply its metaphysical essence, raised to the highest levels" (69: 120; 66: 122f).

During the turbulent 1930s, poetry and art begin to take center stage as Heidegger shifts from the question of the sense of being to the truth of being. According to "Origin of the Work of Art," his first public lecture after resigning as rector, truth inserts itself into the artwork, thanks to art's fundamentally poetic and thus disclosive character. In this way art exemplifies the truth of being as the hidden unfolding of the presence of things. This truth, already indicated by the Greek *a-letheia* (un-hiddenness), is a happening in which being is the hidden unconcealing of beings, the hidden process of bringing them into the open and making them present to Dasein. This process or happening is, as noted above, the appropriating event (*Ereignis*), the mutual appropriation and ground of the relation between being as the presence of beings and Dasein as the being to whom they come to be present. The study of art and Hölderlin's poetry during this period also introduces new themes that concern him in the ensuing decades, e.g. the meaning of things (in contrast to works or tools), the strife of the world with the earth that withdraws from every attempt to grasp it, the significance of art as a *techne* that—in contrast to modern technology—"allows the earth to be earth" and, not least, opens human beings up to a dimension in which they can be addressed by the divine.

From 1936 to 1940 Heidegger completes a major work, the posthumously published *Contributions to Philosophy*, and gives a series of lectures on Nietzsche, later published as *Nietzsche I–II* in 1961. The *Contributions* attempt to prepare the way for a new beginning of Western thinking, one that retrieves what is originary in the first beginning, namely, the way that the clearing in which beings come to be present is itself concealed. This new beginning attempts to come to terms with metaphysics by thinking, not on the basis of some conception of beings in general or some supreme being in particular, but from the historical character of being, i.e. the appropriating event. In this connection Heidegger reads Nietzsche's doctrines of the eternal return and the will to power as the penultimate culmination of Western metaphysics, paving the way to its consummation in modern technology.

An allied tribunal forbids Heidegger to teach in 1945, and, a year later, he suffers a nervous breakdown, requiring hospitalization. In 1951, a year after gaining permission to lecture again, he becomes an emeritus professor. In the immediate post-war period (1947) he settles accounts with existentialism and examines the question of humanism in the light of his thinking. Shortly thereafter, in the face of the challenging, all-enframing character of modern technology, he contemplates a way of dwelling and relating to things and the world via "the fourfold" (earth, sky, mortals, divinities). Complementing this new approach and revisiting themes from the late 1930s, he contrasts meditative, poetic, thankful thinking with the representational and calculative character of modern technological thinking. Continuing his re-reading of Parmenides, he also develops an account of a difference more basic than identity, something unthinkable from the perspective of metaphysics. In 1959 he publishes *On the Way to Language*, the culmination of over three decades of studies. Heidegger gives significantly retrospective lectures and seminars throughout the 1960s (see GA 14, 15), and he also conducts seminars in Zollikon, Switzerland from 1959 to 1969 for a group of psychiatrists and medical students (GA 89). In 1970 he begins arrangements for the Complete Edition of his works, arrangements often criticized for falling short of a critical edition, prompting suspicions about the contents of posthumously published volumes. The first volume—the 1927 lectures, *Basic Problems of Phenomenology*—appears a year before Heidegger dies on May 26, 1976.

By Heidegger's own account, his thinking begins with the question of the sense (*Sinn*) of being, i.e. time (from the mid–1920s to the early 1930s), shifts to the question of the truth (*Wahrheit*) of being, i.e. the history of the clearing that conceals itself (from the early 1930s to the end of the war), and culminates in attempting to hear what language says is the place (*Ort*) of being. There may be other paths to this place (as Heidegger's reading of Eastern thought increasingly makes clear to him), and his own path to it is hardly a necessary one. Yet it is easy to see how this place, characterized as the opening that gathers things together, concludes the path that began with the investigation of time as the sense of being-here (*da-sein*), i.e. being-the-clearing, before turning to the history of the concealment of that sense. The opening withdraws and, in withdrawing, lets things be things and lets us be who we are, i.e. allows us to be humans if we open ourselves to it and let things be themselves. Heidegger's thinking, from beginning to end, aims at transforming human thinking for humans' sake by reminding us that we are the fragile yet potent site of the disclosedness of the being—the presence and absence—of beings. The fragility of the site is all too apparent, overshadowed as it is by the scientific and industrial powers of technological production. Yet this site is potent with possibilities that nothing—no entity, not even the world-industrial complex—can foreclose. For the task of thinking, Heidegger submits, is to think "the possibility of world-civilization ... overturning at some point the technologically-scientific-industrial imprint as the sole measure for human beings' worldly sojourn" (14: 75).

A–Z dictionary

Absence (*Abwesen*)

An absence can be no less gripping than a presence. Moreover, while nothing is fully present to us, whatever is present necessitates the absence of something else and vice versa. In this way, absence and presence are co-dependent. To be is to be present to someone, but never exhaustively. In addition, the presence itself is typically absent from our consideration as we concern ourselves with what is present. By misconstruing how beings are dynamically present and absent, traditional equations of being with presence have led to construing being as abstract and universal, if not simply empty or indeterminable. SZ first attempts to address this tradition by demonstrating how time, including but not equated with the present, provides the sense of being of our being-here (*Da-sein*). Heidegger's mature writings emphasize how Western indifference and obliviousness to being in favor of beings is due to the fact that being (presence) absents itself from the beginning of Western thinking, albeit not without a trace.

Abyss (*Abgrund*)

Considered in terms of the notion of a ground, being has a grounding character but is itself an abyss, i.e. itself groundless. Heidegger makes this point sometimes about being (*Sein*) *simpliciter*, other times about historical being (*Seyn*) as the self-concealing presence of beings to human beings. Historical being as this appropriating event is the ungrounded yet constitutive ground of everything that is (including God and humans) in the sense that whatever is needs it in order to be. Just as the principle that everything that is has a ground (sufficient reason) does not itself have a ground, so being is removed from any ground. In order to think being, it is necessary to make the leap (*Sprung*, *Satz*) from the pursuit of grounds or reasons other than being, since that pursuit amounts to reducing being to an entity or particular being (10: 87, 164–9; 70: 9ff).

Heidegger first broaches the notion of the abyss by way of grounding the essence of grounds in the freedom of transcendence. Every entity has a ground, because Dasein transcends entities, projecting them on to some world, or, equivalently, understands them as being. The transcendence that underlies the transcendental, grounding character of being is grounded in Dasein's freedom. "But as *this* ground, freedom is the *abyss* of Dasein" (9: 174f).

In Heidegger's subsequent attempt to think being historically (i.e. non-transcendentally), the abyss is the "first essential *clearing concealment*, the unfolding of truth." Far from the denial of any ground, the abyss is the affirmation of grounding "in its hidden expanse and distance." The hiddenness of historical being, not supporting itself on any entity and fending off any ground, is an abyss as "the unity of the primordial timing and spacing" and "the site of the moment of the 'between' that Da-sein must be grounded as" (65: 379–88; 66: 99, 131; 70: 53). There are different senses of "abyss" for each beginning of thinking. In the first beginning, the abyss is the "ungrounded [character] of the truth of historical being"; in the second, it is "the appropriated [beginning] of the going-under [*Untergang*]," presence's self-concealing (70: 13). The truth of the appropriating event is the "primordial ground" (*Ur-grund*) that opens itself as self-concealing only in the abyss (*Ab-grund*) (65: 380).

Aletheia

Aletheia, the Greek word for truth, typically stands for the correctness of a thought, perception, or assertion, and, in fact, as early as Homer, a cognate of correctness, *homoiosis*, served as a synonym for it. According to Heidegger, this construal of *aletheia* derives from its more basic meaning as un-hiddenness, where the privative prefix 'un-' apes the corresponding privative Greek prefix '*a-*' in '*a-letheia*' and '*letheia*' derives from words for the hidden or forgotten. For example, "the sun shines" is true in the sense of being correct only if the sun's shining is not hidden. Just as the hidden is hidden *from* someone, so *aletheia* as the unhiddenness of "things" entails their actual or potential presence *to* someone (for Heidegger that someone is *Dasein*). Since "being" stands for this presence of something (together with the absences the presence entails), *aletheia* is at bottom the truth *of* being (*genitivus appositivus*, like the 'city *of* New York'), irreducible to beings or to human beings, to objects or subjects.

Greek thinkers were so taken by *aletheia* as the sheer unhiddenness of things that they equated it with being, so much so that attending to the unhidden thing displaces consideration of unhiddenness itself. The yoking (*zugon*) of *aletheia*—in Plato's Cave Allegory—to the manifest way things *look* in the light marks a key site of its devolution from unhiddenness to correctness (5: 37f; 9: 223–34; 34: 21–112; 45: 180f; 65: 331–5; 66: 109f).

The foundation of *a-letheia* (un-hiddenness) in hiddenness is fatally lost when *aletheia* is translated as *veritas* (truth) and its opposite is no longer the multiple forms of hiddenness but simply falsehood. This hiddenness encompasses the obstruction of some entities by others, observers' shortsightedness, the fading past and the oncoming future, and—ironically—the unhiddenness itself. The essence of *aletheia* (truth in a primordial sense) is neither the correctness of assertions nor the unhiddenness of beings, but the interplay of that hiddenness and unhiddenness or, equivalently, the strife (*eris*) between earth and world. *Aletheia* in this basic sense is the hidden "openness" in the midst of beings that grounds their unhiddenness (65: 339, 342–51, 357).

Letting things present themselves-as-they-are supposes an opening, identified in SZ with Da-sein as the clearing or disclosedness, and thus "the most primordial phenomenon of the truth" (SZ 133, 220f). This openness amounts to nothing if things are hidden from us. *Aletheia* as this unhiddenness is "a determination of *entities themselves* and not somehow—like correctness— a character of *an assertion about* them" (45: 121). Truth as correctness accordingly "stands and falls" with truth as the unhiddenness of entities (45: 20, 96–103, 129ff). Far from ignoring bivalence, this account of truth as the struggle of unhiddenness and hiddenness, in advance, as it were, of any human shortcomings, provides a way to explain it (9: 191). Some critics (e.g. Jaspers, Tugendhat) charge that the interpretation of truth as sheer disclosedness forfeits its specific meaning, where correctness (bivalence) is fundamental. Yet errancy is inherent in any human disclosedness; we are in the untruth as much as in the truth (SZ 222f; 9: 196ff). Moreover, to apply the notion of correctness to truth as unhiddenness is itself a category mistake since correctness presupposes unhiddenness and not vice versa (65: 327).

In a late address, in contrast to his practice for three decades, Heidegger proposes holding off from construing "truth" (*Wahrheit*) as a translation of *aletheia*. In light of the traditional equation of truth with correctness, he concedes that "*aletheia*, unhiddenness thought as clearing of presence is not yet truth," though he continues to insist that the correct correspondence presupposes it, "since there can be no presence and making present outside the realm of the clearing" (14: 86; 15: 396).

Anaximander

Anaximander, one of the thinkers of the first beginning, is the author of the oldest surviving Western philosophical fragment, a saying (*Spruch*) that is typically translated: "That from which things come to be gives rise, too, to their passing away, *according to necessity; for they pay one another recompense and penalty for their injustice, according to the order of time.*" According to Heidegger, the fragment speaks, not simply of things in nature, but of entities as a whole, thereby undercutting the objection that the fragment's mention of justice is anthropomorphic, illegitimately importing a moral notion into a non-moral sphere. Instead the fragment is about how being, signaled in the first clause, imparts itself to beings described in the second clause. Though the saying announces the difference between being and beings, that difference is subsequently overlooked because being conceals itself in the process (5: 363ff; 78: 159, 211–16).

Heidegger reads Anaximander's fragment, like those of Parmenides and Heraclitus, as launching Western thinking, yet before its captivation by the enormous power of Platonic and Aristotelian metaphysics. Heidegger accordingly reads the fragment eschatologically, as superseding all subsequent thinking and gathering into itself what is ending and what is coming as the destiny of historical being. What warrants this critical engagement with Anaximander is the possibility the engagement presents for unleashing "another destiny of being" (5: 335).

Whatever else Anaximander's fragment means, it signals that to be is to be in motion, coming to be and passing away. Rejecting the dichotomy of being and becoming, Heidegger insists that being, in essence, bears and stamps becoming (5: 343). A gloss of a verse from Homer confirms that the Greeks originally understood being as an emerging-and-disappearing presence. In being, so understood, presence and absence are joined at the hip, the presently present emerging into unhiddenness from hiddenness and passing in turn into it (5: 347–50).

Against the backdrop of this understanding of being, Anaximander's fragment says that beings are "out of joint" (in contrast to the usual translation "for their injustice"). This cannot mean that they are no longer present or that they are occasionally out of joint. Instead, it says that they are out of joint as such, which entails that there must be some sense of being right (not out of joint) that holds for them. Beings are between coming to be and passing away, and "this 'between' is the fit [Fuge] according to which what whiles away is respectively fitted, from its arrival here to its passing away" (5: 355; 78: 172). Being between in this way is the being that is imparted to them.

Yet though this joint or fit (where presence and absence meet) constitutes the being of beings, beings are also out of joint (Un-fug) insofar as they insist on taking themselves as exceptions to their transitional state and, hence, doing so in reckless opposition to other things. The fragment is thus telling us that things both are and are not out of joint. They have a tendency to be out of joint by rebelling against the fitness of presence and absence that is their being, the being that usage imparts to them. Yet this tendency is subordinate to that fitness itself, and, indeed, to be themselves, beings must turn back (verwinden) the disorder by coming to terms with their absence and that means, too, allowing for other things to come to themselves, to "be a while" themselves (5: 372; 51: 94–123).

Animals (*Tiere*)

Neither irrational beasts nor sophisticated machines, animals have a way of being that is instructively different from being-human. Aristotle already appreciated rudiments of this difference in terms of the difference between the human *logos* and animal voices (18: 17, 55, 99, 111, 238f). Thus, being alive is not the same as being on-hand or handy, but it is also not the same as being-in-the-world, since the world is essentially tied to human freedom (SZ 50; 25: 20; 28: 189; in contrast to an earlier gloss of *zoon* (living) as "a manner of being and, indeed, being-in-the-world," see 18: 18, 30). At the same time, the only path to determining the ontological status of living things is through a "reductive privation on the basis of the ontology of Dasein" (SZ 194).

Animals are "world-poor" in comparison with humans, though the notion is used only for the purpose of "comparative illustration," not for affirming a hierarchy. An animal dispenses with the world in contrast to a stone that is worldless, incapable of even dispensing with something like a world. Unlike stones, they have access to their environment (*Umwelt*)—but such an environment or, better, such surroundings (*Umgebung*) do not constitute a world. Instead of comporting themselves to a world, they behave toward their surroundings, and this behavior (*Benehmen*) is based upon a complex relation of their drives to their surroundings—and only the surroundings—which dis-inhibit (*enthemmen*) those drives and the facilities based upon them. In the process, animals are continually drawing circles around themselves, not in the sense of encapsulating themselves, but in the sense of opening up or, better, struggling to open up a sphere "within which this or that disinhibiting factor can disinhibit" (29/30: 370).

In keeping with our necessarily privative approach to animals, Heidegger characterizes the animal's relation to its surrounding as "captivation" (*Benommenheit*), a term he also uses to characterize Dasein fully in the grip of its concerns (29/30: 153, 376f; SZ 61). Thanks to this captivated behavior, animals do not relate to beings as beings. The animal lacks this elementary "as" structure (29/30: 361; see ibid., 345, 367, 372, 416, 496; 54: 237f). An animal's openness to its surroundings is not to be confused with the openness of human beings to a world. The captivated character of animals underlies their world-poor character, rather than vice versa (29/30: 393f, 509). Instead of being able to relate to things as they are, animals are driven from drive to drive, in what amounts to a continual process of eliminating what it is that inhibits them (29/30: 362–8). By contrast, humans form a world, a world that only is what it is in this process (29/30: 413f). "World is always *spiritual* world. The animal has no world, not even an environment [*Umwelt*]" (40: 48; 65: 276f).

Anxiety (*Angst*)

In everyday life we are immersed in things handy and relevant to one another in a system of relevance (meaningfulness) that is ultimately in place for our sake. As we move from project to project, we find nothing that is not part of some context of relevance in the purposeful world of our concerns. For example, as we get in a car to drive somewhere, everything in the car has a purpose, as does the car itself, the road on which we drive, and so on. When we arrive at our destination, e.g. our workplace, we find another set of handy things, each part of a complex of mutual relevance that has some ultimate relevance. Angst hits us when suddenly it dawns on us that being-in-the-world as such, as the ultimate relevance and purpose of anything handy, cannot itself be correspondingly relevant or purposeful. Angst discloses—preconceptually—that the world that makes the handiness of things possible is itself "nothing" handy (SZ 184–91, 341–45). (In a complementary way, angst also reveals the nothing in the sense of the slipping away or nihilation of all entities; see 9: 111–18).

Equivalently, angst is the experience of the meaninglessness of existence. Since all our involvement and everything we experience within-the-world, from the simplest implement to the most organized means of assessing and shaping public opinion (the phenomenon of the *They*), *is for existence*, everything within-the-world, too, becomes utterly insignificant (nothing) to us in the grip of anxiety. If being at home in the world means having a purpose within it, like the relevant implements that we use and produce, the experience of angst is an "uncanny" experience, the experience literally of "not being at home."

Anxiety is "fundamental" and "exceptional" because in it Dasein confronts itself and, indeed, as a whole. Although anxiety can be sudden, it is "always already latently" determining being-in-the world, inasmuch as Dasein's absorption in the *They* is a way of fleeing from itself, from its ability to be authentically itself. Because anxiety confirms that Dasein's fallenness is a flight from its capacity for authenticity, it is also liberating, bringing Dasein back to the "individual" possibility that it "always already" is, the thrown possibility of being authentic.

Heidegger compares and contrasts anxiety with fear. As a disposition, fear also discloses Dasein to itself, its way of "being-in," and what it fears. We fear something threatening within-the-world, something that approaches us from a certain direction with the potential to harm us in a determinate way. Fear is guided by circumspection and Dasein's everyday concerns (SZ 141). So we fear precisely what is detrimental to us in and on account of our concerns. We can also fear "for" others. By contrast, what is threatening in anxiety is nothing within-the-world at all; far from approaching from some direction or other, it is nowhere. For obvious reasons, circumspection loses its bearings in anxiety. Dasein experiences anxiety over its *individual* being-in-the-world as such and precisely on account of it. Just as our concerns with what there is within-the-world presuppose being-in-the-world, so "fear is angst that has fallen prey to the 'world,' angst that is inauthentic and hidden from itself" (SZ 189).

The analysis of angst serves as the template for the structural analysis of the unity of existentiality, facticity, and fallenness in care (SZ 191f). It also figures prominently in the analysis of authenticity. Dasein's thrownness into death "reveals itself to it [Dasein] more primordially and penetratingly in the disposition of angst" (SZ 251). Here, too, Dasein is confronted with nothingness, not in the sense of the absence of the relevance of what is handy or on-hand but in the sense of the possibility of Dasein's impossibility (SZ 265f, 308). The call of conscience is the call "determined by angst," a call to Dasein's capability of being "revealed in angst" (SZ 277). The resoluteness that, hearing conscience's call, anticipates death, is precisely a "readiness for angst" (SZ 297, 301, 322).

Appropriating event (*Ereignis*)

Heidegger uses *Ereignis*, "the leading term" of his thinking since 1936, as a metonym, if not a synonym for historical being (though he later warns that this characterization itself can be misleading) (9: 316; 12: 248f; 14: 26f). The appropriating event appropriates being (the presence of beings) and Dasein to one another, by opening up a clearing for particular beings to be present to Dasein. Opening up that clearing coincides at once with bringing (*über-eignen*) beings into their own (their being), and with grounding Da-sein, since the "da" signifies "the appropriated open—the appropriated clearing" (70: 46; 71: 211). Yet the appropriating event itself keeps to itself, it withdraws, and this withdrawal is part of what is peculiar to it (14: 27). The appropriating event determines time, including the withdrawal of the having been and the withholding of the future, and, by the same token, "disappropriation [*Enteignis*]" is inherent in it (14: 28).

Thinking this *appropriating event* is hindered by a tendency to think of it as being, when in fact it is "essentially other than because richer than any possible metaphysical determination of being" (12: 248; 70: 17). Indeed, "being vanishes in the appropriating event" (14: 27). Hence, rather than think the appropriating event as being, the task is to think historical being ("being itself") as the appropriating event that grounds the clearing (the *da*) and thus unfolds (*west*). What is grounded—being, Dasein, and their mutual appropriation—is not separate from the appropriating event; insisting on the simplicity of the latter, Heidegger stresses that only within it is there a clearing (Dasein) at all or any particular being (70: 17, 117; see, too, 11: 45; 12: 248; 65: 247, 256, 470; 66: 100; 67: 62; 70: 16; 71: 192).

Ereignis can no more be translated, Heidegger contends, than the Greek *logos* or the Chinese *tao*. In ordinary German *Ereignis* signifies an event. However, since it opens up time–space altogether, in advance of any reckoning with time, it is not an occurrence *in* time. Taking it as something taking place readily lapses into thinking of it as a particular being, when in fact the relation of any particular being to its being only arises from out of the appropriating event (70: 17f). At the same time, the appropriating event is intimately tied to the happening of historical being, i.e. the dynamic of making a clearing while all the while hiding. So, too, it is related to the first beginning and the transition to the other beginning of Western thinking. In these ways, some of the term's ordinary significance carries over (11: 45; 65: 472).

In Heidegger's earliest lectures, he glosses *Ereignis* as a meaningful event in contrast to a passing incident. Moreover, he does so by employing the hyphenated verb *sich er-eignen* to mean not simply "to happen" but "to make something one's own" (56/57: 75). In the *Contributions*, in addition to employing this transitive use to characterize the mutual appropriation of historical being and *Da-sein*, he also elaborates the meaning of *Ereignis* in terms of notions with cognate roots, e.g. "ownmost" (*Eigenste*), "property" (*Eigentum*), "ex-propriating" (*Ent-eignung*), "taking possession" (*An-eignung*), "dedicating oneself to" (*Zu-eignung*), "handing over" (*Übereignung*) (71: 147–70). In the 1960s Heidegger himself suggests *appropriement* as a possible French translation (15: 365). These considerations speak strongly in favor of translating *Ereignis* as "enownment" or "appropriation."

Yet he also warns against relying too heavily upon the sense of 'own' (*eigen*) in interpreting *Ereignis*. Instead, he hearkens back to its etymological root, not in the subsequent sense of being one's own, but in the original sense of coming into view and being "eyed" (*eräugen*), an eye-opening ostension or clearing (71: 184; 12: 260; 11: 45). Thus, by opening up the clearing, the appropriating event brings things into view, making present the presence of beings to Dasein.

The appropriating event does not appear alongside what comes to appear in it. Just as what opens up things to us and us to things is not itself necessarily opened up in the process, the appropriating event conceals itself. Bestowing (*ver-eignend*) and handing itself over (*übereignend*) to Dasein, dedicating itself (*zueignend*) to Dasein, and taking possession (*an-eignend*) of Dasein, the appropriating event opens up human beings to "having to preserve, lose, inquire into, and ground the truth of historical being" (71: 190). In this process, the appropriating event does not collapse into what is disclosed (*Entbergung*), but is instead preserved in its hiddenness (71: 147–54). Herein lies the mystery of historical being as the appropriating event: by hiding itself, it opens entities or, more precisely, their presence up to Dasein (14: 28).

The appropriating event is *unique* and *simple* (*einfach*) in the sense that what it appropriates to one another (being and Dasein) are inseparable from it. It is *closest* to us since we exist in belonging to it. It is the *realm* "through which being and being human reach one another in their essence" by losing those determinations that metaphysics has lent them. "We dwell in the appropriation, insofar as our essence is given over [*vereignet*] to language." We catch sight of the first, oppressive flash of the appropriating event in the positionality that makes up the essence of the modern technological world and thus the way human beings and being belong together (11: 46ff). Heidegger considers his conception of appropriation (*Ereignis*) innovative. Not even the Greek thinkers of the first beginning broached it. "This clearing itself as the appropriating event remains unthought in every respect" (12: 127).

Aristotle

Heidegger's preoccupation with Aristotle goes back to his late teens, when he received a copy of Brentano's dissertation on the manifold senses of "being" in Aristotle. All but three of the eleven lectures from 1921 to 1927 concentrate largely if not principally on works of Aristotle. He owes his new position in Marburg in part to his 1922 draft, intended for its faculty, of an introduction to a planned monograph on Aristotle (62: 341–419). SZ itself continuously reworks Aristotelian concepts (e.g. *ousia—Anwesenheit, pathe—Befindlichkeit, hou heneka—Worumwillen, pragmata—Zuhandene, logos—Rede, logos apophantikos—Aussage, phronesis—Gewissen, psyche—Dasein in the sense of being in the world*). In 1930 Heidegger revisits Aristotle's accounts of assertion (*logos apophantikos*) in one lecture (GA 29/30) and *ousia* and *aletheia* in another (GA 31), before devoting the entire lecture the following summer to *Metaphysics*, Theta, 1–3 (GA 33). This pre-occupation with Aristotle culminates in the 1939 essay on "On the Essence and Concept of *Physis*, Aristotle, *Physics B 1*," the text that is "the hidden and thus never sufficiently thought-through fundamental book of Western philosophy" (9: 242; 15: 291).

In contrast to Brentano, Heidegger reads Aristotle primarily as a thinker of truth (*aletheia*) rather than of categories. Thus he takes over from Aristotle the notion that beings themselves are unhidden (*on hos alethes*) and that the human soul's ways of relating to beings are, at bottom, ways of revealing them (19: 21–188). He also appropriates Aristotle's way of conceiving assertions, namely, in terms of truth, rather than vice versa. From this perspective, subsequent accounts of truth as a property of an assertion have it hopelessly backwards. Aristotle recognizes that assertions are ways of letting things present themselves of themselves, despite or, rather, thanks to the possibility of mispresenting themselves and the possibility of misuse of the assertion (21: 135, 169; SZ 32f, 226). Heidegger acquits Aristotle of a naïve picture-theory of truth and, while having no more an account of falsehood than Plato does, Aristotle pressed farther by demonstrating how the possibility of falsehood lies, not in our thinking, but in the way beings are (21: 161–8).

Nevertheless, orienting investigations to the derivative sense of the *logos*, i.e. assertions conceived in terms of their synthetic, formal character, removes them from their roots in a primordial, hermeneutic understanding. This orientation, initiated by Aristotle, who fails to inquire into those roots, "precludes any possibility of understanding meaning ... and, in the broader sense, even language" (21: 141f; 29/30: 339f). To be sure, Aristotle countenances a "primordial truth" that need not be given in assertions and can be "seen" or "touched," but this very account exacerbates the problem by identifying truth with the sheer presence or unhiddenness of beings (*Meta.*, Theta 10; 21: 190–4). Moreover, this presence coincides with the categories, the way beings are addressed, thus opening the door to the category-based interpretation of Aristotle and, more importantly, subsequent interpretations of being primarily in terms of categories and only derivatively in terms of truth as *aletheia*.

In early interpretations of the Stagirite, Heidegger contends that, for Aristotle, to be is "to-be-produced." Being in the primary sense is what is not in process of becoming. It is finished, never having been subject to a process or having come to the end of a process. So, too, what is actual is what is potentially usable (the primordial care-based access to it), as though it were made, a product of *techne*. Even though it issues from itself or stands on its own, this self-standing is modeled on *techne* (62: 385, 398; 24: 149–56). Yet in his 1939 essay Heidegger stresses how Aristotle sharply differentiates what is by nature and what is produced. In contrast to artifacts that come from some "producing know-how" (*techne*), what is by nature not only stays within itself but also "returns to itself," even as it unfolds but in no way as a kind of "self-making." *Physis* may be said to produce itself, but this self-producing is a generating not a making (9: 254f, 288f, 293, 299).

Signaling Aristotle's attentiveness to the ontological difference, Heidegger notes in the same essay that *physis* is for Aristotle the beingness, i.e. presencing (*ousia*) of beings, characterized by motion, that stand on their own and lie before us (9: 260f, 266, 281). This presencing, as Aristotle's critique of Antiphon makes clear, is neither a static presence nor mere duration but a process of "coming to be present [*An-wesung*] in the sense of coming forth into the unhidden, placing itself into the open" (9: 272). Constitutive of this process is the thing's form (*morphe*) that corresponds to its *logos*, the way it gathers what is dispersed into a unity so as to be present. *Morphe* is *physis* to a greater degree than *hule* because, while the latter is only the appropriateness for some end or work, the former is the stable state of "having-itself-in-its-end" (*entelecheia*) and "standing-in-the-work" (*energeia*). The movements of an animal, for example, are for its sake, and it takes its stand, as it were, in the way that, in those movements, it makes itself present. In so doing, this "entelechy" makes present the appropriateness of what is appropriate (*dunamis*). At the same time, whenever something makes itself present, places itself in appearance, it also makes an absence present, i.e. an efficacious absence in Heidegger's gloss of privation (*steresis*). "In the 'vinegar' lies the absence of the wine" (9: 297). With this emphasis on the twofoldness of *physis*, Heidegger puts the final touch on his interpretation of Aristotle's *physis* in terms of *aletheia*. "*Physis* is the presencing of the absence of itself, one that is on the way from itself and to itself" (9: 299).

This interpretation places Aristotle's account in very close proximity to Heidegger's own way of thinking of being as the self-concealing clearing, the way that beings come to be present to Dasein. Yet Heidegger concludes the essay by noting that Aristotle's momentous characterization of *ousia* as a kind of *physis* in the *Metaphysics* echoes Heraclitus' more originary account of *physis*, where being—*physis* in the originary sense—is conceived as concealing-and-sheltering (*Bergen*) the unhiddenness of beings (9: 301). This originary sense of being wanes with Aristotle's account of *physis*, as the unhiddenness alone and its constancy—"what sustains itself in the completion" (*entelecheia*, *energeia*)—gain the upper hand, even as *physis* conceals itself (66: 366f, 378, 381, 397; 76: 36–40).

Also coming under criticism is Aristotle's conception of time as "the number of movement with respect to the before and after." Despite its rigor and recognition of the necessity of the counting soul, it remains an interpretation of the common pre-scientific understanding of time as a sequence of "nows" and, consequently, fails to broach the timeliness of human existence that it supposes (21: 263–9; 24: 327–62).

Art (*Kunst*)

Philosophical study of art in Germany before Heidegger focused mainly on questions of aesthetics, the subjective experience of a work of beauty, where the affective experience itself—on the part of the audience (Kant) or the artist (Nietzsche)—dictates in the last analysis whether the work is beautiful or not, whether it is art or not. The work itself is nothing more than a thing or an instrument, the material in an object formed by the aesthetic experience for the subject. (Even in Hegel's aesthetics, where art is the sensuous display of the absolute, what makes something an artwork is its non-contingent, sensuous capacity to convey a spiritual content to our minds and spirits.) In addition to its subjectivity, two other aspects of an aesthetic approach to art are noteworthy: first, aesthetics arises, as Hegel recognized, only in the wake of great art or at least when it has passed its prime and artworks are museum pieces, and second, in reducing what makes something an artwork (namely, its beauty) to the aesthete's experience (in Nietzsche's case, the artist), aesthetics separates art from truth, denying it the possibility of telling the truth (5: 21–6, 67; 6.1: 74–91, 117ff; 65: 503f).

In "Origin of the Work of Art" Heidegger takes aim at this aesthetic approach by observing that the artist is an artist because of the work just as much as the work is a work because of the artist. So, too, any account of aesthetic experience must piggyback on an account of the artwork. "The origin of the artwork and the artist is art" (5: 2, 44f). Aesthetics' tendency to understand the work as a thing is misconceived not only because of the opacity of things as such but also because a work is not an implement outfitted with some aesthetic quality. A work of art (e.g. van Gogh's painting of peasant shoes) brings out in its own way the presence (being) of beings, their truth. That truth places itself into the work (5: 25, 73f).

That truth is neither otherworldly nor eternal. As exemplified by the Greek temple, a work of art establishes a world on earth for a particular, historical people. More than anything we can touch or perceive, the world is the open-endedness of the times and spaces of things. At the same time, the artwork places that world squarely on the earth. While sheltering what emerges from it, the earth shatters every attempt to penetrate it and, in that sense, it is inherently at odds with the world (5: 33). The artwork sets forth the earth in just this way. While material disappears into the implements made of it, the impenetrable yet "inexhaustible fullness" of the earth is on display in the artwork. In contrast to the way the produced character of a tool uses up the earth, the artwork "frees [the earth] to itself" (5: 34, 52).

The truth that inserts itself into the artwork is the essential strife between world and earth, through which each asserts itself. The essence of truth consists in the primordial struggle between unhiddenness and hiddenness, epitomized by the strife between world and earth. By embodying this strife, the artwork is one of the ways that truth as that primordial struggle—in the guise (*Scheinen*) of the beautiful—happens (5: 42f, 48f; 4: 162, 179).

Artworks are created. While the artist disappears into the artwork, the artwork's created character consists in (a) providing the transforming line and shape of the struggle between world and earth, and (b) standing out as created. The more purely the artwork exhibits these created characteristics, the more it "transports us from the realm of the ordinary" and "transforms the customary ties to the world and the earth." In this sense, art is always creative, a beginning. "Art is history in the essential sense that it grounds history." Artworks need, in addition to creators, those who preserve it, i.e. not connoisseurs or curators, art historians or critics with taste, but those who are willing to stand fast in the artworks' transforming truth. Together, the artworks' creators and preservers make up "the historical existence of a people" (5: 54ff, 63–6).

All art is poetic in a broad sense (*Dichtung*), not to be confused with poesy, i.e. poetry in a narrow sense (*Poesie*). This poetic character of art arises from the fact that language first brings beings as such into the open. Without language, there is no openness of beings or, for that matter, of what is not a being. "Language itself is poetry in the essential sense," and there is poesy because "language preserves the original essence of poetry." Each art is "its own respective poetic composing within the clearing of beings that has happened already and unnoticed in language" (5: 62).

Like Hegel, Heidegger is interested only in "great art" and accepts that the present technological age, as the culmination of metaphysics, confirms Hegel's thesis that, as far as its highest vocation is concerned, art is a thing of the past (5: 26; 74: 198). However, he leaves open the question of whether art is at an end, adding that what matters is attaining "a completely different 'element' for the 'becoming' of art" (5: 67b). Meanwhile, reflection on what art might be depends completely on the question of being. Art is neither an appearance of the spirit nor an accomplishment of culture but instead belongs to the appropriating event, on whose basis alone the sense of being can be determined (5: 73). Nietzsche takes art to be a higher value than truth and the antidote to nihilism but only because he mistakenly approaches art aesthetically and equates truth with correspondence (6.1: 73ff, 142f, 150–5, 570–5; 66: 30–40).

Art continues to play a salient role in Heidegger's later writings, though the concern for poetry remains paramount. At the end of his technology essay, he claims that the decisive confrontation with technology must take place in art as a realm akin to, yet fundamentally different from technology (7: 36; 10: 31, 51–60). During this time, however, he also sees a strong convergence between his work and the paintings of Cezanne and Klee. In the mid–1960s Heidegger turns his attention to sculpture in particular. In 1966, at the opening of a solo show of works by the sculptor Bernhard Heiliger, he delivers "Remarks on Art—Sculpture—Space" (St. Gallen, Switzerland: Erker, 1996). A year later he gives an address in Athens on "The Origin of Art and the Vocation of Thinking" in *Distanz und Nähe: Reflexionen und Analysen zur Kunst der Gegenwart*, (ed.) Petra Jaeger and Rudolf Lüthe (Würzburg: Königshausen und Neumann, 1983, 11–22), and in 1969 he publishes the essay "Art and Space" (13: 203–10; 74: 185–206).

Assertion (*Aussage*, S: statement)

Assertions point to something and, by way of predication, determine it as such-and-such, allowing us to communicate as much to one another. Though Heidegger discusses assertions before discourse in SZ, this threefold structure—ostensiveness, predication, and communication—is essential to discourse. These structural components are inter-connected; i.e. assertions have to be about something, but they are not about it irrespective of the specifications that certain predications entail and, indeed, commonly entail, i.e. for the purposes of communication.

Drawing extensively on Aristotle's account of *logos apophantikos*, Heidegger attributes this structure to the fact that assertions can be true or false (SZ 218; 29/30: 441–89). By making it possible for things to present themselves for what they are, assertions differ from other forms of speech (questions, exclamations, commands) (17: 19–28; 20: 181; 21: 129). Assertions accordingly presuppose truth: "The assertion is not the primary place of truth, truth is the primary place of the assertion" (SZ 226; 21: 135). Integral to understanding and interpretation, assertions are existentials, basic revelatory ways of being-in-the-world. Hence, it is a category mistake to take it as something simply on-hand, like an object found in nature. Nonetheless, the assertion written down in a sentence is capable of being observed and conceived in this way. Logic mis-construes the phenomenon of assertions in this way (38: 1–5, 10).

Like any interpretation, assertions are existentially grounded in a "mostly inconspicuous" forestructure. We use something *as* a certain implement in view of *what it is for*, how it fits into a full complement of implements and the purpose for which we utilize them. For example, we use and thereby interpret something as a device for hammering. This "as" character, rooted in what something is for, constitutes the hermeneutical as-structure of circumspective interpretation. Assertions build on this as-structure by making aspects of it explicit.

"Making explicit," however, can take place in different ways. There are, for example, many gradations between theoretical assertions and assertions made in the course of circumspective interpretation (SZ 154–8; 21: 156n. 8). Such considerations obviously become crucial to Heidegger's own project in SZ, replete as it is with theoretical assertions. How can any theoretical assertion be made about Dasein without mis-construing it as something on-hand? At the end of his 1925 lectures Heidegger accordingly distinguishes two sorts of assertions: worldly assertions about the on-hand and "phenomenologically categorial" or "hermeneutical" assertions. Despite having the same structure as worldly assertions, the primary sense of hermeneutical assertions is not to point to something on-hand, but to make it possible to understand Dasein (21: 410, 410n. 1). Yet in later years Heidegger concludes that any sentence in the form of an assertion proves a hindrance to speaking of the appropriating event (14: 30).

As-structure (*Als-Struktur*)

In using something for hammering, I take it and thus, in a sense, "interpret" it as a hammer. This as-structure need not be asserted in the process, and, indeed, a theoretical assertion itself modifies that structure. This modification corresponds to a difference in the respective forestructure, i.e. what we have before us and in advance, what we are looking for, and our pre-conception. In our circumspective, prepredicative interpretations, we are dealing with something handy. When it becomes an object of a theoretical assertion, it becomes something simply on-hand. We attend to what it is and what its properties are, in view of simply observing it and no longer in terms of using it circumspectively in some relevant context. "The primordial 'as' of an interpretation (*hermeneia*) which understands circumspectively we call the >existential-*hermeneutical* 'as'< in contrast to the >*apophantical* 'as'< of the assertion" (SZ 158). The form of the apophantical 'as' (e.g. S is P, Fx, or x as F) is derivative of the more basic, *hermeneutical* understanding (the "hermeneutic-as," e.g. handling *x as F*) (21: 143–61; 29/30: 416–507, see esp. 456). Animals lack the "as-structure" altogether, i.e. the very structure that is the key to understanding the copula and relating to beings as beings (29/30: 416, 484).

Augustine

"The force of existing that gushes forth [from the *Confessions*] is in fact inexhaustible," Heidegger writes a friend in April of 1933, adding that he finds it most fruitful to start with Book Ten (16: 75). Not surprisingly, his 1921/22 lectures on Augustine are devoted to this book, though they are also replete with references to Augustine's corpus. The early lectures sow the seeds of several themes in his existential analysis: the burdensomeness of being (*oneri mihi sum*); the questionableness of "my" existence (*mihi quaestio factus sum*); the necessity of temptations (*nescit se homo, nisi in tentatione*); the three temptations (flesh, curiosity, pride) as evidence of human dividedness; the inauthenticity of pride (*timeri et amari velle ab hominibus*); the tendency to become dispersed into the crowd (*defluximus in multa*); and the existential imperative of resoluteness (*per continentiam ... colligimur et redigimur in unum* (60: 205–9, 229–41). The notion of life as a constant trial (*tota vita tentatio*) is "the basic sense of experience of the self as *historical*" (60: 263).

Yet ironically, in Heidegger's eyes, Augustine falls prey to the very aesthetic beguilement against which he otherwise rails. For the basic characteristic of Augustine's stance towards life is enjoyment, the object of which is God, "beauty so old and new." By subordinating the truth to the experience of a subjective state, the fulfillment of desire, this *fruitio dei* stands in opposition to authentic self-possession (60: 256f, 271). While advising against equating Augustine's *fruitio* with Plotinian intuition, Heidegger also cautions against presuming that one would be able to strip away the Platonic cast of Augustine's thought "in order to be able to attain the authentically Christian." In this connection, and in a lucid sign of his conversion from Catholicism, Heidegger cites favorably Luther's contrast of the *theologian of the cross*, seeing things the way they are, with the *theologian of glory*, marveling at the world's wonders but blinded by them, thinking that he sees God through them (60: 272, 279–82).

Authenticity (*Eigentlichkeit*)

Dasein relates to its being as the possibility that belongs to it more than anything else does, and yet as something it is capable of losing or attaining. Authenticity and inauthenticity are modes of being that are grounded in the fact that each Dasein is its own respective possibility (SZ 42f, 53, 232). While Dasein is initially and for the most part inauthentic, having lost or not yet found itself, authentic existence modifies—without detaching itself from—the They (SZ 128, 130, 175–9, 181). In its absorption in the They, Dasein turns away from itself and flees its authentic capability of being (fleeing, too, the angst that reveals its freedom to choose itself, i.e. to be authentic or inauthentic) (SZ 184–8, 191). Dasein's disclosure of itself with respect to what is most its own is the "authentic disclosure," showing "the phenomenon of the most primordial truth in the mode of authenticity" (SZ 221).

The possibility that Dasein shares with nothing else and that is most its own is its death, the possibility of its impossibility. Authentically relating to this possibility is not evading but anticipating it. Anticipating death as our defining possibility discloses our finitude but also enables us to become free for it and, hence, free to understand and choose authentically among finite, factical possibilities. Breaking the hold of any obdurate identification with possibilities either previously attained or awaited, it also guards against being with others inauthentically, by way of either mistaking their possibilities for ours or foisting our possibilities upon them. Arousing us from the inertia of merely conforming, resolutely anticipating death brings us face to face with the possibility of being ourselves, each on his or her own in a "freedom for death," unsupported by anything we undertake with one another. In the German term translated as "authenticity," namely *Eigentlichkeit*, lies the root term for "own" (*eigen*), and, indeed, to be authentic is precisely to own up to oneself, not least, as a "being towards death" (SZ 259–66).

Conscience attests to this authentic capability, calling Dasein to take responsibility for itself in the wake of its existential guilt, namely, the fact that, while not responsible for being here, it is singularly responsible for choosing certain possibilities over others. In contrast to an existence completely absorbed in the They, an authentic existence listens to itself, to the call of its conscience. To understand the call of conscience, listening to it without distortion, is to want to have a conscience or, equivalently, resoluteness. Resoluteness is the "authentic disclosedness to which Dasein's conscience attests in itself" (SZ 297).

Before we have even come of age, we have fallen prey to forces of assimilation. We seemingly make choices all the time, but it is not clear that we are doing any more than going through the motions since the choices are made under the sway of some group (the They). In other words, we have not really chosen to choose but instead enacted choices that we expect are expected of us, accommodating and inhabiting shared perspectives just because they are shared. In order to make choices in an authentic way, it is necessary for us to make choices conscientiously, i.e. on the basis of who we are as someone with the responsibility of making them—and remaking or retracting them, precisely in view of the possibility of our impossibility. To choose to choose in this conscientious way (or, equivalently, to want to have a conscience) is to be resolute—and to be resolute is to exist authentically (SZ 336).

There is a distinctive transparency and constancy to being authentic, to assuming responsibility for ourselves concretely (ontically). "The more authentically Dasein is resolute ... the more unambiguously and non-contingently does it find and choose the possibility of its existence. Only anticipating death drives out any contingent and 'provisional' possibility. Only being-free *for* death, provides Dasein the goal in an unqualified way and plunges existence into its finitude" (SZ 384, 305). With finitude comes the possibility of "taking back" or "giving up" any specific resolution (SZ 264, 308, 391). To be resolute in a manner that anticipates death is to come back *repeatedly* to oneself and one's factical situation ("dependent upon a 'world' and existing with others"), disclosing the respective possibilities of the situation "*on the basis of the legacy*" that one takes over in being thrown into the world (SZ 383; 64: 117, 122f).

One challenge for Heidegger's treatment of authenticity is accounting for the basis of the choice, even as it chooses to choose. If that basis, e.g. some reason or belief, is drawn from the averageness of everyday Dasein, then the authenticity of the choice seems questionable. Some interpreters countenance this enabling role of average everydayness in Dasein's capacity to be authentic, while others contend that the authentic choice to choose prescinds from any such norm, thereby inviting the charge of decisionism. Both approaches are problematic. The former seems to violate the indexicality of Dasein's authentic choice, i.e. the fact that its choice to choose is made in view of its projection of its death, not shared with any other Dasein. The latter approach renders authenticity an unmotivated spontaneity, a kind of moral luck.

In Heidegger's later writings he returns briefly to the theme of authenticity, as the center of gravity shifts from existential analysis to thinking being historically as the appropriating event. In this context authenticity is "the origin of the historical selfhood of the human being. Appropriated into the truth of historical being, the human being is now itself a human being." The crucial difference is whether the human being is responsive to that truth, responsibly corresponding to it, or pursues some self-made task stemming from a metaphysical-anthropological, willful subjectivity in the form of an "I" or "we" (71: 154–61).

Basic concept (*Grundbegriff*)

Basic concepts are determinations of the domain of a subject matter underlying all the thematic objects of a science. The research producing fundamental concepts yields an ontological interpretation of the beings making up the domain (SZ 10). Heidegger subsequently emphasizes how they comprehend the whole in an explicitly reflexive way, incorporating the existence of the one who comprehends: "No concept of the whole without inclusion of the philosophizing existence" (29/30: 13). The inclusion is existential. Basic concepts grasp the ground, knowing the ground on which one stands and where decisions are made. This knowing, more basic than any willing and more intimate than any feeling, is itself a stance and lays a claim upon us (51: 3). (For lectures on "basic concepts," see GA 18, 22, 29/30, 51).

Beginning (*Anfang*)

The start (*Begin*) of something in time is different from the "inception" of time–space itself, i.e. *the* beginning (*Anfang*) that, while taking hold from its inception, is still coming to us, in and through what it began. A synonym for "beginning" in this latter sense is the "primal source" or "sustaining origin" (*Ursprung*) —from which and through which something is what it is. As a name for "the truth of historical being," the beginning (*Anfang*) is the appropriating event that opens up the clearing for the presence of beings, concealing itself in the process. In this respect, the beginning coincides with historical being's "going-under [*Unter-gang*] into the departure [*Abschied*]," the grounding that turns away from all grounds, i.e. the abyss. Thinking historical being and the beginning as the appropriating event (*Ereignis*) is "the authentic thinking and the only 'actual' leap." It is a process of winding back and coming to terms with historical being (*Verwindung des Seyns*) while also safeguarding it into its departure. In the departure, what is explicitly said is not historical being "but the appropriating event of the beginning that can no longer be addressed as historical being," where not only beingness but being must be left behind (39: 3f; 70: 10f, 21–5, 54f, 83–7, 106; 71: 182; 51: 86f).

At the most basic level, as suggested above, there is only one beginning. Nevertheless, as early as the summer of 1932, Heidegger distinguishes between the first beginning and another beginning, "a *recommencement* of the *originary* beginning" (35: 99). The thinkers of the first beginning are Anaximander, Heraclitus, and Parmenides. For with them thinking begins, i.e. being is first thought and questioned, and, in our understanding of being today, we are ourselves "built" on what they had asked about being. "Insofar as we exist, that beginning *is always still happening.* It is *having been* but not past—as having been, it essentially unfolds and retains us contemporaries in its unfolding essence" (35: 98; 71: 61, 64).

These thinkers of the first beginning experienced that historical being is without the support of any entity, that it illuminates what there is, even while it itself hides, taking leave in the process, and this experience is the originary appropriating event. They experience *physis* as unhiddenness and hiddenness, but without inquiring into its ground and beginning, i.e. *aletheia* as the process of disclosing the unhiddenness, removing it from its sheltering hiddenness. Instead *physis* as the ever-emerging and re-emerging presence of beings appears as though it were constantly present.

What remains hidden from these first thinkers in the unhiddenness of *physis* is that withdrawal, that way of going back into itself (*Insichzurückgehen*) that allows what emerges to be unhidden. They suppose but do not themselves ground the determination of *physis* as *aletheia*, thereby setting the stage for its re-interpretation, i.e. for metaphysics (65: 185f, 195; 71:15f, 27f, 41, 56–71, 181–5). The common thread of metaphysics is an understanding of being as a standing presence, typically derived from a preeminent being, yet common to all particular beings (from Plato's timeless ideas to Nietzsche's will to power). At the end of metaphysics, there are only beings, and being is "empty smoke and an error." The truth (as unhiddenness) is a character of beings as such (so, too, truth as correctness is a determination of beings transformed into objects of judgments) (65: 185, 191f; 70: 55f).

By contrast, in the other beginning, the truth is recognized as the truth of historical being, namely, the appropriating event itself, opening up the presence of beings and Dasein to one another. The other beginning returns to the first beginning, precisely by way of distancing itself from the latter in order to experience and retrieve what began in it (65: 185). The other beginning requires a leap from the first beginning, i.e. there are no mediating principles to permit its derivation from the first beginning. Nonetheless, making the leap requires preparation, and this preparation takes the form of the end of metaphysics. This end of metaphysics, which coincides with the notion that everything is useful and producible thanks to being nothing but willful centers of power, ushers in the experience of the devastation of beings (things and nature) (70: 55f, 86f, 107, 110).

The world's present planetary–interstellar condition is "European–Western–Greek" through and through. This condition can change only thanks to some greatness that was spared at its inception, the beginning that fatefully (*geschicklich*) determines our age. There is no returning to this beginning, no eliminating it, but the greatness that was spared in that beginning comes only to those who do no longer remain "in its Western isolation." "It opens itself to the few other great beginnings that belong with its own to the same beginning of the in-finite relation in which the earth is contained" (4: 177). On the one hand, the first beginning does not exhaust the greatness of the beginning; it allows for another beginning, one that unleashes that greatness spared in the first beginning. On the other hand, the other beginning can no longer remain fixated on its "European–Western–Greek" beginning (4: 177, 179).

Being (*Sein*)

Whatever we are dealing with, whatever we find in our paths, by the very fact that we deal with it, we take it as something rather than nothing. We accordingly distinguish between whatever else we may say of an entity and its being—just as we distinguish "Fx" from the quantified sentence "∃x(Fx)." In order to designate being in contrast to beings (entities, *Seiendes*), Heidegger uses the term *Sein*, the nominalized form of the German infinitive for "to be." The fundamental question is: What is the sense of being? The tendency to understand being as presence, while ancient, seems to be unfounded, not least because it trades on an unquestioned dimension of time and proves unable to countenance the ways that absences (such as the past and the future) are part of the sense of what is. What something is corresponds to what is primordially true of it, i.e. the way it comes—always more or less, for a while, never completely—into the clear out of absence. Herein lie the rudiments of the sense of being: a temporal, hidden interplay of the presence and absence of beings.

Heidegger arrives at this provisional understanding of being through existential analysis, i.e. the analysis of the being of being-here (*Dasein*), the particular being to whom being matters. Even if we restrict the meaning of "being" to the presence of beings, this meaning entails what they are present to: *Dasein*. The difference between beings and their presence is not produced by our being-here. Yet without the disposed understanding of being-here, there may still be beings but there would be no presence (or absence) of them, no being. Being-here discloses the being of beings, including its own, by way of caring about its being-in-the-world, and, without its distinctive timeliness, being-here would not care. Accordingly, time is the sense of being.

Heidegger came to see at least three basic, closely related problems with the foregoing account. First, the foregoing analysis starts out from the distinction between being and beings. While the

distinction seems warranted, it relies upon something that is neither
being, so distinguished, nor beings and that yet somehow underlies
them, namely, their differentiation. Moreover, a transcendental
analysis of Dasein does not by itself provide the ground of this
differentiation. Second, the foregoing analysis suggests, paradoxically if not inconsistently, that its conclusions are timeless, that the
ways we think about being are not themselves part of our history.
Third, the foregoing analysis does not stress the fundamental
feature of being, namely, that it conceals itself more than it reveals
and, indeed, withdraws precisely in disclosing beings. "The unhiddenness of beings, the daylight afforded it, darkens the light of
being" (5: 337).

In order to be able to think the difference between being
and beings as something that itself *is* and, indeed, in historical
terms as something that happens (*geschieht*) thanks to this self-
concealing, Heidegger introduces an archaic term, *Seyn* ("historical
being"), and an ordinary term for event, *Ereignis*, to which he
assigns the extraordinary meaning of "appropriating" or "opening
up." Historical being happens as the hidden appropriation of
the presence of beings and Dasein to one another. On the one
hand, this hiddenness amounts to being's abandonment of human
beings (*Seinsverlassenheit*), underlying their obliviousness to it
(*Seinsvergessenheit*). On the other hand, in concealing itself,
historical being shelters yet untapped possibilities. Thus, positionality, which is the essence of modern technology, characterizes
an epoch of historical being, where historical being's way of
concealing itself both underlies the danger of the utter obliviousness to it and shelters possibilities of saving it. Being is thus not
the unconditioned or absolute, nor is it what is respectively conditioned by human beings. It is, however, the appropriating event in
which beings and being-here first emerge as themselves; it creates
and makes nothing (70: 175).

Being is the most empty and yet fecund, the most common and
yet unique, the most intelligible and yet hidden, the most worn-out
and yet the source of every being, the most relied upon and yet
an abyss, the most said and yet silent, the most forgotten and yet
recollection itself (recollecting us into and towards beings), the
greatest constraint and yet liberating (51: 68, 49–77; 71: 48). In an
attempt to ward off the almost inextirpable habit of representing
being as something standing somewhere for itself and occasionally

confronting human beings, Heidegger crosses out "being" and notes that the four points of the cross refer to the four regions of the fourfold (9: 411).

In a late seminar Heidegger suggests that the sentence "there is being" can simply mean that there are *beings* or that beings *are*, i.e. that they are present, thereby inviting the sort of metaphysical interpretation of being as the presence of beings. However, the sentence "there is being" can also point to what lets beings be present, what allows for the presencing. With this third meaning, the term "being" gives way to "appropriating event," that is to say, "being [the presence of beings] is appropriated [or opened up to Dasein] by the appropriating event" (15: 364f).

Being-here (*Da-sein*)

Dasein is "the good German translation" of *existentia*, the traditional Latin term for whatever is on-hand or present (65: 296; 71: 208). Departing from this traditional usage, Heidegger characterizes Dasein as that entity whose being is at stake, at issue for it. Though this use of *Dasein* is supposedly untranslatable, Heidegger trades on the way it combines the verb "to be" (*sein*) with an adverb for place (*da*) and the way its significance is inherently related to that of "existence" (which he also conceives non-traditionally). The adverb *da* typically means "here" or "there," as in "Here is the weed" (*Da ist das Unkraut*). However, we find ourselves to be here in a way not reducible to merely occupying a space. To be-here is to experience a world opening up, in which entities and even objects have a place. Accordingly, Heidegger urges his readers to understand *da* not as a spatial adverb but as signaling the disclosedness or, equivalently, the clearing (*Lichtung*), in which entities are present or absent (SZ: 133; 15: 204; 65: 296, 298; 71: 211). As the clearing, Dasein makes spatial orientations possible (being here or there in their usual senses) and renders things accessible in the light and hidden in the dark. "*Dasein is its disclosedness*" (SZ 133). Unlike the beams of a flashlight or rays of the sun, Dasein does not disclose by virtue of anything other than itself. Disclosing in this fundamental, self-referential sense distinguishes being-here (*Dasein*) from being-handy (*Zuhandensein*),

or simply being-on-hand (*Vorhandensein*). (Since Heidegger
sometimes singles out the "*da*" of *da-sein*, it is necessary to use
"here" as its translation, though with the understanding that, as
in the German, it signifies Dasein's disclosedness. "Being-here"
seems more apt than "being-there" because the former more
closely echoes ordinary usage in Heidegger's region of Germany
and because it conveys the nearness and transparency of existence
in ways that "being-there" does not.)

"Dasein determines itself as an entity in each case on the basis of
a possibility that it is and somehow understands in its being. This
is the formal sense of the constitution of the existence of Dasein"
(SZ 43). The phrase "in each case" here indicates that Dasein
relates to its existence always as its own and that it exists in the
first-person as a "who" not a "what," though it may do so authentically or inauthentically. Depending upon the context, *Dasein*
may designate this manner of being or the entity with this manner
of being. Accordingly, being-here is not identical to being-human.
The analysis of Dasein is thus distinct from traditional studies of
human nature (e.g. anthropology, biology, psychology), especially
since they pre-emptively construe the human as something on-hand
in nature, ontologically undifferentiated from any other natural
formation or reality.

While being-here and the human being, though conceptually
distinct, overlap in SZ, Heidegger develops their contrast in later
works, contending that we, as humans, are not yet here (*da*), i.e.
not yet the disclosedness. Dasein is "the ground of a specific, future
[way of] being human" (65: 300). "The human being *is* futurally,
in that it takes over being the clearing [*Da*], provided that it
conceives itself as the guardian of the truth of historical being, a
guardianship that is indicated as 'care'" (65: 297, 302–26, 487ff).
In SZ the Da of Dasein is conceived as the clearing or the open, but
as such it falls victim to its transitional role between metaphysical
and post-metaphysical thinking (SZ 305). Thus, for example, as the
condition of the possibility of the presence and absence of entities,
it serves a function similar to a transcendental subjectivity, a point
of convergence with Kant that Heidegger exploits but later recognizes as metaphysical and thus fatal (66: 146; 71: 141, 213). "Yet
Dasein overturned all subjectivity, and historical being is never
an object; only entities are capable of becoming objects and even
here not all of them" (65: 252; 71: 303, 488f). Whereas it was

already clear in SZ that Dasein can never be encountered as an entity simply on-hand, the *Contributions* signals its future status as the entity that does not allow everything to become an object. "The Da means the appropriated open—the appropriated clearing of being" (65: 296ff, 318; 71: 211). Historical being as the appropriating event appropriates Dasein, opening it up to its truth as the clearing that allows beings to be present to Dasein, but remains itself hidden. Dasein's "essence belongs entirely to historical being" (70: 129). "In being-here, beings become themselves and are thus shaped into historical being" (71: 210). In the Zollikon Seminars, Heidegger emphasizes that Dasein must always be seen as being-in-the-world, concerned with things and caring for others, standing in the clearing for the sake of what concerns it and what it encounters.

Being-in-the-world (*In-der-Welt-sein*)

A metonym for "Dasein," "being-in-the-world" signifies the holistic or unified phenomenon in terms of which Heidegger explicates Dasein's worldhood, who Dasein is (particularly in its average everydayness), and the basic existentials (the ways it is in the world). "Being-in-the-world is, to be sure, an a priori and necessary constitution of Dasein but is by no means sufficient to determine fully its being" (SZ 53, 351). As the locus of Dasein's concern or what it takes care of (*Besorgen*), being-in-the-world captures Dasein's facticity and thrownness, how it is unthematically immersed in what is handy (SZ 56ff, 65, 76, 105, 108, 113, 135, 172, 191f, 252, 331). Everyday being-in-the-world is fallen, seductive, sedating and alienating (SZ 176ff). "As being-in-the-world Dasein exists factically with and alongside beings it encounters within-the-world" (SZ 333). It is in terms of being-in-the-world that Dasein is fated, worldly, and historical (SZ 380, 383f, 388, 393).

Being-with (*Mitsein*)

Dasein is with others from the outset, indeed, so much so that, for the most part, it does not distinguish itself from them. The world of Dasein is a *shared world* (*Mitwelt*). Each Dasein is, from its own

vantage point, being-with others (*Mitsein*). Insofar as it is encountered within the world by another Dasein, it is being-here-with it
(*Mitdasein*). That is to say, others are being-here-with Dasein, and,
like Dasein, their being-here-with does not have "the ontological
character of something on-hand along with it within a world." Just
as Dasein typically understands itself on the basis of its world, so
the being-here-with of others is typically encountered "at work,"
i.e. from the standpoint of what is handy within-the-world. "This
being-here-with of others is only disclosed in an inner-worldly way
for a Dasein ... because Dasein is in itself being-with." This being-
with determines Dasein existentially even in the factical absence
of others. Being-with and the facticity of being-with-one-another
are not grounded in the co-occurrence of several subjects on-hand.
Others can encounter Dasein as being-here-with them only insofar
as Dasein of its own has the essential structure of being-with.

In contrast to concern (*Besorgen*) for what is handy, i.e. to
taking care of one's concerns or business, taking care of others and
concerning oneself with them (in negative as well as positive senses)
is solicitude (*Fürsorge*). The latter term can also mean "welfare,"
a social institution that is grounded in being-with and motivated
by the typically deficient yet everyday modes of solicitude such as
neglect or indifference (reinforcing the interpretation of others' being
as the "sheer on-handness of several subjects"). Just as working with
what is handy in the context of concern is guided by circumspection
(*Umsicht*), so solicitude is guided by degrees of considerateness
(*Rücksicht*) and acceptance (*Nachsicht*) of others. The possibilities
of solicitude lie within a spectrum between two extremes. *At one
extreme*, solicitude "can as it were take away the other's 'care' and put
itself in its place in the context of some concern, *leaping into* its place
for it." The displaced other becomes dependent and dominated, a cog
in the machinery of some work-world concern, retreating in order to
take over the result of the concern as something finished and available,
but not of its doing. *At the other extreme*, solicitude "*leaps ahead*, not
in order to take away the other's 'care' from it, but to first give it back
authentically as such." This latter solicitude is authentic care, i.e. the
care for the other insofar as she exists and not insofar as she takes care
of something within some concern. "This solicitude... helps the other
become transparent to herself *in* her care and *free for* it."

Dasein exists essentially for the sake of itself, but, since it is
essentially being-with others, "Dasein is essentially for the sake

of others." In Dasein's being-with, it primordially understands the others as being-here-with it. This understanding is the ground for any knowledge of another, for making another's acquaintance, or for sympathy with another (SZ 118–25).

Biology (*Biologie*)

In Heidegger's earliest articles, taking on Darwin-inspired biologists such as Ernst Haeckel from a Catholic perspective, he argues for the autonomy of organisms as well as the need to understand the complexity of their interaction with the environment. In SZ he states that the path to an ontological determination of the living— "neither purely being-on-hand nor also Dasein"—is a "reductive privation on the basis of the ontology of Dasein" (SZ 10, 50, 194). He pursues this determination in his 1929/30 lectures. There he targets Darwinist and mechanist approaches to organisms as well as neo-vitalist approaches based upon Kantian purposiveness or Aristotelian *entelechy*. He draws on Driesch's concept of "holism" (*Ganzheit*) but also criticizes Buytendijk's view that an animal is in its surroundings almost as though they were its body. Instead he turns to the work of Baer and, above all, Uexküll's exploration of animals' distinctive "environment." All the while he emphasizes the privative character of the analysis, since our access to animals is neither a case of being-with-one-another (reserved for *Mitdasein*) nor a case of simply being-alongside something handy or on-hand. Instead we have to transport ourselves into the animal's life (29/30: 309, 335, 380f; 76: 66f).

In keeping with Heidegger's rejection of purposiveness, he contrasts the finished and prepared character (*Fertigkeit*) of human productions with the facility (*Fähigkeit*) of organisms. What machines and organisms have in common is a kind of service-ability. Echoing Aristotle, Heidegger distinguishes between an artifact prepared to serve a purpose beyond itself, available apart from the process that produced it, and a living organism's self-serving facilities that never exist apart from the organism interacting with its surroundings. Drawing on Uexküll's research on amoebas, Heidegger asserts that the facilities enable and even render necessary the possession of organs rather than vice versa.

In other words, it is not that an animal can see because it has eyes but rather that it has eyes because it can see. An organism has organs because it has certain facilities, rooted in drives and urges, through which the organism—as long as it is uncurbed, uninhibited—advances and regulates itself of itself, opening up its surroundings in the process (29/30: 319–35, 342; 26: 102f, 113). This process is one in which the animal is "captivated," as surroundings unleash its circle of drives and the animal proceeds to eliminate what unleashes it. Heidegger refers to this basic conception of captivation as "the first conception, on the basis of which every concrete biological question can first be established" (29/30: 377). Six years later he voices skepticism about the viability of biology as an understanding of life as long as biology derives its legitimacy from science in the grips of modern processes of "machination" (65: 276). As for versions of biologism, they are all forms of metaphysics, the metaphysics of power and machination (46: 215f; 65: 173).

Bodiliness (*Leiblichkeit*)

Sartre and Löwith head a list of critics who charge Heidegger with neglecting the body in SZ. Heidegger himself confesses that he found the theme "the most difficult," and at the time of writing SZ he did not know what more to say beyond the few lines devoted to it (SZ 108; 89: 292). Even in his early lectures, he affirms how life-experiences are given through necessary relations to bodiliness (56/57: 210; 18: 199). And later he asserts that Dasein is factically split off into a body, by virtue of its thrownness. Heidegger justifies neglecting to treat the body in more depth, by contending that clarification of Dasein's basic structures, in a bodily and sexually neutral way, is a condition for a phenomenology of the body (26: 172ff; 89: 202). Not fundamental ontology but metontology, the "metaphysics of Dasein," would be the likely place for thematizing the body (26: 174, 202). In the Zollikon Seminars Heidegger addresses bodiliness in several respects: its dependency upon Dasein's spatiality, its irreducibility to corporeality, its absence and remoteness, its way of being both here and there at once, its dynamic character of "bodying forth" and relation in that respect to the self (89: 105, 109, 111, 126f, 244, 294; see, too, 65: 275f). Yet Heidegger continues to differentiate being-in-the-world from our way of being bodies: "Bodying-forth is inherent in being-in-the-world as such. But being-in-the-world is not exhausted in bodying-forth" (89: 244; see, too, 15: 235ff).

Boredom (*Langeweile*)

Boredom is, literally, "a long while" (*Langeweile*). Time is oppressively prolonged in three distinct ways, yielding three forms of boredom: being bored by something, being bored (or, more literally, boring ourselves) with something, and profound boredom. In each case, the time that we are ourselves is neither filled-up nor fulfilling. Thus, we may be bored by a train station, vainly trying to pass the time by counting its windows, as we wait for the next train. We may also be bored with a dinner party, where (in contrast to the first form of boredom) the entire event is a way for us to kill time (our time). In this second form of boredom, the emptiness of the time springs, not from some object or setting (e.g. the train station where we tarry), but from our decision to immerse ourselves in the predictable, dull rituals of the dinner party, while leaving our authentic selves behind and abandoning ourselves to the meaninglessness of time without a past or future.

In profound boredom, we are bored by everything, including ourselves, and nothing in the world matters. The time of beings as a whole is startlingly empty. In contrast to boredom's other forms, we do not try to fight it by distracting ourselves, since there is no point in doing so. Whereas the time that stands still when we are bored by something or by others (in the first two forms) is some relative time period, in profound boredom it is time as a whole that is boring. Yet, like any refusal, this sweeping refusal of significance also reveals unexploited possibilities and brings Dasein face to face with its self (not its ego) and its temporal freedom. For Dasein's prospects of liberating itself lie in its capacity for resolute self-disclosure in the moment (*Augenblick*). Whereas the moment cannot be heard in the past-times marking the first two forms of boredom, the third form compels us to hear it. What it says (albeit ironically by refusing) is the authentic possibility of Dasein's existence, the moment of resolutely disclosing, seeing and acting in a world of significance (29/30: 115–249; also 9: 110).

Building (*Bauen*)

Building in the "authentic sense" is not a means to dwelling but rather is itself already a way of dwelling, a way of being on earth (as respective etymologies of the corresponding German terms suggest). Hence, it is impossible to ask, let alone decide, what it means to build "as long as we do not consider that every act of building is in itself a way of dwelling." As a way of being on earth, dwelling is being at peace with the free sphere that safeguards each thing in its way of essentially unfolding, as a gathering of earth and sky, divinities and mortals. To build a bridge, for example, is to erect a distinctive place where earth and sky, divinities and mortals come together as one, and where that fourfold unity directs the process of building, its erection of places and arrangement of spaces. In keeping with the ancient sense of *techne*, such building "brings the fourfold *here*" into the thing built and "brings the thing as a place *forth* in what is already present, for which space is now made by this place." The things built in this way (*die Bauten*) safeguard the fourfold, and "this fourfold safeguarding is the simple essence of dwelling." By the same token, "*we are able to build only if we are capable of dwelling*" (7: 148–63).

Care (*Sorge*)

Being matters to Dasein. This mattering shows up in the way that Dasein is always ahead of itself as already being-in-the-world. It exists, projecting possibilities for itself, but always factically, i.e. within a holistic framework of meaningfulness, signaling what things are for. Absorbed in the world of its concerns, Dasein also finds itself always already alongside what is handy within-the-world. *Being ahead* of itself, *being already* in a world, and *being alongside* implements within-the-world—Dasein's existentiality, facticity, and fallenness respectively—make up its ontological structure. "The being of Dasein means being-ahead-already-in (the-world) as being-alongside (entities encountered within-the-world). This being fulfills [realizes] the meaning of the term *care*, that is used [here] in a purely ontological-existential sense. This meaning excludes any ontically meant tendency of being, such as worry or carefreeness" (SZ 192, 284). Because Dasein is essentially care (*Sorge*), it has concerns (*Besorgen*)—i.e. it concerns itself with what is handy—and it has solicitude (*Fürsorge*)—i.e. in both senses of the expression, it "takes care of" others. "Care is always, even if only privatively, concern and solicitude" (SZ 194, 266, 298, 300). It is a complex but fundamental existential–ontological phenomenon, more basic than any theory or practice, any willing or wishing, any drive or urge. In other words, it is "a priori," what is presupposed "in the most primordial sense" (SZ 193–96, 206, 228). Being towards death is grounded in care, and the call of conscience is the call of care, a call out of the uncanniness of being-in-the-world (SZ 252, 259, 277f, 286). And yet care can be inauthentic or authentic. "But resoluteness is nothing but the authenticity of care itself, cared for in care and possible only as care" (SZ 301). Selfhood can only be existentially read off "the authenticity of Dasein's being *as care*" (SZ 322). From the fact that *being ahead* is grounded in the future, *being already* in the "having been," and *being alongside* in making present, Heidegger infers that "the primordial unity of the structure of care lies in temporality." Dasein is, at bottom, care, and the sense of care lies in temporality (SZ 234, 326f).

The notion of care surfaces less frequently in Heidegger's later thinking, though when it does, he continues to understand it as a basic feature of Dasein, albeit within the context of historical being as the appropriating event. As such, care shows us to be "*seekers, preservers, guardians*" of the truth of historical being. Grounded in reserve, it is "the anticipatory decisiveness" for that truth (65: 17f, 35, 294; 52: 181).

Celan, Paul (1920–70)

Celan was a Romanian-born poet who, thanks in no small part to speaking Yiddish and German at home, became a major German poet and a professor of literature at L'École Normale Supérieure in Paris. His parents perished in German concentration camps, and he himself served in a labor camp for eighteen months. In chilling, memorable verses—such as "He unleashes his dogs on us and sends us a grave in the sky ... death is a master out of Germany" (*Der Tod ist ein Meister aus Deutschland*) from his *Todesfüge*—he bears moving witness to the tragic events surrounding the war. From the early 1950s until his death he was an avid student of the work of Heidegger as was Heidegger of Celan's poetry. Beginning in 1957 the two engaged in a sustained correspondence, intriguing and even puzzling particularly for what was left unsaid between the thinker who embraced National Socialism and the poet who could not stop re-living its horrors. They met four times, once professionally at a conference on language (the source of Heidegger's "The Way to Language"), and three times in Freiburg (including two visits at Heidegger's hut in Todtnauberg) during a period when Celan was intermittently hospitalized for mental illness. In retrospect Celan, back in Paris, found the first visit disappointing, though it led to his poem "Todtnauberg" (1967), in which critics have searched for clues to the precise meaning of the disappointment (the lack of admission of remorse on Heidegger's part?). Nonetheless, two cordial meetings ensued. Their last encounter, again preceded by hospitalizations of Celan, was on March 26 at a public poetry reading in Freiburg. On the night of April 19–20 Celan took his life. Despite the fact that Celan's poetry has enormous affinities with Heidegger's writings, it remains distinctive, setting the stage for considerable contemporary European debate about the task of poetry and thinking in the present.

Circumspection (*Umsicht*)

"The most acute manner of merely *looking upon* the so-and-so constituted appearance of things can not discover what is handy. The view of things, looking-upon [them] only 'theoretically', dispenses with the understanding of handiness." This remark suggests that, in order to transition from seeing implements the way we do in using them to the way we see them apart from that use, we must undergo a Gestalt-shift. We are hardly blind to implements when using them. "Circumspection" refers to how one sees one's way *around* things practically, fitting ourselves into the

complex ways implements refer to one another for some intermediate purpose (*Um-zu*) (SZ 69).

Clearing (*Lichtung*)

Dasein is disclosedness in the sense that it is illumined (*erleuchtet,
gelichtet*), not by something else, but such that "it *is* itself the
clearing." Descartes' talk of *lumen naturale* (the natural light of
human understanding) is based upon Dasein's being the clearing
for light and dark alike (SZ 133). In Heidegger's late works, the
emphasis is on the clearing of being, to which Dasein belongs, and
in this context he often differentiates the clearing from any sense
of light or lighting. "As long as one thinks in a physicalist way,
the fundamental character of the clearing, that lies in advance of
the light, is not seen" (15: 231, 262; 54: 217f). The clearing is the
"free region" where things are present, coming across or standing
opposite one-another. It is the "open" or "openness" that affords
any possible appearing and showing. Heidegger draws on the
metaphorical sense of "clearing" that stands literally for a glade.
Despite the closeness of the German words for clearing (*Lichtung*)
and light (*Licht*), a glade can obviously be quite dark. So while
"light can fall upon the clearing ... and in it the brightness can
play with the dark," the light presupposes the clearing and not
vice versa. "The clearing is the open for everything that comes to
be present and absent" (14: 80f). At times, however, Heidegger
continues to associate "clearing" with "light" (5: 40ff, 61; 7: 259;
9: 331, 365).

The clearing underlies metaphysics, without being thought itself,
though Parmenides, a pre-metaphysical thinker, experiences it as,
and names it, *aletheia*. "The peaceful heart of the clearing is the
place of the stillness out of which there is the likes of the possibility of the co-belonging of being and thinking, i.e. presence and
perceiving" (14: 84). Since any possible claims on what is binding
are grounded in this co-belonging, the importance of thinking
aletheia as the clearing is patent. "Only because the essence of
being is *aletheia*, can the light of the light come into prominence"
(54: 218). Just as the *aletheia* is the struggle in which what is hidden
from us becomes unhidden, so the clearing is a timing as well as a

spacing (14: 81; 16: 630f). The fact that philosophy as metaphysics thinks what the clearing affords but not the clearing itself is due to the fact that the clearing is not only a clearing of what is present but also a clearing of the self-concealing presence (14: 88). A human being only is by moving from herself to something completely other than herself, i.e. "the clearing of being" (15: 386f). The clearing is the end of Heidegger's analysis of truth, as the un-grounded ground—or, in other words, the grounding abyss (*Ab-grund*)—of the other levels of truth. "*The essence of truth is the clearing for the self-concealing*" (65: 348). The self-concealing rages through the clearing, and, only if the ensuing struggle between hiddenness and unhiddenness happens and in its wholeheartedness dominates the "here" (*Da*), is it possible to succeed in moving out of the domain of sheer manipulation and towards the steadfastness of being-here (*Da-sein*). "Thus, truth is never only clearing, but unfolds as hidden just as primordially and wholeheartedly with the clearing. Both, clearing and hiddenness, are not two but the essential unfolding of the one, the truth itself." This unfolding or becoming of truth is nothing less than the appropriating event itself (65: 273, 329f; 66: 84f, 108–14, 314).

Conscience (*Gewissen*)

Conscience is the silent call of Dasein *from* its They-self, i.e. its absorption in the They, *to* the capability-of-being that is its alone as being-in-the-world. To the extent that Dasein is constantly listening to the din of the They, the call of conscience interrupts it. Conscience in this sense is an existential, a primordial phenomenon of being-here, a way Dasein discloses itself to itself. "In conscience Dasein calls itself ... The call comes *from* me and yet *over* me" (SZ 275). Neither God nor some anthropological, biological, or psychological factor, this one calling is Dasein itself. The call comes from the uncanniness of being thrown as an individual self into the world, something not determinable by anything worldly. Hence, insofar as it is ordinarily wrapped up in the They, the call comes as alien to Dasein. The call's uncanniness is the basic mood of the angst that brings Dasein face to face with the nothingness of the world and with its own individual capability-of-being.

The call of conscience in the existential sense summons Dasein to the fact that it is guilty in a primordial sense, not by virtue of something (some being) it owes others, but by virtue of existing or, in other words, by virtue of something it owes itself in existing. Each of us has been thrown into the world as the sort of being who, without having chosen to be at all, individually projects some possibilities rather than others. We are *not* the ground of our being, and we are the ground of *not* being some possibilities. As a thrown projection, situated between these two nullities (not the ground in one respect, being the ground of not projecting some possibilities in another), our existence is accordingly shot through with a distinctive, individuating indebtedness and responsibility. Being thus indebted and responsible simply by virtue of existing is being guilty (*Schuldigsein*) existentially.

One cannot choose not to have a conscience, but one can choose to want to have one. To understand conscience's call is to choose to want to have a conscience or, equivalently, to let oneself silently act on oneself on the basis of being-guilty in the existential sense. Letting oneself so act on oneself enables Dasein to be responsible and testifies to its authentic capability-of-being. In understanding conscience's call, the mood is one of uncanniness at being completely by oneself, i.e. the anxiety of conscience (*Gewissensangst*). Conscience attests to the authentic disclosedness in Dasein, as Dasein silently projects itself onto its ownmost being-guilty, all the while prepared for angst. This authentic disclosedness is resoluteness (SZ 295ff; for a later, critical take on "conscience" in connection with conscious certainty, see 67: 188).

Consciousness (*Bewusstsein*)

Beginning with Descartes, modern philosophy conceives consciousness, and so also self-consciousness, as fundamental and, in some sense, a priori. This conception is mistaken since consciousness, like intentionality, rests upon a more basic phenomenon: the comportment of Dasein as a being-in-the-world, which in turn supposes the clearing, Dasein's sojourn in the open. The idealism of modern philosophy is tied to its commitment to taking consciousness as fundamental (SZ 49, 62, 203, 207, 212, 363n; 89: 226). In Heidegger's first Marburg lectures he examines how consciousness came to be the theme of then present-day phenomenology, particularly given the absence of such a notion among the Greeks. He finds the answer in the kind of suspect care that underlies phenomenology and has a history that goes back to Descartes' philosophy and its medieval roots (17: 47, 106f).

Constancy (*Ständigkeit*)

Dasein is authentic to the extent that it constantly and resolutely projects itself on to the possibility of no-longer-being-able-to-be-here. Both the constancy of the self and the possible lack of the same (*Unselbstständigkeit*) require an existential–ontological inquiry since it is the only adequate access to the problems they present (SZ 117). Inauthenticity and a lack of self-constancy are characteristic of a self-identification with one's everyday, more-or-less anonymous social world, the They. So, too, there is a "constancy" nearest at hand, that is an inauthentic way of being-with. This inauthentic constancy is betrayed by a troubling obsession with maintaining a distinctive sort of distance (*Abständigkeit*) from others (catching up with them or keeping them down). The preoccupation with this distance runs hand-in-hand with everyday Dasein's comforting, inconspicuous immersion in the They. Through involvement in common, interchangeable practices (like using public means of transportation or information) and by relying exclusively upon the accessibility and acceptability of public criteria and interpretations, Dasein in its everydayness is no different from anyone else. Accordingly, the "'constancy' nearest at hand" is marked by a certain averageness, a leveling down of possibilities, and its publicity or public character that also accommodate Dasein's lassitude, relieving it of the burden of being.

Though this inauthentic constancy, absorbed into the They, is not the constancy of the self, it remains an existential (something Dasein does and discloses). Nonetheless, Dasein's ontological distinctiveness lies in its capacity for being constant in its selfhood. Dasein is ontologically different from the real and the on-hand, inasmuch as its standing or constitution (*Bestand*) consists, not in the substantiality of a substance, but in the "self-standing character" (*Selbständigkeit*) of the existing, caring self (SZ 303,

322). In Heidegger's later writings he emphasizes the related concept of steadfastness (*Inständigkeit*).

Conversation (*Gespräch*)

Glossing Hölderlin's verse "we are *a* conversation," Heidegger observes that "the being of humans is grounded in language, but this really happens only in conversation" (4: 40; 38: 24). In the "heavenly conversation" between humans and gods at a feast, each speaks from the heart about matters of fate, in contrast to matters that can be mastered, and, as a consequence, they speak to each other wholeheartedly, i.e. as friends. Just as language has its origin in such a conversation (feast), so, too, the conversation "makes" for friends rather than vice versa, "bringing them into their authentic essence, for which they do not of themselves and never directly suffice." Constantly threatened by prattle (*Geschwätz*), conversations do not always succeed, but when they do, they are poetic (52: 157ff, 162ff).

Correspond (*Entsprechen*)

"Correspondence" can be used to translate *Übereinstimmung* or the Latin *adequatio* (in *adequatio rei et intellectus*) to designate the truth-defining relation between things and understanding (judgment, proposition, representation, etc.). Truth as correspondence is derivative of truth as unhiddenness. However, "to correspond" is also a translation of another German word, *ent-sprechen*, which signifies listening to what language says. "The human being speaks only because he corresponds to language," where language is not the expression of thinking but the house of being, the place for thinking. "Language is the originary dimension within which humanity in general is first able to correspond to being and its claim, and, in corresponding, to belong to being. This originary corresponding, explicitly carried out, is thinking" (12: 29f; 11: 25f; 79: 71).

Curiosity (*Neugier*)

In SZ Heidegger characterizes curiosity as the everyday sort of *seeing* that is characteristic of the way the *They* discloses in general. This characterization draws upon Augustine's account of the temptation of curiosity as a *concupiscentia oculorum*, a craving on the part of the eyes, i.e. the desire to look in the sense of merely taking something in (*Nur-Vernehmen*). This tendency arises, Heidegger contends, when, in periods of repose, Dasein is no longer bound to the workworld and concerns itself only with the possibilities of seeing the world simply as it appears. Curiosity is thus Dasein's everyday tendency to let itself be carried along solely by the way the world appears. Exploiting the German etymology of the term, a combination of the new (*neu*) and avarice (*Gier*), Heidegger notes the specific restlessness that characterizes curiosity. It is a restless search for the new by jumping hastily from one thing to the other in a constant state of distraction rather than tarrying among things and wondrously contemplating them. Accordingly, the curious becomes dispersed among ever new possibilities, while never dwelling anywhere (*Aufenthaltslosigkeit*). Augustine is again the source of the related notion of dispersal into a plurality as falling away from one's proper calling and oneness (with God).

Danger (*Gefahr*)

By putting everything on order in a standing reserve, the positionality (*Ge-stell*)—the essence of modern technology, the destiny of being in the present epoch—completely neglects things and is oblivious to the world, i.e. to itself. It "stalks" the truth of being or, as the German word may also suggest, puts it behind or after everything else (*nachstellen*). This stalking (or "entrapment" as it is also translated) is the innermost essence of the positionality. All the positionality's ways of positioning and positing (*stellen*) beings (at the cost of their being) go into this stalking, and together they are the danger (79: 53). Since the positionality is nothing less than the hidden unfolding of historical being itself (the way beings are present to us and the way we relate to them in the present), the positionality is obliviously, vainly stalking itself. "In this respect, what is most dangerous about the danger consists in the fact that the danger conceals itself as the danger that it is" (79: 54). So, too, since the corresponding distress is also not experienced, the lack of distress is what is genuinely distressing.

Nonetheless, there are characteristic marks of the danger. The fact that millions perish in concentration camps, suffer and die of hunger, or languish in poverty are telltale signs that the danger remains concealed, because it continues to be distorted and obscured by the essence of technology, i.e. positionality. Another sign is the tendency to grapple with technology by technological means alone, thereby reinforcing the hiddenness of its essence and origins, while underestimating its power. "Technology is in its essence neither a means to some purpose nor is it itself a purpose ... The essence of technology is historical being itself in the essential shape of positionality. But the essence of the positionality is *the danger* ... not as technology but as historical being. The presence of the danger is historical being itself insofar as it entraps the truth of its essence with the forgottenness of this essence" (79: 62; 5: 280f, 292–6).

Darwinism

While the young Heidegger, defending Catholicism, criticized versions of the theory of descent (partly on scientific grounds), he later criticizes Darwinist emphasis on self-preservation, an emphasis made with a view to "an economic consideration of the human being." To construe self-preservation and adaptation as the relation between things on-hand (where one of the things is the environment) fails to do justice to animal or to human reality. In contrast to Darwinism's economic approach, Heidegger proposes an "ecological" approach (glossing the concept of the biologist Franz Doflein): "The word 'ecology' comes from *oikos*, house. It means research into where and how animals are at home, their manner of living in relation to their surrounding," not to be confused with a world or comporting themselves to a world. Crucial to Heidegger's criticism is an emphasis on the complex roles played by the organism's drives and facilities in interaction

Death (*Tod*)

Every moment that we are alive, death is a constant and definitive yet undetermined possibility. We cannot somehow overtake or outrun our death; we cannot even experience it as a particular entity (*als Seiendes*), and no one else can die our death for us. Death is definitive as the possibility of the end of any other possibility we might have. Yet it escapes the realm of what we can take care of (*Besorgen*) as well as the field of our solicitous relations with others (*Fürsorge*). Like a great love, it is most intimately ours—and yet not of our choosing (SZ 234–40, 250f, 257ff, 263). At the same time, it is a possibility that we are likely to ignore, elude, and conceal—underscoring our cognizance of its status as our pre-eminent possibility (SZ 252–5). "Death as Dasein's end is the possibility of Dasein that is most its own, not shared, certain and, as such, undetermined, and not capable of being overtaken" (SZ 258f, 263ff).

Because the "*existential* concept of death" pertains precisely to what belongs to us each individually (in the first person, as it were), it is not to be confused with the deceased (*Verstorbene*), the perishing (*Verenden*) of something alive, the demise (*Ableben*) of others, or the absence of what is "not yet." In regard to the deceased, our loss is not theirs nor can it be, since death in the existential sense is not shared. We are *in stricto senso* never on-hand but always "here," whereas the corpses that we come to be in perishing are precisely not "here" (SZ 241). In other words, dying is not perishing because perishing entails the accessibility of what perishes as something on-hand, *ante mortem* and *post mortem* (SZ 248). Biological–physiological, medical, psychological, biographical–historical, ethnological, and theological studies of death investigate Dasein's demise, an "intermediate phenomenon," co-determined by conceptions of perishing and the existential conception of dying. Death is also not anything like the absence of what is *not yet* the case—an unpaid bill, a full moon, a ripened fruit—since these are endings of something on-hand or handy. "In death Dasein neither is completed nor has it simply disappeared, nor has it become finished at all or fully accessible as something handy" (SZ 245).

Death is the possibility of being-here that is "most its own" (*eigenste*), precisely as "the possibility of no-longer-being-able-to-be-here" (SZ 250). Dasein projects this possibility *nolens volens*, even if by way of repressing it. Hence, to be-here authentically, Dasein has to project this possibility explicitly for itself. It has to "anticipate," literally "run ahead into" (*Vorlaufen in*), its death—again, not as something that can be actual for it or that it can make actual, but precisely as the possibility of the absence of its possibilities. Anticipating this defining possibility discloses the finality and finitude of existence, enabling us to become free for it. With this freedom for death comes a freedom to understand and choose among finite, factical possibilities authentically. Anticipating death is also liberating in the sense that it breaks the hold of any obdurate identification with some previously attained or expected possibilities. Being free for this ultimate possibility also serves as a check against being with others inauthentically, i.e. mistaking their possibilities for ours or foisting our possibilities on them (SZ 264). Anticipating death as Dasein's uniquely defining possibility exposes any forlornness on its part and confronts it with the possibility of being itself, without the support of any concerns or solicitude, "cut loose from the illusions of the They" (SZ 266).

Though the topic of death becomes less central in Heidegger's later works, he continues to draw on the liberating character of its anticipation. "In the unusualness and uniqueness of death, what is most unusual in all beings, historical being itself, opens itself up. But in order to be able to intimate something of this most primordial connection ... the relation to death itself ... the anticipating had to be made apparent ... not so that the mere 'nothing' is attained but the reverse, so that the openness for historical being might open itself completely and on the basis of what is most extreme" (65: 283ff). Whereas anticipating death is previously synonymous with Dasein's authenticity, in the *Contributions* "carrying out this being-towards-death is only necessary in the context of the task of laying the ground for the question of historical being's truth," i.e. "it is a duty only for the thinkers of another beginning" (65: 285). As the departure from beings, death also brings Dasein nearest to the nearness of the clearing of historical being (71: 193f; 70: 138f). Death is also "the shrine of the nothing...that unfolds as being itself" (79: 18).

Decision (*Entscheidung*)

Whereas resorting to a lottery is a way of evading a decision (in effect, a decision not to decide), to umpire is to embrace decision-making. In genuinely, i.e. non-arbitrarily, deciding, an umpire "becomes who he is supposed to be, *he* becomes *he himself*," since he is not this self prior to the decision. The decision is pre-reflective in the sense that, ignoring any relation to egoistic considerations, proclivities, and prejudices, he decides "completely on the basis of what he is supposed to decide" (38: 70ff). While being authentic is analogous to being an umpire in this sense, there is a crucial difference between an umpire's decision and the decision of who we are. With the umpire's decision, the matter is ended but the decision of who we are entails an ongoing decisiveness.

In lectures in the summer of 1934, following his resignation as rector, Heidegger speaks of genuine decisiveness in the context of higher education as a decision against traditional university practices and policies (including the division of faculties) and for "the authentic task of higher education," a task that he regards as coinciding with the national socialist revolution of the preceding year. He lambasts mere appearances of decisiveness, e.g. the rector appearing in a Nazi para-military uniform instead of traditional academic apparel, yet leaving the same old university practices in place. Continuing those practices is not a genuine decision but amounts to "closing oneself off" from what is genuinely happening. Genuine decisiveness is the same as "opening oneself" to it, i.e. *resoluteness* (38: 75–7).

Two years later Heidegger addresses the theme of decision, playing again on its etymology, only this time in the context of inquiring into the essence of historical being as the origin of the de-cision or division (*Ent-scheidung*) of gods and humans. While unorthodox to a fault, this use of the term (flagged by the hyphen) underscores the fact that the most basic sense of decision is not human or divine, and that human decisions are only authentic by corresponding to the primordial de-cision. It is scarcely possible to approach decision without reference to human choice. Indeed, this reference, he avers, proved to be a stumbling block to conceiving the SZ account of resoluteness as truth in the sense of openness. However, the de-cision is not fundamentally "moral-anthropological" or "existentiel"; it has "nothing in common with ... making a choice." Instead it is that division of gods and humans that lets the appropriating event of the open come into play, the open as the clearing for the self-concealing and what is yet un-decided. This de-cision thus makes room for a further decision, namely, the decision of owning up, or not, to this primordial de-cision. That further decision is also not so much a choice as it is a wholeheartedness that supposedly coincides with thinking and corresponding to the truth of historical being.

As a means of preparing for this impending decision, Heidegger lists several either/or decisions that spring from it "as historical necessities" (e.g. "whether the human being wills to remain a subject *or* grounds being-here," "whether art is an exhibition of lived-experience or the setting-into-work of truth," "whether the human being in general even dares the decision *or* whether he leaves himself over to the undecideness that the age takes as the 'pinnacle' of 'activity'"). What is common to this imposing list is *the one decision*, namely, whether historical being definitively withdraws, "whether this withdrawal ... becomes the first truth and another beginning of history" (65: 87–91, 93, 103; 40: 84).

That one decision requires human beings, both "the future ones" and those who prepare for them. The future ones include the few individuals who are the founders in poetry, thinking, deed, and sacrifice; the groups who in alliance with the founders make out "the laws for recasting beings"; and the many with a common historical ancestry. The agreement between the individual, the groups, and the many is dominated by the respective way that being is present to Dasein, and in the latter a "primordial gathering" is prepared. In and as this gathering, a "people" becomes historical (65: 96ff). The decision is not one of self-preservation, not least because to make the people's preservation the goal is to confuse a condition for setting a goal with the goal itself. Not a culture or world-view but only the truth of historical being is decisive (65: 97ff, 102f).

Descartes

Heidegger's first Marburg lectures contain his most extensive account of Descartes' philosophy, as a "decisive turning point in the history of philosophy," albeit only in the way that the present-day interprets itself under the dominance of theoretical knowing. Relying mostly on Descartes' *Meditations* and *Regulae*, Heidegger traces "the field of being disclosed by [Descartes'] care about known knowledge" and, with it, Descartes' account of the cogito, truth as certainty and its criterion both back to Aquinas and forward to Husserl (17: 128ff; 23: 105–44). Heidegger contends that, despite laying claim formally to the cogito "as absolute being," Descartes not only fails to inquire into its specific being but from the outset blocks any possible way of determining it. Nor does he recognize the need for its determination, since the *cogito* is certain (*esse certum*) and one with the creator (*esse creatum*) (17: 252f). Presumably much of the material from these lectures was planned for the Second Section of Part Two of SZ (SZ 40).

Though Part Two was never published, Heidegger devotes an entire section of Part One to the Cartesian ontology of the world in terms of *res extensa* due to its sharp contrast with his analysis of worldhood (SZ 89–101). While Descartes characterizes finite beings as created substances, whose substantiality consists in thinking or extension, he excuses himself from asking what substantiality or the infinite, uncreated being is (SZ 93f). In addition, without due warrant, he privileges mathematical knowing as "the sole and genuine access" to beings, such that only what is accessible in it "*is* in the authentic sense." In effect, as can be gathered from his translation of the sense of hardness into resistance (as a permanence in an extended place), he does not let innerworldly entities indicate their manner of being but instead "dictates" to the world what it authentically is, i.e. "constant onhandness." In the process, he blocks any path to understanding being-in-the-world (SZ 95–8).

In 1933 Heidegger offers a strident rebuke of the standard picture of Descartes as "the radical thinker" who places philosophy and science on a completely new footing, liberated from "the darkness of the middle ages." Descartes' radicalism is an "illusion," and his alleged new beginning is in reality "the commencement of a further essential degeneration of philosophy." The methodical character of the doubt serves a mathematical method that has pre-determined "what truly is" and harbors no doubts that the ground of knowledge must be simple and accessible to intuition. Yet the presupposition that philosophy should be subject to the mathematical method is "arbitrary, not justified by Descartes in any way." Equally unjustified is the presupposition that the doubt leading back to "the indubitable onhandness of the I that thinks" is the primordial way for a human being to come to itself. So, too, Descartes simply presupposes that the "consciousness of the I has priority over the being of the self." Moreover, by making the I into a *subjectum*, Descartes appropriates the medieval sense of the term, signifying what, lying immediately before us, cannot be doubted. Before Descartes, *subjectum* stood for anything on-hand; with Descartes "the 'I' becomes the exceptional subject with respect to which the remaining things first determine themselves as such ... becoming objects" (36/37: 37–46; 41: 106; see, too, 5: 98ff; 14: 76–9; 41: 98–108; 42: 50–61; 88: 71–95).

Destruction (*Destruktion*, S: destructuring)

Heidegger's earliest sketches of phenomenology include the notion of dismantling the preconceptions that stand in the way of authentically appropriating factical existence (58: 139; 59: 29). Only by tracing the ways in which we take up phenomena back to their historical roots is it possible for phenomena to present themselves as what they are (64: 75f). Because our experiences are always wrapped up in a foregoing interpretive context, formed by our language and traditions, phenomenology is necessarily destructive. It investigates what "foreconceptions" dominate an account, but it does so with an eye to determining the extent to which they are explicitly lifted from a pre-theoretical, basic experience as opposed to being made to correspond to theories already at hand (59: 93).

Such destruction of the tradition is necessary, thanks to Dasein's tendencies to equate its manner of being with that of things within-the-world and to accept tradition. Working against these two tendencies provides the structure, respectively, of the two parts of SZ, though Heidegger never publishes the second part, the aim of which was to be the explicit destruction of the tradition. The planned destruction was to begin with the Greeks who conceived being in terms of nature (the world as *physis*) as the overriding, i.e. present presence of things, a conception that is fatal to understanding—among many other things—the temporal and historical character of Dasein's being. It is essential to the project of fundamental ontology that we achieve transparency about its history. This task, guided by the question of being, is "the destruction of the transmitted content of ancient ontology ... to arrive at the original experiences from which the initial and subsequently leading determinations of being were acquired" (SZ 22).

Heidegger later criticizes the naiveté of this "ontological destruction" for its failure to recognize how being itself, far from presenting itself transparently, in fact conceals itself (15: 337, 395). Nonetheless, the destruction—precisely by dismantling the ways the ontological tradition obscures "the originary dispensation of being as presence"—affords a preliminary insight into the history, i.e. the destiny of being (14: 13).

Difference (*Differenz, Unterschied*)

The difference between being and beings is the most essential difference. In Heidegger's ontological–transcendental period, the difference is ontological. Whatever particular, innerworldly beings we are concerned with, theoretically or practically, we in some sense transcend them by understanding what it means for them to be. The "ground of the ontological difference" lies in "the *transcendence* of Dasein*," the way it is always in motion beyond beings, not to another entity, but to the world (the very sense of Dasein as being-in-the-world). Dasein's timely projection of its world (the unity of its temporal horizons) provides the sense of being that enables its inter-actions with innerworldly beings (9: 123, 134f; 24: 322; 27: 223).

In the *Contributions*, Heidegger considers transcendental conceptions of the ontological difference inadequate, since they cannot escape conceiving the difference between being and beings in terms of differences between particular beings. This way of conceiving the difference shows its metaphysical pedigree, since metaphysics thinks of being exclusively from the standpoint of beings. (The history of metaphysics is a history of disempowering being in favor of the limitless primacy of beings; 65: 427f, 449). The ontological difference, i.e. the metaphysical differentiation of being from beings, precludes any account of their unity and continues to treat being itself as a particular being (65: 250, 424).

At the same time, the ontological difference remains an "unavoidable" means of passage to the truth of historical being. The task of thinking is to grasp the ontological difference's origin and unity in the hidden difference of historical being and beings, the essence of which is the appropriating event (65: 272, 250, 423, 426, 467). The ontological difference is thus, in an important sense, provisional and transitional. Thinking must begin with this difference on the way to an initial clarification and then "leap over" this differentiation into its origin and unity (65: 207, 251, 451, 469). The key to thinking the difference in non-metaphysical terms is to recognize that it is not the result but the ground of thinking (70: 70–4).

In 1941 Heidegger observes that "historical being 'is' itself difference and never … one of the two differentiated" (70: 76). Similarly, in 1957 he notes that what matters is thinking "the difference *as* difference" (11: 56, 59). We only think being fundamentally when we think it in its difference from beings and vice versa. This difference cannot be represented since the attempt to represent it leads to construing difference (*Differenz*) as a relation (*Distinktion*) that we produce. The difference is instead something that we find in advance of representing. What we find is that being "comes over" beings, disclosing them, and by this means the unhiddenness of beings "arrives." This "coming over" and this "arrival" coincide; it is not as if there is being without beings or vice versa. Moreover, being in this context is not a universal; "there is being" only in this and that historical character. "Being in the sense of coming-over and disclosing, and beings as such in the sense of the self-concealing arrival unfold (as so distinguished) from the same, the dif-ference [*Unter-schied*]." This difference grants the "between" that both holds the coming-over and arrival apart and keeps them related to one another (11: 68–73; 12: 22–30).

Dilthey, Wilhelm (1833–1911)

Dilthey is known for his revival and development of hermeneutics as well as his attempt to provide a critical foundation for the humanities' method of sympathetically understanding (*Verstehen*) lived experience, in contrast to the natural sciences' method of explaining (*Erklären*) external reality. Dilthey does not provide a systematic account of his work, but this alleged weakness, Heidegger submits, is indicative of his strengths, especially since he at times countenances the "historically *conditioned* character" of what traditional philosophers posit as absolute. From the outside Dilthey's main interest lies in grounding the humanities, yet he achieves much more. His achievement can be gathered from his remark that "thinking is bound by an inner compulsion to life, it is itself a form of life." Regarding the humanities as a "further development of factical life-experience," Dilthey recognizes that "life can be interpreted on the basis of itself." Thus Heidegger touts and draws upon Dilthey's philosophy for its promise of tackling "the problem of lived experience in an actually primordial way," for "understanding the entire world from life," and for interpreting life as "an efficacious context." Nonetheless, Heidegger criticizes him for letting a reified construal of life (the concern with questions of "constitution") insinuate itself into his philosophy. As a result, Dilthey sees the phenomena "only from the outside, albeit not from the outside in terms of nature but from the outside in terms of the history of spirit" (59: 152–68; 56/57: 163–6; 5: 99f).

Disclosedness (*Erschlossenheit*)

"Phenomenological truth is the disclosedness of being" (SZ 38). The disclosedness of being contrasts with the discovery (*Entdecktheit*) of beings (SZ 200f, 203, 210, 220–8, 297, 420). Dasein is able to discover entities and features of them (ontic truths) only because it is disclosedness itself or, equivalently, the clearing that enables the encounter with particular beings (SZ 133, 182). Disclosedness is not knowledge or willing since dispositions and moods can disclose to being-here "that it is and has to be" while leaving its whence and wherefore completely in the dark (SZ 134–7). Understanding discloses to Dasein its way of being (including its meaningfulness, what it is for-the-sake-of, and its capability-of-being) (SZ 143–7). "As existentials, disposedness and understanding characterize the primordial disclosedness of being-in-the-world" (SZ 148, 160, 182). In the final chapters of SZ Heidegger analyzes the timely character of disclosedness in general, the disclosedness of the world, the workworld, and the environment in particular (SZ 335–52, 356, 364–8), as well as the disclosedness of one's historical situation and destiny (SZ 384ff, 397). Dasein can only take time for itself and even lose time because a time has been allotted to it as "an ecstatically extended timeliness" whose disclosedness is grounded in that timeliness (SZ 410).

Discourse (*Rede*)

Discourse or talk (an alternative translation) is an existential, i.e. it is constitutive of the way Dasein exists and discloses itself. The basic existentials in SZ—one's disposition and understanding—reside within an intelligibility that has been articulated in discourse even before it is interpreted. Equally as basic as any existential, "discourse thus already underlies interpretation and assertion." We exist as discursive beings and, in and through that discursiveness, what it means to be (including to be this or that, even ourselves) discloses itself to us.

Heidegger accordingly dubs discourse "existential language," i.e. the process of speaking and listening to one another, in which our existence is disclosed to us. What is articulated in discourse is a "sense" (*Sinn*). What is sorted out is a "whole of meaning" that can in turn be broken up into meanings (*Bedeutungen*). Discourse meaningfully articulates or sorts out the intelligibility of being-in-the-world (SZ 162). Language (*Sprache*) is discourse's specifically worldly being insofar as, once spoken or put into words, it can become something handy within-the-world. However, language can also be treated as something on-hand in nature and culture, open for inspection like any other natural phenomenon or cultural artifact.

Discourse always sorts out meaningfully the intelligibility of being-in-the-world, particularly in our shared concerns, and, in that sense, it is invariably *about* something. Not only determinate assertions, but wishes, commands, and recommendations are about something. Its structure includes (1) being about something (*Worüber*), (2) what is said as such (*Geredete*), (3) communication (*Mitteilung*), and (4) conveying or making itself known (*Bekundung*). These four existential characters make language possible (SZ 162f).

The roles that hearing (*hören*) and keeping silent play in discourse illustrate its connection with understanding and intelligibility. For example, when we did not hear someone correctly, we often say that we did not understand her. When we do hear, it is in virtue of the fact that we already have an understanding. Thus, "we never hear noises and complexes of sounds" but instead "the motorcycle ... the north wind, the woodpecker tapping, the crackling fire" (SZ 165). So, too, when we hear someone speaking, we hear, not so much the vocalization, but what they are saying. But while being rooted in understanding, hearing also makes plain the shared character of understanding—even within a single Dasein. Thus, Heidegger notes that hearing (or listening to: *hören auf*) is Dasein's openness for others. But he adds that it is also Dasein's authentic openness to its ownmost potential, in the sense of "hearing the voice of the friend that each Dasein carries within herself" (SZ 163). At the same time, being-with establishes itself in listening to one another, where hearing can lead to obeying and hearkening as well as to tuning others or oneself out.

In SZ Heidegger singles out two modes of discourse: the everyday sort of discourse, namely, idle talk or palaver (*Gerede*), characteristic of the fallenness of the They, and conscience, the exceptional mode of discourse that calls Dasein from "the public idle talk of the They" to its authentic self. In idle talk, hearsay, and quick reads, keeping informed about what is said as such and passing it on take precedence over concern for what the discourse is about. "Idle talk is the possibility of understanding everything without a foregoing appropriation of the matter" (SZ 169). Whereas in idle talk Dasein overhears itself, listening only to the They-self, conscience calls Dasein silently to its self, to the capability of being that is most its own (SZ 269ff, 277, 296).

Disposedness (*Befindlichkeit*, MR: state of mind, S: attunement)

Dasein always already finds itself disposed to being one way or another. When we ask someone how he is, we are asking how he feels, and how he feels—his mood—corresponds to his disposition. The German word translated "disposedness" is constructed from the verbal construction *sich befinden*. The query *Wie befinden Sie sich?* means simply "How are you?" or, more literally, "How do you find yourself [to be]?" Disposedness is a *basic existential*, a way of being-here that discloses its way of being to it. Disposedness discloses Dasein's thrownness, its being-in-the-world as a whole, and its openness to the world (SZ 137, 340). The first basic existential treated in SZ, disposedness is the primary indicator of existence. In contrast to "I think, therefore I am," it would be more correct to assert "I feel, therefore I exist." How Dasein is disposed brings it "more or less explicitly and authentically face to face with its 'that it is and that, as the entity that it is, it has to be in its potential-to-be'" (SZ 276). As a basic existential, disposedness is constitutive of existence generally. Understanding, for example, is always disposed; even indifference is a way of being disposed. We are typically (ontically) familiar with modes of disposedness in the form of moods or affects, which are accordingly originary and disclosive in a holistic way. For example, while fearing makes up who we are, and discloses something essential about us, it does not do so apart from the fearfulness of the situation and the threats within it. A mood or affect is constitutive of our being-in-the-world as a whole. As early as 1929 Heidegger dispenses with the term *Befindlichkeit* in favor of mood (*Stimmung*) while retaining key features of the original analysis sketched above. (In 1941, Heidegger acknowledges that his SZ conception of *Befindlichkeit* coincides with his later account of *Stimmung*; see 70: 131).

Dwelling (*Wohnen*)

Dwelling is "*the basic feature* of being, in keeping with which the mortals exist" (7: 163). Though Dasein's "being in" is already linked with dwelling in SZ (SZ 54), Heidegger's later work places the emphasis on dwelling as mortals' manner of "being on earth" and so, too, under the sky and before the divinities, since each of these four (earth, sky, divinities, mortals) entails the others. More precisely, "by *dwelling*, mortals *are* in the fourfold," safeguarding each in its distinctive unfolding as one (7: 152). This dwelling takes place precisely where mortals are, namely, among things. Inasmuch as dwelling safeguards the fourfold by bringing it to bear on things, dwelling is a kind of building, cultivating things that grow and erecting things that do not. Thus, things built, e.g. bridges, are places that allow for the fourfold, while also arranging and safeguarding it. This safeguarding is "the simple essence of dwelling" (7: 161). Thinking, like building, belongs unavoidably to dwelling, and yet neither thinking nor building is sufficient for dwelling as long as they are pursued apart "instead of listening to one another" (7: 163).

Epoch (*Epoche*)

In a twist on the Stoics' and Husserl's use of this term (to designate a suspension of judgment), "epoch" signifies how being "keeps to itself" or "holds back," but in such a way that a world "suddenly and unexpectedly" opens up and lasts for a time (5: 337f, 265, 371). Because being (the presence of beings) withdraws, beings are left as the exclusive standard for being (6.2: 347, 440). As a result, each epoch necessarily misnames and misconstrues being by thinking it in terms of beings or, what is the same, failing to come to terms with its withdrawal. While there is a tradition from epoch to epoch and their succession is not contingent, they are not derivable from one another. Instead each springs from the same hidden source (10: 135f; 14: 12f). Each epoch is a way that *presence* transmits itself to Western humanity (15: 367). The process by which being presents itself as the objectivity of objects, but in essence withdraws from us, specifies a new epoch of the withdrawal, i.e. modernity (10: 83, 90, 101). The appropriating event that consummates the forgottenness of the essence of being determines the present, technological epoch in which being unfolds as positionality. "It is the epoch of the complete neglect of the thing via positionality" (79: 51). "The danger is the epoch of historical being," i.e. its withdrawal, "unfolding as positionality" (79: 72).

Errancy (*Irre*)

Dasein errs, passing by the mystery of being, while insistently turning to what is accessible. Yet this erring is not a matter of occasionally going astray. To the contrary, *"the errancy* is inherent to the Da of Dasein," the "space" that opens up as the interplay of unhiddenness and illusion. Errancy is not an error or mistake in thinking or representing within some already secured region of objects, though it is the ground of such inevitable errors. The ground of errancy is "the primordial, originary hiddenness, in whose regions knowing does not reach because it is excluded from the clearing." Errancy is the concealment of being from Dasein, and this concealment is essential to the event that appropriates them to one another. In other words, "the errancy itself is the clearing of historical being," and, far from being opposed to truth, it is "the appearing of the truth itself in its own essence." This errancy, grounded in being's hiddenness, gives rise to a raft of errors from the most ordinary oversights to the most decisive blunders in human history. At the same time in the errancy, being's hiddenness becomes apparent. Thus, errancy also creates the possibility for human beings to lift themselves up, "by experiencing the errancy itself and not mistaking the mystery of being-here" (5: 337; 9: 196f; 40: 116f; 66: 259; 69: 150; 71: 93f). "How does it come about that human beings misconstrue historical being so much? Because they must be exposed to beings in order to experience the truth of historical being. In this exposure, beings are the truth, the open and they are this because historical being unfolds as the self-concealing" (65: 255).

Essence (*Wesen*)

Phenomenologists are concerned with the discernment of essences. Heidegger is no exception, though he also argues that any such discernment is grounded in existential understanding (SZ 147). From beginning to end, his writings are replete with references to essences and what is essential. Yet the first use of the term in SZ is in scare quotes ("Dasein's 'essence' lies in its existence"), already suggesting an uncomfortable reliance upon its traditional significance as *essentia* (SZ 42, 133, 214; 9: 327). In "On the Essence of Truth" Heidegger argues that this question is bound up with the question of the truth of essence (just as later the essence of language becomes a question of the language of essence). In contrast to the traditional understanding of essence as whatness or reality, he proposes understanding essence "verbally," in terms of the clearing that is the basic feature of historical being (9: 201; 12: 166).

In the late 1930s Heidegger revisits the question of essence. For the Greeks, universality (holding for many) is a consequence, not the genuine mark, of an essence. Instead "essence" is synonymous with the "being-*ness* of a being," conceived as what is constantly present and unhidden, i.e. what constantly shows itself, affording a look (*eidos*) of itself and enabling a representation or perception of it. Alternatively, the essence is what something truly is, what it is in truth. Thanks to this conception, Plato and Aristotle were able to identify the essence (beingness) of being respectively with *idea* and *ousia*. The *idea* is the essence of a being because it is the presumed, dominating look that a being presents and that we have in view, albeit not thematically, whenever we relate to that being. Similarly, the *ousia* is the essence because it is *to ti en einai* (the what it already was [for something] to be), what is presupposed by anything else that may be said of that thing (what in a certain sense the respective thing already "was" before it became the individual) (45: 58–75; 65: 288). This conception of the beingness of beings runs counter to contemporary sensibilities, where reality is identified, by contrast, with the individual on-hand here and now. Nevertheless, even today when essences are investigated, the investigation focuses on the whatness of beings while "bracketing" the on-handness, the actuality of the respective individual beings (45: 71).

Heidegger agrees with the Greeks that essence is not a concept or empty universal but what is most essential to being (45: 30, 37f). At the same time, his rejection of the Greek identification of being with beingness in the sense of constant presence demands a re-interpretation of the concept of essence. The Greek sources of the concept of essence explain his contention that the question of truth's essence entails the question of essence's truth. For Heidegger truth is *aletheia* in the sense of the emergence of unhiddenness from hiddenness. That is to say that truth is not unhiddenness itself. "The 'essence' of truth is a happening that is more actual and more effective than all occurrences and facts, because it is their ground" (45: 44).

"For essence—verbally understood—is indeed only the way something is, how it is." It is "the ground of the inner possibility of what is initially and in general taken as familiar." Whereas traditional notions of essence serve the pretense of being independent of being, the verbal understanding thinks the essence on the basis of historical being, i.e. the appropriating event. How one conceives essence depends upon how one understands being and truth. If being is projected as a constant presence or as timeless, essence is determined accordingly. However, if being is projected as temporal, then essence is itself timely (9: 186; 49: 60f, 68f; 65: 288f). Heidegger uses *wesen* as a verb, e.g. *Seyn west als Ereignis*, i.e. "Historical being unfolds as appropriating event," or *Die Wahrheit "ist" nie, sondern west*, i.e. "The truth never is, but unfolds instead" (65: 342, 344). He also employs *Wesung*, e.g. *Wesung ist die zum Seyn gehörige, ihm entspringende Wahrheit selbst*, i.e. "the essential unfolding is the truth itself, inherent in historical being, springing from it" (65: 247, 258f, 262f, 351, 388). "The happening of the truth of historical being ... is the essential unfolding" (65: 288), "the essential unfolding of the 'here' [*Da*] (the clearing for the self-concealing) (65: 330). By no means universal, *Wesung* determines what is essential in the sense of what is "primordially-unique" (65: 66). Historical being essentially unfolds only in the moment where Dasein leaps ahead into the appropriating event (65: 75; 7: 44; 12: 190).

Ethics (*Ethik*)

If ethics is study of the good life or of the principles of right and wrong, the existential analysis of SZ is not an ethics. However, it does present reasons to be wary of theories of value not founded upon the way human beings are with-one-another (SZ 99, 286). Moreover, by differentiating authentic and inauthentic ways of being-with-one another, namely, liberating and domineering relationships respectively, the existential analysis provides the rudiments of an ethics. For example, being-with-others, not to be confused with being-alongside anything else, is a condition for sympathy rather than vice versa. Similarly, the ontological analysis of Dasein yields existential conceptions of phenomena presupposed by ethics (e.g. conscience, freedom, responsibility, authenticity, and selfhood). Hence, the existential analysis in SZ, while presumably neutral on questions of the good and the right, has implications for ethics, demonstrating that (and, to an extent, also how) the ontology of Dasein, not that of beings on-hand, is the condition of the possibility of morality (SZ 286, 293).

A year after the publication of SZ, Heidegger introduces metontology as the inquiry that turns from fundamental ontology to beings as a whole, in light of the fact that the understanding presupposes the factical existence of human beings, which in turn presupposes the factual on-handness of nature. "Here, too, in the domain of metontological-existentiell inquiry, is the domain of the metaphysics of existence (here the question of an ethics may be raised for the first time)" (26: 199, 136). Yet this passing mention bears no fruit, as Heidegger aborts the project of metontology.

Ethical concerns permeate his thinking in the fateful early 1930s. He extols pure willing as the basis of Kant's categorical imperative (31: 284f) and portrays knowledge of "the spiritual-political mission of the German people" as the "demanding knowledge of what must be *before* anything else and *for* everything else, if the nation should grow into its greatness" (36/37: 4). Later in the decade, he criticizes the traditional equation of being with presence for its inability to countenance what ought-to-be (*das Gesollte*) and value (40: 205–11). He also identifies the nihilistic effects of equating being with power and the will to power in the form of machination, the gigantic, and their political expressions (Americanism, Bolshevism, and National Socialism). Since that equation is rooted, not in human failing, but in historical being's self-concealment, thinking the latter is diagnostic. Yet it is also key to human liberation, i.e. to human beings becoming who they authentically are, namely, being-here, standing with gratitude, steadfast reserve, and humble awe in that appropriating event. Eschewing "metaphysical explanations" of human beings as sinners or beyond good and evil, Heidegger identifies "the nobility of the poverty of the historical essence of the human being," namely, dispensing with beings, guarding historical being as the appropriating event (the self-concealing clearing) (65: 491; 66: 148; 69: 110f; 70: 113, 132; 71: 212f).

Heidegger's post-war discussion of dwelling poetically and thinking outside positionality as the essence of technology continues this call to being-in-the-world in a way at odds with the notion that everything is useful (i.e. a potentially useful part of a standing reserve). The supreme human action is thinking authentically, and authentic thinking consists in corresponding to a *claim* that being makes on us (12: 30, 166, 169f). Acknowledging the pressing question of ethics, Heidegger notes its traditional connection with ontology. Looking to the Greek meaning of *ethos* before such disciplines arose, he notes that *ethos* is the familiar human abode that is also the open region for the unfamiliar divine presence. If, in keeping with this basic sense of *ethos*, "ethics" means considering this human abode, "then the very thinking that thinks the truth of being as the originary element of the human as ek-sisting, is in itself the primordial ethics" (9: 313, 356).

Everydayness (*Alltäglichkeit*)

Heidegger orients the existential analysis of Dasein to everydayness as the way of being that is nearest to us, yet repeatedly skipped over. Everydayness is Dasein's inconspicuous, average way of existing, the way it is "initially and for the most part" (SZ 16f, 66, 370). "All existing as it is" comes from and goes back to Dasein's everyday, indifferent way of being, dubbed its "averageness." Not a mere aspect of Dasein, everydayness embodies "the structure of existentiality a priori" (SZ 43f, 50). Dasein's concern, circumspection, the inconspicuous context of its implements, and its spacings are all part of its average everydayness (SZ 73, 81, 105ff). In Dasein's everydayness it is predominantly "captivated" (*benommen*) by its world, and the They is "who" it is (SZ 113f, 127f). Idle talk, curiosity, and ambiguity characterize how Dasein is its Da everyday, namely, as fallen. "Fallenness is a basic type of being of everydayness," i.e. a lost, inauthentic everydayness, so much so that authentic existence is a modification of fallen everydayness (SZ 175, 178–81, 313, 376). "Everydayness takes Dasein as something handy that is procured [*besorgt*], i.e. administered and reckoned away" (SZ 289). Everydayness has an obvious temporal sense. It makes up how we comport ourselves day after day and "as a rule." An entire section of SZ (§ 71) is devoted to "The Temporal Sense of the Everydayness of Dasein" (SZ 370ff).

Existence (*Existenz*)

"Existence" can be a translation of the Latin *existentia*, traditionally signifying reality or being-on-hand. Since being-on-hand is essentially not being-here (*Dasein*), Heidegger reserves the Latin term for this traditional significance but employs 'existence' exclusively for Dasein. More precisely, existence is the being Dasein always comports itself to, one way or another. "The 'essence' of Dasein lies in its existence." Dasein invariably understands itself on the basis of its existence as the possibility of being itself or not. Existence can be authentic or inauthentic accordingly. This possibility is "ontically" decided by the respective Dasein, guided by an "existentiel" understanding, without need for the theoretical transparency provided by "existential" analysis and understanding of the structures of existence (which together make up the "existentiality of existence"). Whereas fundamental ontology is grounded in the existential analysis, the roots of the latter are ultimately "existentiel, i.e. ontic." Existentials are the characters of Dasein's being that make up its existentiality. Since Dasein is its disclosedness, existentials at once constitute-and-disclose existence as Dasein's being (SZ 12f, 42f, 53, 183ff, 201, 212, 232f, 260, 298, 302f, 304). "The primordial ontological ground of Dasein's existentiality is *temporality*" (SZ 234). Existence is in motion, but its motion is not the movement of something on-hand. Instead it is the happening that determines existence as historical (SZ 374f, 382, 386).

Categories are the other basic possible ways of characterizing being. The problem of categories—not least their plurality and difference from other ways of speaking about being (particularly in the context of Aristotle's metaphysics)—profoundly affected the young Heidegger. However, since categories historically derive from the ways of addressing and passing judgment on what is encountered within-the-world, i.e. beings other than Dasein, he distinguishes existentials sharply from categories. Whereas categories answer to the question of what (in the broadest sense) something is, when we come across a stranger we are more likely to ask who, not what, she is (SZ 44f, 56, 88, 143).

Being-in, being-alongside, concern, solicitude, world-hood, the They, possibility, and sense are examples of existentials. Death, conscience, and guilt are existential phenomena (SZ 240, 270,

317). At times Heidegger identifies disposedness and understanding as the two fundamental existentials (SZ 134, 143, 148, 150, 160, 336). Yet truth is a fundamental existential as well (SZ 297). Discourse is a primordial existential (SZ 161, 165), and fallenness is an existential mode of being-in-the-world (SZ 176). All four (disposedness, understanding, discourse, fallenness) are Dasein's "most general structures" (SZ 270). Existence itself is an existential determination, as are facticity and fallenness, and all three together, as a unity, make up the fundamental ontological character of care (SZ 191ff, 249f, 284, 316, 328, 350).

"The substance of the human being is not spirit as the synthesis of soul and body but existence" (SZ 117). To many of Heidegger's contemporaries, this observation suggested parallels with Kierkegaard's and Jaspers' conceptions of existence. However, the "existentiel" concept of existence in their thought concerns the human self as an entity, "insofar as it is interested for its own sake as this entity." By contrast, the "existential" concept of existence in SZ concerns the human self, "insofar as it is related, not to a self as an entity, but to being and the relation to being." That relation is ec-static or "ek-sistent." That is to say, by projecting being on to time and standing out in the openness of time, Dasein is exposed to the unhiddenness of beings as such (49: 39, 45, 53f, 60). To be sure, for the most part, we are immersed in beings, an immersion that Heidegger calls "insistence" (*Insistenz*). While "the essence of the human being consists in its existence," existence is not a given but something that human beings can come to. In order to make the transition to existence (i.e. to ek-sistence in contrast to insistence) human beings must be transformed by it, and this transformation is a matter of letting be, i.e. freedom (9: 189f, 35: 78, 85ff, 90–93). Since Jaspers' publication of his "Philosophy of Existence" (1931), Heidegger substitutes "steadfastness" (*Inständigkeit*) for "existence" in the "dictionary of thinking" (49: 54; see, however, 6.2: 432–5, 437f).

Facticity (*Faktizität*)

In Heidegger's earliest lectures he attempts a phenomenological analysis of life in terms of the largely pre-reflective, self-referential experience of a world of meanings and relations. "Facticity" designates that world of meanings and relations, which is undetachable from life itself (58: 101–10). "Factical life in its facticity, its richness of relations, is what is nearest to us; we are it itself" (58: 175). In contrast to a matter of fact in the sense of *factum brutum* (such as the fact that something on-hand is a certain mineral), facticity includes "the being-in-the-world of an 'inner-wordly' being but in such a way that this being can understand itself as bound up in its 'destiny' with the being of beings that it encounters within its own world" (SZ 55f, 135). Not something that is given in an intuition, Dasein's facticity disperses it into specific ways of "being-in," and, while its thrownness signals the "*facticity of being handed over*" to itself, both what it is capable of being and its way of "being swept up into the whirlpool of the They's inauthenticity" are inherent to its facticity. "Dasein exists factically," and, together with existence and fallenness, facticity is a "fundamental ontological character" of Dasein as care. Also inherent in facticity are various ways of being "closed off" and "covered up," accounting for the fact that Dasein is equiprimordially in the truth and untruth (SZ 55f, 135, 145, 179, 181, 191ff, 222, 229, 276, 284, 298, 316, 328).

Fallenness (*Verfallen*, MR: falling, S: falling prey)

A basic existential, fallenness is Dasein's everyday propensity to become absorbed into the world into which it has been thrown, i.e. the world of its concerns (*die besorgte >>Welt<<*), and to lose itself in the They, the public ways of being with one another where idle talk, curiosity, and ambiguity are the norm. "Fall" here does not suppose a state before the fall, as in the fall of original sin. Moreover, far from being something on-hand to which Dasein relates, the world is part of Dasein's being or, more precisely, its projection. Nonetheless, by falling prey to it, Dasein "falls away" (*abfällt*) from itself. As such, fallenness makes precise what it means to be inauthentic, to fail to be oneself (SZ 176). In falling prey to the world, Dasein is in motion, constantly being seduced (tempted), tranquilized (sedated), alienated, and ensnared by the They. In this movement within its own being, Dasein plunges into the groundlessness of everyday existence, though the plunge itself is hidden by public interpretations of existence. This plunge is a vortex, constantly tearing Dasein away from its authenticity, but a vortex inherent to its thrownness and facticity (SZ 176–9).

Fate (*Schicksal*)

Fate is Hölderlin's name for historical being; as such, it is "the uncanny that is always annoying to everything small and calculating" (39: 229). Fate seems blind only because we are blinded by the fact that, trying to fit it into our calculations, we confront it merely as the unpredictable. For thinking that only calculates, fate must be an impenetrable cause or its effect. In stark contrast to this sort of thinking, Hölderlin names and thinks the essential ground of fate as *wholeheartedness*. The appropriating event of the fête brings everything apt into harmony with fate; the fête is the time-space and the "most wholehearted balance, since each 'is, as it is'" —and by no means devoid of difference (52: 92, 98). The holiday celebrates this balance in advance as the uniqueness that, like the feast itself, is nothing common in the sense of something used, needed and calculable. By contrast, it has is own way of remaining, though it is also fundamentally different from any interruption of work; it is an expecting (52: 93F).

Fit (*Fuge*)

The fit stands for the limits under which an entity enters into appearances, enabling it to display itself for what it is. The fit is dynamic, as in the case of the fit of a plant and soil, fish and water, giving rise to talk of fitting (*Fug*) and fittingness (*Fügung*). The fit fits presences and absences together into a movement, just as a fugue fits movements together within a single movement. Philosophy is a fugue or fit in beings that avails itself of their truth, where the availing (*Verfügung*) fits itself to historical being (65: 45). *Fug* translates the Greek *dike*, a metaphysical not a moral concept, signifying the way the overwhelming force displays itself, its sway, and forces everything to fit in and fit themselves to it (40: 169).

Explaining why Plato contends that philosophers should reign, Heidegger observes: "Knowing *dike*, the laws of the fittingness of the being of beings, is philosophy" (6.1: 168). As the dynamic interplay of presence and absence at once, the fit is a *logos*, a gathering in which things are differentiated and thus articulated. The fit of things gathers them together into presence that "whiles away" (5: 368f). Similarly, the holy sends (*schickt*) the divine and the human their places, and this sending "fits" the relations of the holy to gods and humans and, vice versa, the relations of gods and humans to one another and this relatedness to the holy. "The unity and simplicity of these primordial relations is the fit that fits everything and in each respective case determines what the fitting [*Fug*] is. We call the fit [*Fuge*] historical being, within which every entity unfolds" (52: 100; 6.1: 171).

Formal indication (*formale Anzeige*)

In Heidegger's Marburg years as well as in lectures given before and afterwards in Freiburg, he describes his concepts as "formal indications" and his method as one that "formally indicates" the phenomena in question. Philosophical discourse is exposed to an "essential misinterpretation of its content," the view that everything, insofar as it has been articulated, is something on-hand. With the aim of "being able, at least relatively, to elude" that misinterpretation, Heidegger takes philosophical concepts as formal indications. A formal indication is a way of pointing to existential phenomena, roughly fixing their preliminary senses and the corresponding manner of retrieving those senses, while at the same time deflecting any "uncritical lapse" into a conception that would foreclose pursuit of their genuine sense. Formal indications accordingly have a "referring-prohibitive" function. Their "fundamental sense" is based upon the insight that, while any interpretation must emerge from our original access to phenomena, existential phenomena are not given to us directly. Hence, they need to be indicated but in a purely formal, revisable fashion. The sense of a concept as a formal indication is less a matter of content than a matter of enactment or performance (*Vollzugssinn*). The formal indication also gives notice that the sense of access (*Bezugssinn*) to the phenomena is not originally theoretical. Formal indications in this dual sense are requisite for philosophy since it is necessarily reflexive, requiring a retrieval of what is not given directly. This retrieval, moreover, is not possible without a transformation of the philosopher herself. Whereas our tendency to plunge into the usual, ostensive ways of considering things makes formal indications possible and necessary, philosophy runs counter to this plunge that is, in effect, our "ruin." (9: 9ff, 29, 65f; 29/30: 422, 430f; 31: 20; 60: 62–5; 61: 19f, 32ff, 42, 51–4, 59–62, 80, 131–55). In SZ Heidegger employs the notion of a formal indication—but without any explanation (SZ 52f, 114–17, 179, 231, 313ff). Examples of formal indications are the concepts of existence, caring, comportment, life, death, facticity, the "I," the "am" of "I am," ruin, nothing, and philosophy.

Fourfold (*Geviert*)

Fourfold is a useful but mildly misleading translation of the neologism *Geviert*, misleading because Heidegger stresses the "onefold of the Four." Heidegger introduces the fourfold by way of identifying "dwelling" with "being on earth." Being on earth, being "beneath the sky," "remaining before the divinities," and "belonging together with other human beings" all entail one another. Yet the fact that we are already thinking the other three whenever we think one of the Four does not mean that we are considering how they are onefold. In order to consider how earth and sky, divinities and mortals form the one-fold of the Four, it is necessary to see them as constituting things. Heidegger discusses bridges and a jug as examples of "things" that, each in its own way, gather the fourfold together and precisely *are* the place of this gathering (7: 154–60, 168–79).

"Mortals *are* in the fourfold, in that they *dwell.*" This way of dwelling is itself a fourfold safeguarding: freeing the earth to itself (the antithesis of subjecting and exploiting it), allowing the heavens and their times to take their course (the antithesis of today's rest-less 24/7), awaiting the divinities and their grace (the antithesis of making gods for oneself or serving idols), and guiding mortals to a "good death" (the antithesis of making death as the empty nothing into a goal or blindly staring at it as the end). Yet what ties this fourfold safeguarding into a unity is the way that dwelling brings it to bear upon things—something that happens only if things themselves are allowed to unfold in their own essential way (7: 151ff).

In the early 1940s Heidegger assigns the world a place in a fourfold relation that also includes earth, divinities, and humans (70: 157). By the end of the 1940s, however, the world embraces a fourfold, historical structure, consisting of a constellation for earth and sky, divinities and mortals, something that may or may not happen.

Heidegger reads "Hölderlin's Earth and Heaven" as the poet's commemoration of Greece as a unity of the fourfold (though Heidegger does not name it so in the essay): the earth as the structure for the heavens, manifesting the divine, all appearing in a special, philosophical light to humans who think and write poetically. In this unity of heaven and earth, gods and humans, each is in-finitely related to the other without being centered in any of them. These relations are expressed in the voices of all four, resonating in one another, while "destiny gathers together the entire infinite relation in these four voices." Destiny is their "all-gathering in-ception" (*An-fang*). The inception (beginning) is something that persists only as long as it is coming (*Anfang bleibt als Ankunft*) (4: 170ff). In this sense the fourfold remains the beginning that is still coming. The East—Greece as the "morning land"—is the great beginning, and the West only is by becoming what the East can come to. Heidegger asks whether the West in this sense still exists (given that it has become Europe). The earth and heaven of the poem have vanished, the in-finite relation of the fourfold seems destroyed where everything is made available and on order. But perhaps it is not destroyed; perhaps it has never made its appearance in our history and is at most blocked and refused. In this case it would remain for us to ponder this refusal and listen to it where it is spoken of, namely, in Hölderlin's poem (4: 176).

Freedom (*Freiheit*)

Heidegger returns to the theme of freedom repeatedly during his career. Three different senses of "freedom" are patent: (1) existential freedom (the freedom to choose to be oneself), (2) transcendental freedom (freedom as the origin of grounds), and (3) liberating freedom (freeing humans to Dasein). Following reviews of these three senses, this entry ends with a gloss of Heidegger's remarks on freedom in the history of philosophy.

(1) *Existential freedom.* Dasein has the freedom to choose to be itself, i.e. to be authentic or inauthentic (the so-called freedom of the They-self), albeit always within the boundaries of its thrownness and finitude (SZ 188, 193, 228, 232, 262, 276, 285, 366, 384). "Dasein can only be free in its positive possibilities when the idle talk that covers things up has lost its effectiveness and the 'common' interest has died out" (SZ 174). In SZ Heidegger conceives of freedom in two ways, existential and existentiel, the former as the condition of the latter (SZ 193, 199). Dasein has the freedom to choose itself only by "being-free" for this freedom, and being-free for it coincides with being-free for "the authenticity of its being as a possibility that it always already is" (SZ 188, 191, 285, 312). In order for Dasein to be authentic and, thus, existentially free, it must be free for its most defining possibility, its death (SZ 144, 188, 264, 384f). Being free for death consists in anticipating death as the possibility of the end of all one's possibilities. Anticipating this possibility enables Dasein to be free for "authentic existentiel possibilities," i.e. it makes existentiel freedom possible (SZ 193, 199, 262, 285, 312). Being free for its death (existential freedom) entails a choice on Dasein's part, a choice that comes with hearing the call of conscience (SZ 288). To be resolute is to hear Dasein's silent call to choose to be oneself as the entity responsible for the choices it makes—not in the abstract, but in terms of the factical possibilities that it projects. Resoluteness is accordingly "the existentiel choosing of the choice to be oneself" (SZ 270). Having itself chosen the world—more precisely, the "for-the-sake-of which" (*Worumwillen*)—that underlies its meaningful involvement with what it encounters and uses, resolute Dasein is free for it (SZ 298).

(2) *Transcendental freedom.* A few years after the publication of SZ, Heidegger hearkens back to this grounding sense of freedom in relation to the world. However, in the later context, the freedom that he analyzes as the origin of grounds is in no way an "act of will" (9: 163, 162–75, 185–91). Freedom is the origin of grounds insofar as it forms that "for-the-sake-of" (*Umwillen*) which Dasein engages things, namely, the world. Freedom projects and holds the

world up against it, enabling human beings to obligate themselves,
i.e. to become "free selves." "The surmounting of [beings] to
the world is freedom itself" (9: 163f; 26: 238f, 246ff). Only by
surmounting, i.e. transcending beings in terms of its world, is
Dasein able to relate to them and to itself (27: 306). Freedom in
this basic sense, i.e. making up Dasein's transcendence, is not a
special sort of causality but instead a freedom *for* grounding in
general, whether as founding, occupying some basis among beings,
or justifying (where these types of grounding are themselves freely
done based upon freedom in the basic sense). So, too, freedom is
the origin of the principle of sufficient reason (*Satz vom Grund*)
that we are then free to abide by or not. But as the transcendental grounding of these ways of grounding, freedom is not to
be mistaken for any of them. It departs from all such grounds as
the abyss (*Ab-grund*) of Dasein. Yet it has this abyss-like character
precisely in factically existing, "thrown as a *free* capability-of-being
among beings." In other words, Dasein's freedom is always that of
a being thrown into the world, and it is not free from that freedom
(9: 163–75; 76: 60f).

A similar, albeit even more nuanced structure holds for
the relation between freedom in this basic sense and truth as
correctness. Truth as the correctness of an assertion or perception
holds only if we free ourselves for a binding orientation, e.g.
asserting or perceiving how something presents itself. But this
condition is only met by being free for something appearing
(something manifest) in an open region. Freedom in this sense
makes correctness possible because its own essence is taken from
"the more primordial essence of the uniquely essential truth,"
i.e. *aletheia* (9: 185ff). Correct assertions correspond to what
manifestly appears, the entity that is respectively "open in a
comportment that stands open. Freedom for what manifestly
appears in the open lets the respective entity be the entity that
it is" (9: 188). Not to be confused with indifference, being free
in this sense of letting entities be what they are means actively
engaging oneself in the open region in which entities come to
stand. Being free in this fundamental, alethic sense is thus not
the same as the absence of constraints or the capacity to do one's
will. Prior to negative and positive senses of freedom, it is "the
disclosure of beings as such, through which the openness of the
open, i.e. the 'da' is what it is." By first placing before him some

possibility for choosing and imposing upon him some necessity, this disclosure frees a human being to "his 'freedom'" (9: 189f).

This last remark demonstrates once again how Heidegger roots the freedom to choose in a more basic freedom, one that coincides with Dasein's unchosen transcendence and disclosedness. Accordingly, he observes that human beings do not possess freedom so much as freedom—"the exposed, disclosing Dasein" —possesses them. There is no history without this freedom, and all comportment (*Verhalten*) is relative to this freedom, precisely, as the reservedness (*Verhaltenheit*) that has endowed human comportment with "the inner direction for representing the respective beings in a way that corresponds to them" (9: 189; 26: 247). At the same time, against the backdrop of letting things be, human beings can also distort and cover things up. Moreover, although Dasein, in its comportment to beings, discloses beings as a whole (not to be confused with the sum of known entities), it tends to overlook or even forget this unhiddenness in its preoccupation with knowing and technically mastering beings. Constantly attuned to beings as a whole, it is then attuned to them as something indeterminate, even indeterminable. This way of being attuned is not nothing, but "a concealment of beings as a whole" (9: 193).

Hence, in its basic freedom, Dasein both "discloses and hides" beings as a whole. However, it does so in a way that secures the hiddenness (primordial un-truth) that is older than any distortion or manifestation of this or that being and older, too, than letting be. For this letting-be and, with it, the truth as un-hiddenness presuppose the *mystery*, namely, the concealing of what is hidden as a whole. Once again, absorbed with what is at any moment apparent, accessible, and manipulable, human beings are prone to forget the mystery which, in turn, leaves them to their own devices (9: 194ff).

Freedom is distinctively human. The self-movement of merely living awakens the illusion of freedom. While the living move about in a field of play whose limits they can move at will, they remain subservient to utility and its enhancement. In short, mobility is confused with freedom. In contrast to an animal's captivation by its surroundings, Dasein is free, transcending entities (including itself in a way), thanks to an openness that it founds and occupies (9: 165–71; 29/30: 401, 408f, 496ff). This connection between freedom and experience of a distinctly human free space (*das Freie*) is iterated in the early 1940s: "The human being must first come into the free space in order to be able to let entities everywhere in the open be what they are as entities" (54: 213). Both being "free from" and being "free for" presuppose a free space (clearing, opening) (54: 221f).

(3) *Liberating freedom*. From the early 1930s, in keeping with a new emphasis on human beings' historical potential for being-here, Heidegger characterizes freedom in terms of liberation (*Befreiung*). The human transition to being-here is a transition to "letting be: freedom." The freedom is a liberation from being-sheltered (*Geborgenheit*) to "existence, understanding of being, *being*." It happens only in the way one comports oneself to beings and to oneself. Not ethical or religious, this freedom is equivalent to "letting be." There is freedom "only on the basis of and as liberation" that can be guided only by existence and what has priority in it: "the understanding of being and what manifests itself in it." In this way Heidegger ties existence to freedom and freedom to the understanding of being (35: 92f). Similarly, after characterizing freedom as the liberation into the struggle for the essential transformation of human beings into Dasein, he writes: "Freedom—is liberation of the essence of the human being, liberation is the steadfastness of Dasein" (71: 113).

In 1941 lectures Heidegger contrasts the illusion of freedom with authentic freedom. The former derives from the sense of having space that one can move within and expand according to one's needs. To be unencumbered in this way appears as freedom when it is in fact subservience to the demands of utility. There is, by contrast, another stance, dispensing with calculations of utility and limiting itself to the essential. This limitation is "liberation" to the "vast region" (*Weite*) of what pertains to the essence of the human being, the region in which alone a "realm" (*Reich*) can be grounded, namely, where "the historical human stands out into an open, while subordinating everything needed and useful to it" (51: 4f). Only where there is freedom in this sense is the beginning of history—and thus its future—present as such (51: 16). We are handed over to this freedom in the thinking that lets be known that there *is* something that need not be productive or useful in order to be (51: 10). To think being in contrast to beings is to be transported into their confrontation with one another, but also to be liberated to "the belongedness to being." "This liberation liberates in this direction, that we are free, opposite beings, we are free 'towards' them, 'free' from them, free 'before' them and in their midst and thus we ourselves are able to be ourselves. The transporting into being is the *liberation* to freedom. This liberation alone is the essence of freedom" (51: 68).

(4) *Freedom in the history of philosophy.* While metaphysics hampers Kant and Schelling from asking the relevant questions, Heidegger applauds both for appreciating the centrality of the question of freedom for the question of being, its conceptual elusiveness, and the fact that there is nothing higher, nothing freer than "willing one's own essence," or, equivalently, the resoluteness and steadfastness that spring from "the decisiveness of one's own essence" (31: 299ff; 42: 185f, 267–70, 281). In lectures on Schelling's treatise on freedom, Heidegger identifies seven concepts of freedom: initiating something oneself, being free from something (unbound), being free for something (self-binding), controlling oneself, determining oneself autonomously, being capable of good and evil, and being indifferent (in-decisive) (42: 144f, 152f, 167, 177f). Human freedom corresponds to the penultimate concept, the decisiveness for good and evil, a decisiveness that is a knowing, certain of its own essential necessity and authentically willing (42: 270–4).

Not to be overlooked is Heidegger's review of the early modern, Scholastic debate over semi-pelagianism, as a backdrop for Descartes' account of the possibility of error. "In contrast to the Protestant doctrine of belief (*Luther*, De servo arbitrio, 1525), where human freedom is absolutely suppressed, the *Jesuits* [especially Molina] attempted to magnify human freedom." After tracing the rebuttal of Molina by the Jansenists in the spirit of Augustine (authentic freedom lies not in *indifferentia*, but in submitting to God's will), Heidegger adds that, as Aristotle discovered, the indifference in question is to be found in human willing, though it is not "*constitutivum* of *libertas*" (17: 153–6).

Future-ones, the (*die Zukünftigen*, also "the ones to come")

If human beings are to be transformed into being-here, and, what is the same, if the truth of historical being is to be grounded-and-sheltered, then there must be those few individuals who create this possibility. While identifying Hölderlin as the most futural, Heidegger does not place himself explicitly among the future ones. However, he does situate his thinking in the space of the beginning of their knowledge. Such knowledge begins "with genuine historical knowledge," i.e. knowledge of the hours of the happening that first forms history. "Our hour," Heidegger observes, "is the age of the going-under [*Unter-gang*]." Those who make the leap into the other beginning must "go under" in the essential sense of "anticipating what is coming (the future) and sacrificing themselves to it as their future, invisible ground" (65: 96, 397).

George, Stefan (1868–1933)

Stefan George heralded a post-modern restoration of Germany, first and foremost as a spiritual realm (*Reich*), guided by the poet–artist. The circle around George revived interest in Hölderlin against the background of Nietzsche's writings, a revival that resonates strongly, as do many themes from George's poetry, in Heidegger's work. In George's *Blätter für die Kunst* (1919) and later in the anthology, *Das Neue Reich* (1928), he published "The Word," a poem that Heidegger examines (together with other George poems) in two essays from the late 1950s: "The Essence of Language" and "The Word." Heidegger glosses the confidence exuded in the first three stanzas as typifying the notion that words are names that make what is already present available for representation (12: 212f). The second three stanzas, however, depict the poet experiencing that the absence of the word entails the absence of things. Hence, the poem's final line: "where word breaks off no thing may be." Far from being merely "means to exhibiting what is at hand," "words first lend presence, i.e. being, in which something appears as an entity" (12: 214). With this experience, the poet "renounces" any claim to have control over "the words as names for posited entities" (12: 215). Yet the poet does not remain silent. Instead he "says," indeed, "sings" this self-denial, thereby signaling a new relation to words, a relation that, in truth, is anything but a self-denial. The poet thus manages to sing—and the singing is itself a *laudatio*—by corresponding to "the mystery of the word," namely, that it "bethings" or, less obscurely, "that it first lets the thing be as a thing" (12: 216f, 220f).

Gigantic (*das Riesige*)

As the modern age races to its consummation, "with a speed unknown to the participants," the gigantic makes its appearance, though it reveals itself not as itself, but through its *shadow*. This shadow (sometimes mistakenly equated with "Americanism") is the overcoming of the planet by the world. The airplane's reduction of great distances and the radio's means of bringing "remote worlds in their everydayness" into our own wholly other everydayness are expressions of the gigantic. In the gigantic looms a danger. "As soon as the gigantic in planning and calculating and adjusting and making secure shifts out of the quantitative and becomes a special quality, then what is gigantic, and what can seemingly always be calculated completely, becomes, precisely through this, incalculable. This remains the invisible shadow that is thrown over all things, if the human has become a subject and the world a picture" (5: 95).

While the Greek determination of beingness (in terms of *techne* and the *idea*) set the stage for this turnover of quantity into quality, the modern systematic process of representing entities as objects, without regard for specific spatial things and relations, introduces the gigantic. For representing objects in this way finds no limit in the given. To the contrary, for it "everything is humanly possible" as long as it is so represented, namely, as a calculable object whose conditions—also part of the calculation—are furnished in advance. Hence, the emergence of the gigantic coincides with the dominance of representing as such (where the world is a picture) and the objectification of entities. At the same time, however, the gigantic is being's abandonment of beings, though the abandonment goes unrecognized, since representing clings to beings, sealing itself off from being or, at most, allowing it to hold as the most general, the emptiest representation. Nonetheless, albeit unbeknownst to itself, the gigantic is the incalculable, and, as such, it is one of the resonances of historical being (65: 135ff).

Heidegger recounts various ways in which the gigantic takes hold: slowing down history (while avoiding essential decisions), making everything homogenous and public (while destroying every passion for essential gathering), claiming naturalness in the appearance of the logical (while removing the question of being from questions worth asking), and reducing beings as a whole under the guise of their limitless expansion (while asserting the ability to dominate unconditionally, where nothing is impossible). As the unconditioned dominance of representing and producing, the gigantic brings to completion the basic, metaphysical stance of human beings. Neither in control of itself nor cognizant of the truth of historical being, the gigantic is the denial of the latter in favor of "the rational" and "the given" (65: 441f).

Ground (*Grund*)

SZ is concerned with the basic question (*Grundfrage*) of all ontology, with Dasein's basic structures (*Grundstrukturen*) and basic constitution (*Grundverfassung*), and with determining Dasein's being on the basis (*Grund*) of its being-in-the-world (SZ 52f, 56, 231). The existential analysis repeatedly "grounds" one phenomenon or structure (e.g. knowing, a work, concern, referring, relevance, spatiality, solicitude, circumspection, interpretation, talking and hearing, logic, urge, discovery, reality, dying, certainty, care, disposition, understanding, historicity) in another (SZ 61f, 70, 76, 78, 85, 104f, 113, 121, 138, 147f, 164f, 194, 203, 211f, 252, 256, 328, 340, 386). Dasein's being is disclosed to it in a primordial sense in angst as a "basic disposition" (*Grundbefindlichkeit*) (SZ 188ff). Existential guilt is "being the ground for a nullity," and Dasein is the "thrown ground," whose self consists in taking over being this ground (SZ 283ff). The establishment of these multiple sorts of grounding is couched within a project of demonstrating an overriding, fundamental ground: "The primordial existential ground of the existentiality of Dasein is *temporality*" (SZ 234, 304).

Despite these frequent and many-layered references, Heidegger does not thematize ground as such in SZ, beyond one passing comment. The comment is, however, revealing. The sense of being,

Heidegger comments, can never be set in contrast to beings, or to being, as something that carries beings "since 'ground' is only accessible as sense" (SZ 152). Thus, a ground is not a carrier that could presumably be described independently of what it carries. Sense constitutes at once both the way something presents itself to us and the way we attend to it (or, in traditional phenomenology, the intentional act and the intentional object). In this constituting manner, the sense grounds the entire phenomenon. The sense is irreducible to the act or to what affords itself to/in the act, and yet it is also inseparable from both. The ground is accordingly the sense that constitutes and makes sense of the existential structures of being-here. Time is the ground, so construed, of existence. (For Heidegger's account of the metaphysics of the principle of sufficient reason—*Satz vom Grund*—see 26: 136–70).

In the transitional essay "On the Essence of Ground," Heidegger characterizes Dasein's self-disclosing transcendence, the way it surmounts things "for-the-sake-of" its world, as freedom (9: 165, 170; 26: 276–83). Freedom, so construed, is the origin of ground altogether, in the sense of three equally primordial forms of grounding: founding, occupying, justifying. Founding is the projection of a world as what things are for-the-sake-of (i.e. Dasein itself). This founding coincides with already occupying a position among things in the sense of being absorbed by them. The coinciding entails both an excess of possibilities beyond those possessed or explicitly projected by Dasein and a withdrawal of possibilities. This excess and withdrawal, in addition to signaling the finitude of freedom, also gives rise to the why-question ("why this and not that?"), a question that presupposes an understanding of being (9: 169). This understanding is unveiled in transcendence, lying at the base (*zugrunde*) of all comportment with beings. "The essence of ground is this threefold dispersal of grounding, springing forth transcendentally," namely, in the projection of the world, the absorption in beings, and ontological justification of beings (9: 171).

By the end of the 1930s Heidegger calls into question his earlier treatments of ground, as talk of ground in the form of Dasein's freedom and transcendence gives way to talk of grounding in the form of the abyss of the appropriating event (66: 94; 67: 61–8). "What justifies [*be-gründet*] everything and gives the reason or ground [*Grund*] for everything is itself the ground" (51: 2). Heidegger appeals to a dictionary account of grounds: foreground, background, middle ground. These together constitute a space, though he adds the proviso that the spatial character be stripped off. "Ground here is the taking up that gathers out of itself, the gathering in itself that affords the open, in which all entities are. >>Ground<< means being itself and this is the beginning" (51: 88).

In the 1950s, after suggesting a way of understanding being as the groundless ground (Abgrund), Heidegger seemingly reverses ground (pardon the pun), stating that any concern for grounds reiterates the old metaphysical questions and runs counter to genuine thinking. The way things come-into-their-own (their appropriating) affords more than any acting, causing, grounding. So, too, the principle of sufficient reason (the claim that everything has a ground or sufficient reason) reinforces the seemingly empowering hegemony of technological thinking. Yet the principle itself is without a reason or ground, pointing to the need to take the "leap" (Satz) from this manic pursuit of reasons for beings and into being itself, being that is without a why. "The leap, however, is the leap from the principle of [sufficient] reason as a principle about beings into the principle as speaking [Sagen] of being as being" (10: 116; 12: 247; 67: 61–6).

Grounding, the (die Gründung)

The title of the fourth and longest movement of the *Contributions to Philosophy*, "The Grounding" refers to historical being's grounding of the abyss of the "In-between" as its truth. The "In-between" here is the time-space clearing "in the midst of" and "among" beings, the juncture of the back-and-forth ecstatic movement of the *da*, the "here," in the transition from the first to the other beginning. "What matters is moving the human essence into being-here" (65: 371f). "Grounding" is, Heidegger notes, ambiguous. On the one hand, it denotes the appropriating event as the grounding truth of historical being, the happening of its hiddenness as a clearing. On the other hand, it denotes taking over this ground in the sense of letting it prevail and building on it. Only in so fathoming (Er-gründung) the appropriating event, "does the steadfastness of being-here succeed in the manners and on the paths of the sheltering of the truth into beings" (65: 307f).

Accordingly, "The Grounding" principally concerns the themes of being-here, truth, time–space, and sheltering (65: 291; 66: 117, 321; 69: 132; 71: 205f, 209).

Being-here. Historical being (the unhiddenness of beings that withdraws) comes to this truth only on the basis of those who are-here. Being-here (*Da-sein*) is in this sense the ground of the *truth* of historical being, a ground necessitated by the basic experience (*Grunderfahrung*) of historical being as the appropriating event. As this grounded ground (the thrown projection), being-here transforms human beings—and every relation to beings—from the ground up. It is the ground of future human beings as seekers of historical being, preservers of being's truth, and guardians of the stillness of the passing-by of the last god (65: 293f, 305). Being-here also coincides with the crisis between the first and the other beginning. While in the first beginning 'Dasein' means what "unfolds, emerging unhidden of itself," in the other beginning it is not the manner of actuality of any being but instead "the being of the here" (*das Sein des Da*), namely, "the openness of beings as such as a whole, the ground of *aletheia*, thought primordially" (65: 296). Being-here is also the "between" between humans and divinities, and the "instance-between" (*Zwischenfall*) into which human beings must be moved in order to become for one another and become themselves—become selves (65: 293–7, 311f, 317–25).

Truth. Truth belongs to this grounding because it *is* as Da-sein. Truth, in this essential and primordial sense, is not correctness but the clearing of historical-being, as the openness in the midst of beings that is itself hidden. In this context Heidegger traces decisive conceptions of truth—truth as idea and yoke (Plato), as certainty (Descartes), and as life and the will to power (Nietzsche). *Aletheia*, the Greek term subsequently translated "truth," literally means the unhidden, and, in awe of this unhiddenness, subsequent thinking sets aside the underlying hiddenness instead of contemplating it. Differing essentially from *aletheia* despite its relation to this "truth" of the first beginning, the truth grounds as the clearing for the hiddenness of historical-being. "The clearing for the concealment as the primordial-unified unfolding is the abyss of the ground that the here [*Da*] unfolds as" (65: 350).

Time-space. Time-space is the abyss that both refuses any ground and yet, as such, is "an exceptional sort of opening up," namely, "the first clearing of the open" (65: 380). This abyss first lets the ground—historical being as the appropriating event—prevail as ground in the unity of the timing and spatializing of being-here. As this abyss, time-space grounds the "here" (*Da*) of being-here as the site of the deciding moment (*Augenblicksstätte*), the moment of the decision to shepherd being or not. This site is based upon the basic mood of reserve that comes with the knowledge of the possibility of another beginning. Contrary to any intuition or concept of time or space as something subjective or objective, time-space is based upon the basic mood of this decision. As such it grounds the possibility of the nearness and farness of beings, of Gods and humans, and of decisions regarding them. Ordinary or traditional conceptions of time and space spring from time-space (65: 323, 375, 382ff; 66: 321).

Sheltering (Bergung). The final section of "The Grounding" introduces how being-here in the other beginning shelters historical being and beings. The section corresponds to Heidegger's contemporary lectures on art and his future discussion of things and technology. Thus, historical being's hiddenness is not to be set aside or canceled but preserved by way of a thing, implement, work, deed, or sacrifice that upholds and sustains it in an openness in which that hiddenness (or self-concealing) essentially unfolds. This safeguarding of the hiddenness amounts to sheltering or rescuing its happening by transforming it into the conflict of world and earth (disclosing and concealing), "the preliminary appearance" of the appropriating event's truth. "Waging the conflict sets the truth into the work, into the implement, experiences it as thing, brings it to completion in deed and sacrifice" (65: 389–92).

Handiness (*Zuhandenheit*, MR: readiness-to-hand)

Handiness is the manner of being of implements (tools, equipment) in use, entities circumspectively encountered in the environment (where "circumspection" designates the way we are able, largely unreflectively, to see our way around our work environment, caught up in a particular concern; for example, a driver circumspectively sees the steering wheel, the car accelerating toward him, the bend ahead). Not everything is handy and not everything handy always is so. For example, a car is handy as long as it is in use. But if it breaks down, if the keys are missing, or if a fallen tree blocks the road, the car is simply on-hand. What is conspicuous in the experience of the breakdown, obtrusive in the experience of the missing keys, and obstinate in the experience of the fallen tree is the sudden on-handness of what is otherwise handy. So the difference between being-handy (*Zuhandensein*) and being-on-hand (*Vorhandensein*) is akin to a Gestalt-shift (first you see the duck, then the rabbit, or vice versa, etc.). Perhaps for this reason, Heidegger stops short of assigning an ontological priority to the handy over the on-hand, though he does contend that handiness is the way that entities are defined "ontologico-categorially" as they are "in themselves" and that knowledge must penetrate beyond what is handy in our concern, if it is to expose what is simply on-hand. At the same time, what announces itself in the breakdown is not simply the on-handness of the implement but what it and, indeed, the entire complex of such implements are for, namely, the world. This world is neither handy nor on-hand, but pre-disclosed as part of being-here (*Dasein*) (SZ 71–6). Translators of SZ typically reserve "handy" for the translation of *händlich* (SZ 73), and they translate *Vorhandensein* as "present-at-handness" (MR) or "objective presence" (S), while, as can be gathered from this entry, I render it as "on-handness" or "being-on-hand." In a late essay, Heidegger notes that "handiness as well as on-handness are manners of presence" (14: 11).

Hegel, Georg Wilhelm Friedrich (1770–1831)

Appreciation and criticism of Hegel's thinking can be found in Heidegger's very early work (1: 411), in early Freiburg lectures (58: 1, 12, 97), and in Marburg seminars in 1925/26 and 1927. At the conclusion of SZ, following his account of how timeliness fundamentally enables our "factically thrown existence," Heidegger clarifies his results by both comparing and contrasting them with Hegel's interpretation of the connection between spirit and time (SZ 428–36). In Heidegger's view, no philosopher—before or since Hegel—has taken the history of philosophy more seriously as a philosophical problem than Hegel does (11: 54; 65: 214).

Heidegger's study of art stands under the shadow of Hegel's thesis about the end of art, and he applauds Hegel's insightful treatments of identity and spirit, breaking free of traditional logic (5: 68f; 11: 34, 54f; 40: 129). Nor does Hegel's persistent appropriation of Aristotle's thinking escape Heidegger's attention. All these themes, together with Hegel's appreciation of negativity and the ontological limitations of finite theoretical knowing and subjectivity, suggest wide-ranging affinities between the two philosophers.

Yet, no doubt because of these similarities, Heidegger takes pains to emphasize the differences between Hegel and himself, all the more so as he begins to move from fundamental ontology's framework with its unmistakably Kantian echoes to an attempt to think being historically. As "the metaphysics of absolute knowing," Hegel's philosophy is the beginning of the end and culmination of metaphysics (7: 74). His "onto-theo-ego-logy" has the effect of making finitude disappear, canceling time, and dissolving everything into the absolute (5: 195, 199, 203; 28: 46f; 32: 17f, 92, 180–84). Not surprisingly, despite his multiple uses of "negativity" in the *Science of Logic*, Hegel takes it for granted, leaving it and its origin unexplained (68: 22ff). Like Fichte, Hegel looks for a ground and system where Kant—to his credit—recognizes that there could only be an abyss (15: 298ff). Whereas Hegel focuses on what was thought in the history of philosophy, with a view to superseding (*aufheben*) it metaphysically, Heidegger attempts to "step back" from metaphysics towards what was not thought by it, namely, the difference between being and beings (5: 175; 11: 56–9, 68ff). In 1964 Heidegger notes that for Hegel, "the matter of philosophy as metaphysics is the being of beings, whose presence is in the form of substantiality and subjectivity," and yet Hegel fails to ask how there can be presence at all. In other words, he fails to recognize what presence presupposes: the clearing, the open for everything that comes to be present and absent (14: 77, 81, 86f).

In the absoluteness of subjectification (*Subjektität*), every entity becomes an object, just as nature in the age of subjectivity ("in which the essence of technology is grounded") becomes the object of technological objectification, assaulting things and humans "without distinction." In Hegel's remark that experience is a movement that consciousness exercises in itself, demonstrating the constant presence of the absolute in the process, Heidegger sees "the will of the absolute holding sway." In this way he situates

Hegel's metaphysics of absolute spirit within late modernity's underlying conception of being as will (articulated especially by Leibniz and Nietzsche). This situating also explains Heidegger's contention that the reputed collapse of Hegel's system in the nineteenth century is a myth. After referring to the moment when the technological devastation of the earth is not yet recognized but nonetheless willed, Heidegger observes: "Hegel grasps this moment of the history of metaphysics in which absolute self-consciousness becomes the principle of thinking" (7: 97; 5: 190ff; 7: 74; 9: 432f; 65: 213f).

Heraclitus

"When I am thinking something over," Heidegger confided to a colleague, "it is often as if Heraclitus is standing next to me." Indeed, for the better part of three decades he repeatedly finds inspiration in Heraclitus' fragments (e.g. 7: 211–34, 263–88; 15: 9–263; 36/37: 89–100; GA 55). Heraclitus recognizes the hiddenness that gives meaning to *aletheia* (unhiddenness), as can be gathered from Fragment 16 (how can *physis*, as presumably what never goes under, never hides, be hidden?) and Fragment 123 (*physis* loves to hide). To be sure, Fragment 16 announces the dominant meaning of being as *physis*, supposed by Plato and Aristotle, namely, constant presence (55: 86f, 90, 101; 70: 86). Nevertheless, Heraclitus' pulse is on neither being nor beings as a whole, but on "the hidden essence what is called 'to be'"—indeed, where self-disclosing and hiding are in the closest and requisite proximity to one another (7: 277ff; 15: 343f; 55: 81, 86, 125f, 131–40; 55: 81).

As the reciprocity of self-disclosing emergence and sheltering concealment, *physis* (an early word for being) can also be considered a *harmonia* (Frgs. 8, 54) of opposites held in tension, as in the images of a bow or lyre (Frg. 51), fire (Frg. 66), and the *cosmos* (Frg. 30). Heraclitus thinks being in distinction from beings *before* metaphysics, i.e. before the reduction of being to unhiddenness, to sheer presence (15: 280ff; 55: 76–9, 141–71).

Similarly, in contrast to the metaphysical interpretation of *logos* as assertion, Heraclitus understands it pre-metaphysically as the sheltering and gathering of things, that lets them lie before us in their unhiddenness (Frgs. 45, 50). What is telling in all human relations to beings (the human *logos*) is the hidden and forgotten but constant turn to being (the *logos*) (55: 323f). Herein lies the fundamental discordance of human beings (Frg. 72), turned at once towards and away from the *logos*' absent presence. Heidegger refers to this discordance as strife (*eris*), presumably from Frg. 80, and reminiscent of his comment on Frg. 53, eight years earlier, that "*polemos* and *logos* are the same" (40: 66, 134–43; 55: 317f, 320, 338, 344f).

Hermeneutics (*Hermeneutik*)

When it is unclear how we should understand the meaning of a text, we try to interpret it. Any possibility of interpretation rests on some level of foregoing understanding that the interpretation supplements and develops. For example, we may understand the wording of the book of Genesis or copyright law, but be unsure how to interpret them. Stemming from such theological and legal quandaries of interpretation, "hermeneutics" stands for the theory or practice of interpretation. In the early 19th century Schleiermacher attempts to combine practices of biblical exegesis and classical philology into a single doctrine of the art of interpretation. The effort was at once critical and romantic, generalizing the problem of understanding by searching for its conditions, yet with the conviction that a creative unconscious is at work in gifted individuals.

Dilthey expands hermeneutics beyond oral and textual interpretation to the discernment of meaning as it occurs to individuals ("the greatest reality" of history) precisely as they live their lives in a specific historical setting. "Like the letters of a word, life and history have a sense" (Dilthey, *Gesammelte Schriften* [Stuttgart: Teubner, 1979], 7: 291). Dilthey construes hermeneutics as the analysis of "understanding" and "categories of life," as they take root in quotidian, prescientific practices. Hermeneutics is, he also recognizes, deeply reflexive and engaged. Far from merely confronting something lying "outside" her, the interpreter is herself implicated in the process of interpretation. For this reason, Dilthey explicitly construes his hermeneutics as a replacement for traditional metaphysics, fulfilling the need for metaphysics that Kant considered deeply rooted in human nature. An avid reader of both Schleiermacher and Dilthey, Heidegger proposes yet a further extension and revision of hermeneutics. At the outset of his lectures in the summer of 1923, entitled *Ontology: The Hermeneutics of Facticity*, he traces the term "hermeneutics" back to use of *hermeneuein* to signify a manner of communicating a message or something otherwise inaccessible or hidden (63: 9–14). Heidegger's hermeneutics is not, like Schleiermacher's, confined to interpretation of texts, and it is most decidedly not a hermeneutics of the unconscious spirit speaking through a writer. In contrast to Dilthey's hermeneutics, it is not a hermeneutics of artifacts, historical disciplines, or even life as it is lived but of Dasein. Unlike Dilthey, Heidegger does not oppose historical understanding to explanation in the natural sciences, but instead identifies understanding as a basic existential, presupposed by historical and scientific disciplines alike. Both Schleiermacher and Dilthey develop hermeneutics in the shadow of Kant's epistemological project. Indeed, Dilthey aims at a critique of historical reason, where lived experience, not some decontextualized transcendental self, grounds the interpretation. By contrast, Heidegger's hermeneutics is directed at interpreting, not epistemological conditions, but how "the authentic sense of being and the basic structures of its own being are made known to the understanding-of-being that is inherent in being-here" (SZ 37).

Nevertheless, there are several traditional hermeneutical principles at work in the hermeneutics of Dasein: namely, that all interpretation is rooted in a foregoing understanding, that interpretation is not restricted to language (even though there are no restrictions on discourse or language), that the meaning of what someone does or says may be opaque to her (*mens auctoris* is a poor guide to interpretation since the interpreter can understand a text better than its author does), that interpretation moves in a circle from part to whole and back, from beginning to end and back. Heidegger elaborates this last principle in terms of what calls the "hermeneutical situation," signaling the fact that every interpretation moves within a certain forestructure (*Vorstruktur*), composed of what the interpreter has before her to do (*Vorhabe*) as well as her preview (*Vorsicht*) and preconception (*Vorgriff*) of it. This situation underlies the circular or, better, helical character of interpretation, the "hermeneutical circle." While this process of interpretation is not linear, it is far from being a logical fallacy; "the decisive thing is not to come out of the circle, but rather to find one's way into it in the proper manner" (SZ 153).

The importance of finding one's way into the circle points to another common note in Heidegger's and Dilthey's hermeneutics. They share the overall aim of replacing traditional metaphysics with hermeneutics, precisely by insisting on the historical reflexiveness of existentials (for Heidegger) and categories of life (for Dilthey). Thus, in early lectures, Heidegger identifies hermeneutics as the self-interpretation of facticity: "Hermeneutics has the task of rendering one's own respective Dasein accessible to this Dasein itself in its character of being, to communicate it, and to track the self-alienation with which Dasein is afflicted." The understanding that emerges in this interpretation is "utterly incomparable to a cognitive comportment toward another life." To the contrary, it is no comportment, no intentionality at all, but instead "Dasein's *being-alert* for itself" (63: 15).

Heidegger speaks only infrequently of hermeneutics in his later work, though he gives a clarifying and augmenting retrospective in 1953/54, connecting hermeneutics to "the essence of language as the saying" (12: 90–3, 113–19, 137–44; 66: 325).

Historical being (*Seyn*, also "be-ing," "beyng")

Metaphysics is guided by the question of what beings are or, alternatively, what makes a being a being. The answer to the question—metaphysical being (*Sein*)—amounts to some conception of the being of beings (their beingness) and/or the supreme being responsible for all the rest. This guiding question, like the answer, presumes that "what genuinely is" are beings themselves, regardless of other descriptions of them (e.g. relations, occurrences, classes, norms, etc.). However, metaphysics does not ask the fundamental question: what is being? Nor can it ask this question since any account of being it might give is derivative of whatever beings there are for it. From the earliest Greek conception of the being of beings as *physis* to contemporary accounts of charged particles in a region of space-time, what genuinely is are the beings themselves.

By contrast, Heidegger insists that only historical being *is*, because it is the hidden ground of any attempt to say what there is (65: 473; 66: 192; 69: 141f; 70: 11, 15). Yet it is neither the common feature of all that there is nor does it leave any trace of itself in beings—despite its dependence upon human beings (65: 293; 66: 53, 199–203). Historical being might be construed as a significant part of Heidegger's answer to the fundamental question, what he first dubs the sense, later the truth of being itself—but only if it is kept in mind that historical being, far from being a matter of description or explanation, points to a decision that is yet to be decided. What remains to be decided is "whether human beings dare historical being and thus going-under *or* whether they are contented with beings" (65: 91, 451f, 464; 69: 59f).

The primordial appropriation of beings and Dasein to one another—the presence of beings to Dasein—"happens" (*geschieht*), and historical being is historical (*geschichtlich*) as this happening. However, its happening is not a universal (that would reduce it to transcendent(al), metaphysical beingness). It happens as something that uniquely began (indeed, it is *the* beginning and its essence is the originary beginning) and is still coming to us, provided we are here (*da*) for it (70: 16, 23f). With this robust sense of the historical in mind—not to be confused with a chronological or historical record (*Historie*)—Heidegger identifies the essence of historical being with the essence of history (60: 162; 65: 32f, 451, 494; 69: 136). History as the appropriating event is the truth of *Seyn*, and the grounding of its truth (66: 116; 69: 96, 101f; 71: 180). *Seyn* is translated "historical being" to underscore this pre-eminently historical character in contrast to metaphysical being (being as beingness, *Sein als Seiendheit*). "The understanding of 'being' [*Sein*] is essentially remote from knowledge of historical being [*Seyn*]" (70: 9).

From its first beginning, historical being affords the epochs of its history by withdrawing itself. Every such epoch includes a metaphysical account of a transcendent being or concept of being (beingness) in an attempt to transcend and forego the historical abyss—the abyss of historical being—underlying it. Historical being's other, originary beginning is the appropriating event—"historical being" and the "appropriating event" are metonyms (65: 293; 66: 83, 148; 69: 27f, 106, 108, 116, 146; 70: 10f, 19, 66f). "Historical being is neither 'over' us nor 'in' us nor 'around' us; rather we are in it as the appropriating event" (69: 55). Thinking the other beginning—or, equivalently, knowing historical being as the appropriating event—begins with coming to terms with or getting over historical being's hiddenness (*Verwindung des Seyns*), where "getting over" also means safeguarding it as hidden (70: 19–22, 92, 100). It is one thing to leave historical being in its hiddenness and another thing to experience it as self-concealing. Experiencing it brings beings back within their limits and takes from them the singular priority they seem to have (65: 254). What is at stake is nothing less than humanity's complete abandonment to the devastation of the power of machination, as opposed to the decision to "be here," to carry out and belong to the hidden truth of historical being (65: 254, 489f; 69: 24f, 31). Historical being is poor and unrelated to power or its absence. Instead, it is the utter majesty of not producing or needing to produce anything (66: 287–96; 69: 110f; for eight names of historical being as the appropriating event, dispensing with "any assistance from explanations of entities," see 65: 471).

History (*Geschichte*)

History can stand for a story about the past, a means of recounting something in the past and thereby making it an explicit object of consciousness or knowing. All the while, the past is observed and explained from the perspective of the present. But such recountings and explanations presuppose that something happens. "History" can also stand for what happens itself. Thus we distinguish a historical study from a historic, i.e. history-making event. In a cognate way Heidegger distinguishes history in the more fundamental sense of the term, i.e. *Geschichte* as happening, from historical studies, i.e. *Historie*—and similarly historicity (*Geschichtlichkeit*) from historicality (*Historizität*). History is what happens (*geschieht*) but not, at bottom, in the sense of an occurrence in time. Rather the essence of history is historical being itself, namely, the happening of the appropriation of human beings to the presence of beings and vice versa. This happening has a beginning that is still coming to us and, in that sense, is futural.

We are caught up in history and, hence, it is never an object as the past is for historical studies that chronicle or recount it. "No historian can make out what history is." In contrast to the historian's fixation on the past, the center of gravity of history and its happening is the future placed in our care. Yet it is also something that has long been happening and is still unfolding, albeit in a hidden way. "*The futural is the origin of history.* But the most futural is the great beginning, what—constantly holding itself back—reaches farthest back and at the same time farthest ahead." Since the destiny of all beginnings is to be overtaken and pushed aside by what it begins, the proper relation to the beginning is not conservative, but revolutionary, breaking through the dominance of what has become customary "in order to save the beginning and the future" (45: 40; see, too, 6.2: 20; 38: 79–118; 45: 34–37, 40–3; 52: 132; 54: 94; 65: 32f, 479; 69: 93; 71: 264–71).

Strictly speaking, only human beings have a history. "The happening of history is the happening of being-in-the-world" (SZ 388). Dasein's historicity encompasses the "context of living," extending from birth to death, not as a succession of experiences in time, but as the care that happens "between" (in the sense of uniting) the throwness of its birth and anticipation of its death. In this happening, i.e. in the timeliness that care is, lies the origin of historicity and the place of the problem of history (SZ 373ff, 385). Authentic care, as the resolute anticipation of death, entails taking over the authentic, factical possibilities afforded by Dasein's throwness into the world with others. Seizing upon the finitude of its existence frees Dasein from an endless multitude of inauthentic possibilities and brings it "into the simplicity of its fate," the primordial happening of Dasein. This primordial happening lies in authentic resoluteness as Dasein, free for its death, projects "an inherited yet chosen possibility." These possibilities are part of our shared "destiny" (*Geschick*) since the primordial happening of Dasein is always a shared happening, the happening of a community, a people. "The fateful destiny of Dasein in and with its 'generation' makes up its full, authentic happening." Authentic historicity is grounded in the authentic, finite timeliness that, free for its death, projects the inherited possibility for itself, taking over its throwness in order to be for "its time" in the present moment. Explicitly projecting those possibilities is a repetition or retrieval (*Wiederholung*) of them (SZ 384f).

Whereas Heidegger in SZ raises the prospects of an authentic chronicling of the past in the form of such a retrieval (SZ 393ff), he subsequently pans *Historie* for its objectification of the past (yet another expression of all-objectifying, modern subjectivity), for its metaphysical supposition of determining history on the basis of an ontology of events, and for its attempt to explain the past exclusively from the perspective of the present or, more precisely, from the perspective of the calculating enterprises of the present where everything *is* only in being producible or on order. History only arises when we leap past these misguided attempts to determine history by objectifying past events. These criticisms of *Historie* in the second half of the 1930s have a clearly political bent, as he castigates it as a nihilistic flight from history into the ahistorical where the pre-historical "blood and race become bearers of history" and where the aim is to valorize the present as eternally on-hand and place all objects in the service of *"utilization and breeding"* (6.2: 127, 349f; 65: 10, 148, 493f). (Seeds of Heidegger's subsequent approaches to history, reviewed above, can be found in the explication of six meanings of "history" in his 1920 SS lectures [59: 43–59]; on the relation between history and *Historie* as evidence [*Kunde*] of the former, and between *Historie* and its development into a science of history, see 38: 81–99.)

Hölderlin, Friedrich (1770–1843)

A major German poet from Württemberg and classmate of Hegel and Schlegel in Tübingen, Friedrich Hölderlin started working as a private tutor in 1793 but also attended the University of Jena in 1794. Struggling with mental illness from the late 1790s on, he was admitted into a clinic for the mentally ill in Tübingen in 1806. A year later he was declared incurable and spent the rest of his life in a room overlooking the Neckar River in Tübingen. Little poetry survived these later years, and he was best known in his lifetime for his novel, *Hyperion* (1797/99). However, the odes, elegies, and hymns he produced from 1799 to 1806 exercised a powerful influence on German letters, particularly with Norbert von Hellingrath's publication of his collected works, beginning in 1913.

Aristotle is without doubt the most important influence on the early Heidegger's thinking, but it is Hölderlin who most influences his mature thinking. Hölderlin's poetry is, in Heidegger's own words, "absolutely essential" to his thinking (16: 678). As he puts it in the *Contributions to Philosophy*, "philosophy's historical destiny culminates in the knowledge of the necessity of making Hölderlin's word heard" (65: 421f, 12; 39: 291).

In his 1966 *Spiegel* interview, he states that anyone hearing his first Hölderlin lectures in 1934/35 would recognize them as a confrontation with National Socialism—a claim that has been frequently challenged (16: 664). From those first lectures to essays completed shortly before his death, Heidegger repeatedly returns to Hölderlin's poetry. In addition to three lecture courses (GA 39, 52, 53), Heidegger gives talks in the late 1930s and the war years, publishing them after the war in a collection, first in 1951 and, with newly composed essays, in 1971 (see GA 4). He also completed short essays in 1970 and 1974 (13: 213–20, 231–6), and further unpublished material appeared in 2000 (GA 75). In numerous other writings (e.g. on technology, dwelling, and language), Heidegger appeals to Hölderlin's poetry.

Heidegger repeatedly casts Hölderlin as the poet of poets, pointing the way for thinking the essence of poetry, not as the expression of the poet's experience, but as the articulation and founding of being for a particular, "needy" time (4: 41). Hölderlin manages to write poetically and thus found the same historical being that Heidegger is trying to think historically, from the "appropriating event." Hölderlin's poetry "first determines a new time," namely, "the time of the gods that have flown away *and* of the coming god" (4: 47). So, too, Heidegger attempts to found a new beginning at a time of distress, the time of not only the departed gods but the very abandonment of-and-by being. Just as Hölderlin's poetry is for a future—a "new beginning," the "place of our future historical being"—so Heidegger's thinking aims at preparing for another beginning of Western thinking (39: 115, 122f, 146f, 220–2; 70: 166; 75: 81). In this respect, Hölderlin's basic position is "fundamentally different" from Hegel's "still metaphysical" stance (52: 99). Similarly, a chasm separates Hölderlin from Nietzsche whose notion of the will to power is rooted in modern metaphysics (52: 78, 143).

Hölderlin's thoughtful poetry also serves as a springboard to Heidegger's poetic thinking in other, more specific ways as well. Just as a mood of mourning grounds Hölderlin's "Germanien," so a non-aggressive yet decisive awe (*scheu*) must ground thinking being historically (4: 131; 52: 171f). In addition, Hölderlin's supple way of saying what needs to be said aids Heidegger in his own struggle to say historically (non-metaphysically) what being is. For Hölderlin's poetry exemplifies and thus retrieves the essentially conflicted character of *aletheia*, the struggle between hiddenness and unhiddenness, precisely by hinting at what is hidden and leaving the unsayable unsaid. Fending off any metaphysical backsliding into abstraction, Hölderlin's images and metaphors do not make perspicuous what is intrinsically hidden, even as they gesture toward it. In short, his poetry intimates (*ahnt*) yet preserves the mystery (4: 25; 39: 31ff, 113–20, 250; 70: 157). In a parallel way Heidegger's thinking focuses on the truth of historical being as the self-concealing struggle between hiddenness and unhiddenness, as the way that historical being (*Seyn*) essentially unfolds by refusing to be conflated with any particular being that has been revealed (*Seiendes*) or way that it has been revealed (*Sein*). Thinking must live, no less than poetry, from this indirection.

Inasmuch as Hölderin's poetry founds being as a new beginning by retrieving the struggle inherent in *aletheia*, it points beyond the first beginning (the initiation of metaphysics) to the originary beginning, the appropriating event of historical being that is still coming. In this way Heidegger interprets Hölderlin's poetry as signaling authentic timeliness and history, the time of the always already originary beginning that is still arriving. This founding and originating by way of retrieving is the paradigmatic instance of the unique law of Hölderlin's work. That law is the basic law of history as fate: coming into one's own only by way of critical engagement with the foreign. "There must be the sojourn in the foreign and the estrangement in the foreign so that, in the foreign, what is one's own begins to be illuminated" (52: 175). It is necessary not merely to commemorate and thus preserve the foreign in order to appropriate what is one's own, but to think the place from which "what is coming must first be said and back to which the having been must be sheltered, so that this foreigner itself can be its own" (4: 150). As this last remark suggests, what is essential is how the foreign is to be engaged: unselfishly, wholeheartedly, in a greeting (4: 96; 52: 51ff; see GA 52).

In one way what Heidegger dubs "historical being" and what Hölderlin dubs "the holy" name the same, namely, what essentially unfolds in advance of divinities and humans, what is most proper to the history of the other beginning (70: 157f). In another way, however, they do not name the same since Hölderin does not explicitly think the "in-between" (*Inzwischen*) and the abandonment of beings by historical being. The "in-between" here signifies the time–spatial clearing in which historical being unfolds "amidst" beings as an abyss, yet collapses (*ein-fällt*) into beings (66: 117f, 309, 310f, 321; 70: 66f, 79). Hence, his poetry, despite having overturned metaphysics or at least having become a harbinger for its overturning, stands in danger of being appropriated by it (70: 157f, 160; 52: 143). Nor is this surprising, given Heidegger's remark: "Hölderlin still thinks metaphysically. But he writes poetry differently" (52: 120; 4: 30f, 76; 39: 1, 122; 75: 81).

Heidegger's first Hölderlin lectures (GA 39) take place on the heels of his resignation as rector. His engagement with Hölderlin at this time, he later contends, is part of an attempt to establish an alternative to the purely technological, power-driven conception of Germany's destiny under National Socialism. To support that contention, he could point to depictions of Hölderlin as "the most German of the Germans" (16: 333) and the "founder of German being" (39: 220), together with the observation that the founding is far from being realized, since "the poet of the Germans has not yet become the power in the history of the German people" (39: 214).

Holy, the (*das Heilige*)

The holy in Hölderlin's poetry provides a window into historical being since both words name the same (71: 157). Hölderlin depicts poets as divining and corresponding to nature. Nature is the "all-present," resonating with Greek *physis* and yet different from it. For "the holy is the essence of nature," and it is "older than the ages and above the gods." Nature in this sense is "the originary [*das Anfängliche*] prior to everything," the "all-creative" and "collective spirit" that distinguishes and unifies at once; it is "the open in which everything comes to be present" (4: 59f). Mediating all beings (gods and mortals, heavens and earth), nature as the holy is itself immediate and unapproachable. "The holy places all experiencing outside of what is customary for it and thus withdraws from it the place where it stands. Thus, un-settling in this way, the holy is itself the awesomely unsettling [*das Entsetzliche*]" (4: 63). Because it is only as something that is coming, the poet never represents or grasps it as an object. Still, even the poetic gesture of mediating the holy would threaten it, were it not the case that everything is only by being gathered into the wholeheartedness of the holy (4: 73). The holy is sheer unselfishness, the appropriating event is the holy, fitting gods and humans to itself and to one another (39: 83–7, 223; 52: 77, 100).

Homecoming (*Heimkunft*)

Heidegger glosses the poet's calling as "homecoming" in the Hölderlin-poem by this name. Coming home requires traveling to the origin. Homecoming is the "mystery" of the joy of coming home to the nearness to the origin. "To write poetically means to be in the joy that safeguards in word the mystery of the nearness to the most joyful" (4: 25). The poet has the delicate task of saying yet safeguarding the "mystery," bringing it near us, by keeping it far away. Accordingly, the poet does not name but wordlessly sings or, better, strums the holy. Through the homecoming, the homeland is prepared in its nearness to the origin, though the poet's singing remains to be heard by "the kindred ones." If it is heard and "commemorated" by thinkers, "then there is a homecoming. But this homecoming is the future of the historical essence of Germans" (4: 30).

Human being (*Mensch*)

A human being is not an animal possessing language. A human being's comportment in its world is radically different from an animal's behavior in its surroundings. Theological conceptions of humans as *imago dei* settle in advance the question of the distinctively human way of being. But so, too, do sciences of the human—anthropology, biology, psychology—when they start from the underlying presupposition that human beings are simply entities found on-hand in nature. The traditional, theological, and contemporary scientific conceptions of human beings are all ontologically naïve.

Refusing to countenance any such naiveté, Heidegger finds that what is distinctively human is being-here, i.e. existing in such a way that being is disclosed and matters to it (SZ 25, 41, 133, 165, 196f, 212). Inasmuch as Dasein is—exists as—this disclosedness, "truth, understood in the most primordial sense, belongs to the basic constitution of Dasein ... *'There is' truth only insofar as and as long as Dasein is*" (SZ 226). As Heidegger shifts from a transcendental to a historical understanding of being in the early 1930s, this singular status of the human is in no way diminished. "The question of human being is determined ... *solely* on the basis of the question of *being*. Within the question of being, the essence of the human being is to be conceived and grounded ... as *the site* that being requires to open up. The human being is the here (*Da*), open in itself" (41: 214; 29/30: 531; 38: 34ff). The sense in which being requires the human being to be here (*da zu sein*) is iterated in Heidegger's efforts to think being historically. "Who is the human being? [It is] what historical being uses to sustain the essential unfolding of its truth. As so used, however, the human being >>is<< a human being only insofar as he is grounded in being-here, i.e. becomes himself the grounder of *being*-here, in creating. But historical being is conceived here at the same time as the *appropriating event*. Both belong together: the re-grounding in being-here and the truth of historical being as the appropriating event" (65: 318).

Technology's positionality, the drive to disclose everything as part of a standing reserve, is the greatest danger to the human essence. Yet the same destiny that has given us technology has also given human beings a part in that disclosing. What grants this disclosure (the appropriating event) allows human beings to see and turn towards "the supreme dignity of their essence," which "rests on guarding the unhiddenness and, with it, the hiddenness of every essence on earth" (7: 33; 12: 179). These last remarks stem from 1949, but they echo a refrain running throughout all of Heidegger's writings, namely, the exalted dignity of the human being that lies in being-here, in witnessing and safeguarding truth, not only the unhiddenness of beings but the hiddenness of the disclosure that makes up historical being as the appropriating event.

In light of this elevated if also demanding role of human beings in Heidegger's thinking, the suggestion that his thinking is alien to humanism seems *prima facie* wrongheaded, and

Heidegger says as much (9: 319). Yet he is quick to add that, insofar as humanism is historically rooted in metaphysics or makes itself the ground of a metaphysics, it closes off any possibility of thinking of human beings as being-here. "To this extent the thinking in SZ is against humanism ... because it is does not esteem the humanitas of the human being highly enough." The same holds for existentialism that regards itself as humanism. The SZ claim that "the essence of Dasein lies in existence" has nothing to do with existentialism or Sartre's claim that "existence precedes essence" since Dasein's existence refers not to a subject *pour soi* but to "standing ecstatically in the truth of being" (9: 330, 334). "The human being is not the master of beings. The human being is the shepherd of being. In this ... the human being loses nothing but gains because he attains the truth of being. He gains the essential poverty of the shepherd whose dignity rests on being called by being itself to preserve its truth .... Is that not humanism in the most extreme sense? Certainly, it is the humanism that thinks the humanity of the human out of the nearness of being" (9: 342f).

Husserl, Edmund (1859–1938)

Every semester from the fall of 1921 through the spring of 1924, Heidegger holds a seminar on either Husserl's *Logical Investigations* or *Ideas I*. The investigations in SZ were "only possible on the foundation laid by Husserl," and Heidegger fittingly dedicates SZ to Edmund Husserl "in reverence and friendship" (SZ v, 38n). "Husserl gave me my eyes," he tells his students in 1923, and two years later he adds that, opposite Husserl, he still considers himself a novice (63: 5; 20: 168; 21: 88). Yet in the same lectures Heidegger presents an "immanent critique of the progression of phenomenological research," as a means of freeing up questions Husserl never raises (20: 124). In 1926 Heidegger confides to Jaspers that, if SZ were written against anyone, then it is Husserl.

Even before the completion of SZ Heidegger mounted strident criticisms of Husserl's phenomenology. Husserl fails to probe the meaning of "being," equating it instead with scientific objectivity in the explicit sense of "being an object of or being true for theoretical, scientific knowing" (20: 165; 21: 98). Because he understands subjectivity as the counterpart of nature, he remains in the ambit of the very naturalism he is trying to combat (20: 34–46, 61, 165). Instead of investigating the ontological meaning of "intentionality," Husserl gives it all the trappings of a proto-theoretical, "naturalistic" construction utterly removed from the world in which human beings actually work and live (20: 145–9, 155). Missing is any acknowledgment of our absorption in the world of everyday life. Reminding Husserl of an earlier conversation regarding "being-in-the-world," Heidegger writes to his erstwhile mentor: "Does a pure ego not have, as part of its very essence, a world at all?" (Husserl, *Ideen III*, 274n. 1). Husserl's attempts to elaborate a personalist account of the subject merely exacerbate the problem (20: 165–71; SZ 47). So, too, nothing in Husserl's analyses of time-consciousness corresponds to the temporal significance of the future and death (cornerstones of Heidegger's time-analyses). For all Husserl's astute criticisms of the "tyranny of the now" interfering with appreciation of retention and protention, the now clearly possesses a privileged status in his analysis of time.

Heidegger also criticizes the aim and motivation of Husserl's phenomenology. Husserl's "pre-hermeneutic" phenomenology is primarily concerned with securing known knowledge, and the ultimate motivation for this concern is angst in the face of existence (17: 97; 65: 188). This angst explains Husserl's penchant for modeling philosophy's endgame on theoretical sciences like mathematics and physics as well as his (at least early) obliviousness to the significance of history. It also explains the already noted ontological shortsightedness regarding the question of being in general and the question of the being of intentionality in particular.

Despite these criticisms, Husserl's influence on Heidegger's thinking can be traced to what Heidegger takes to be the three "decisive discoveries" of Husserlian phenomenology: intentionality, categorial intuitions, and the primordial sense of the a priori (20: 34–122). Though Heidegger contends that being-in-the-world is more basic than intentionality, his insistence on understanding being-in-the-world as a "unified phenomenon" iterates Husserl's emphasis on the basic unity of the intentional experience (SZ 53). The intentional experience is a unity of a subject, an object, and a sense (the sense or *noema* is what escaped Brentano, Heidegger avers). In a directly parallel fashion *being-in-the-world* encompasses Dasein's interactions with entities by virtue of disclosing the sense in which they are (SZ 151).

Husserl's doctrine of categorial intuition provided a way of undermining the Kantian insistence that access to being, relation, and other such "categories" can only be rooted in acts of judgment. I do not need to make a judgment that the tree exists; I "see" that it exists (or, equivalently, it presents itself as such), and, only because I see it, can I make that true judgment. To be sure, Heidegger is concerned with understanding and existentials rather than categorial intuitions and categories—because categories correspond to judgments of what is on-hand, whereas existentials are self-disclosive determinations of being-here (SZ 44, 55). Thus, for Heidegger, "phenomenological intuition of essence is grounded in the existential understanding," and our existence is first disclosed to us in moods (SZ 147, 134). Yet, despite these differences, it is clear why Heidegger esteems Husserl's doctrine so highly. For the meaning of "to be" is given-and-realized in an existential—just as it is in a categorial intuition—in an unthematic, prereflective way, recoverable by phenomenological analysis. (The notion of categorial intuition gives way to eidetic intuition, intuition of essences, as the aim of Husserl's phenomenology. Given how overworked the notion of essence is in Heidegger's phenomenology, influence on this level should also not be dismissed, despite Heidegger's efforts to re-think the notion after 1930).

Husserl's third fundamental discovery triangulates the first two, since the primordial sense of the a priori lies precisely in disclosing the categories (senses, essences) constitutive of intentionality. In parallel fashion the existential analysis aims at disclosing the existentials constitutive of existence (SZ 37, 44, 50n1, 194, 197; 20: 34; 21: 410; 15: 377f).

Identity (*Identität*)

The principle of identity is typically expressed by the formula "A = A," but, as philosophers from Leibniz to Hegel clearly recognized, such purely formal equivalence obscures the fact that the principle speaks of the being of beings, namely, of the sameness of each being with itself, indeed, in the sense not of an empty oneness, devoid of any relation, but of a mediation holding sway in the unity. In contrast to these speculative idealists, Parmenides holds, not that identity is inherent in being, but rather that being, along with thinking, belongs to identity, i.e. to "the same" (*to auto*). So, too, being and thinking (the human being) belong to one another, which is unintelligible if we attempt to determine one separately and then bring it together with the other. In order to appreciate this "identity," it is necessary to leap beyond traditional conceptions of being and being-human to a place where neither serves as the ground. This place appears metaphysically as an abyss but is in fact where we already are, handed over to being and vice versa. In the present, being and human beings alike belong to the same all-positioning, technical world, where they are challenged to conform to the hegemony of powers of production (11: 47). What matters, however, is experiencing the identity that underlies that positioning or positionality, i.e. the appropriating event as the identity ("the same") to which being and being-human belong. The experience of this identity, this co-belonging to the appropriating event affords the possibility of turning the positionality back to it in a more originary way, retrieving the positionality from its domination. The appropriating event is the Parmenidean identity to which being and thinking co-belong. In contrast to the metaphysical construal of identity as a property of being, "the essence of identity is a property of the appropriating event" (11: 48; 79: 115–29).

Innerworldly (*innerweltlich*, MR: within-the-world)

"Innerworldly" designates handy and on-hand entities encountered within-the-world by Dasein in contrast to the world and worldhood of Dasein itself (SZ 65). It also distinguishes the way that Dasein is with (*Mitsein*) others in a shared world from the way that, intrinsically within-the-world (*innerweltliches Ansichsein*), others are here with it (*Mitdasein*) (SZ 118, 120).

Jaspers, Karl (1883–1969)

In 1920 Heidegger drafts a critical review of Jaspers' ground-breaking *Psychology of Worldviews* (1919), sending a slightly revised version to him the following year. Heidegger appreciates the concreteness and power of Jaspers' analyses of limit-situations where the unity of a life comes asunder. He touts the work for "making us aware of the problem of existence" in an unprecedented manner (9: 11, 15). Yet he also criticizes the supposedly "formal" character of its observational method and its failure to probe the historical roots and actual motivational basis of the preconception of life at work in the study (9: 22f, 27f)—just as later he takes pains to distinguish his conception of existence from Jaspers and to underscore that his position is philosophically oriented to being and not, like Jaspers, to existence as an entity's selfhood (35: 82–8; 49: 18f, 37–40).

Nonetheless, in an expression of indebtedness to Jaspers' work, Heidegger refers to *Psychology of Worldviews* as "an existential anthropology," showing the possibilities of existential analysis (SZ 249, 301, 338). Though Jaspers never seriously engaged the review's criticisms, a friendship blossomed, albeit with its ups and downs, and Heidegger visited Jaspers regularly until June 1933. However, Jaspers was bitterly disappointed by Heidegger's involvement with National Socialism, including his willingness to discredit opponents with anti-Semitic jargon (as in the case of Eduard Baumgarten, applying for a position in Göttingen). Heidegger stopped writing Jaspers in 1936, remaining silent when Jaspers was removed from his teaching position in 1937. Jaspers' 1945 report to the commission responsible for "cleansing" the university was negative, contributing to Heidegger's forced retirement. The report was probably unexpected by Heidegger since he had himself requested it. Yet in 1947 and again in 1949, thanks in part to the changed situation in Germany, Jaspers urged Heidegger's reinstatement. In 1949 he also initiated a new correspondence that Heidegger welcomed, though they were ultimately unable to overcome their differences, especially since in Jaspers' eyes Heidegger failed to appreciate the extent of his earlier political failings and his responsibility for their consequences. "Since 1933," Jaspers writes Heidegger, "a wilderness has been placed between us that seemed to become ever more impassible with what subsequently happened and was said."

Kant, Immanuel (1724–1804)

Between 1926 and 1936 the list of Heidegger's lectures on Kant's philosophy is extensive: (a) the last third of the 1925/26 logic lectures, his first foray into the *Critique of Pure Reason* (*CPR*); (b) the 1927 lectures, addressing Kant's thesis that being is not a predicate and his differentiation of persons from objects in nature; (c) the 1927/28 lectures, devoted to the B edition of the *CPR*; (d) the treatment of Kant's concept of world in the 1928/29 lectures; (e) the 1930 lectures on Kant's "two paths to freedom" (the Third Antinomy and his practical philosophy); and (f) the 1935/36 lectures on the question of the thing, including an extensive reading of the *CPR*'s Analytic of Principles (GA 21, 24, 25, 27, 31, 41). These lectures, together with his SZ remarks on Kant and, above all, the 1929 book *Kant and the Problem of Metaphysics* (GA 3), reveal an engagement with Kant, whose intensity is rivaled at the time only by his readings of Aristotle. The *CPR* dominates that engagement, and, indeed, taken together, his lectures, remarks, and book provide a commentary on every major segment of the work. At the end of his 1927/28 lectures, he notes: "Some years ago, as I studied the *CPR* again and read it, as it were, against the backdrop of Husserl's phenomenology, it was as though scales fell from my eyes and Kant became for me an essential confirmation of the correctness of the path on which I searched" (25: 431). In SZ he explains the reason for his enthusiasm: Kant is the "first and only one" to have looked to temporality to determine what it means for something to be (SZ 23).

Heidegger takes pains to explain the ontological baggage that hindered Kant from recognizing the implications of his insight. He takes issue in particular with Kant's remark that skepticism regarding the external world is "the scandal of philosophy" and with his failure to move beyond the ontologically deficient interpretation of the "I" as the reality of a *res cogitans* (SZ 203ff, 318ff). Nevertheless, Heidegger also interprets the *CPR* to be laying the foundation for metaphysics by working out the inner possibility of understanding what it means to be and, indeed, doing so on the basis of "time as the fundamental determination of finite transcendence" (3: 232, 243; 21: 306f, 312f; 25: 10, 51f). In these respects he takes Kant's transcendental philosophy to be anticipating and approximating the fundamental ontology of SZ.

As Heidegger distances himself from all talk of a transcending subjectivity, and as his fundamental ontology and metaphysics of Dasein give way to thinking being historically, he spends less time on Kant. Yet he does not completely ignore him, as can be gathered from his 1936 defense of Kant's notion of aesthetic disinterestedness as a kind of letting be (6.1: 106–13), his assimilation of Kant's transcendental method to the Leibnizian principle of sufficient reason in the 1955/56 lectures on the principle (10: 105–18), and his re-visiting of Kant's thesis about being in the 1961 address by that title (9: 445–80). Yet by the mid–1930s Heidegger no longer links his project directly with Kant's critical philosophy (see below).

Heidegger's early interpretations of Kant's critical philosophy remain, nonetheless, instructively idiosyncratic and challenging. Though Heidegger agrees with Neo-Kantian calls for revising the CPR, given its lopsided division (the Logic dwarfs the Aesthetic), he directly opposes their interpretation by adopting a phenomenological interpretive stance that emphasizes the role of sensibility (intuition and imagination) over understanding. Repeatedly citing the opening line of the Transcendental Aesthetic, he insists that Kant's major work is "intelligible only when one … keeps in mind, that for him knowledge proper is intuition" (21: 114f; 25: 83; 3: 243). Heidegger also makes the case that "the productive synthesis of imagination" is the crucial presupposition of the transcendental unity of apperception in the CPR (25: 410f, 421f; 26: 272). He reads the CPR as an inquiry into metaphysics as an investigation of "conditions of the possibility of yielding particular beings" (21: 307; 25: 10, 51f). In Kant and the Problem of Metaphysics, this "problem of metaphysics" is developed into "a fundamental ontology," i.e. the analysis of human existence and its understanding of being as the foundation of metaphysics (3: 232).

In the lectures of the late 1920s, he considers Kant's chapter on schematism—where the question of the categories' temporalization is located—as the "core" of the CPR. In the 1936 lecture, no doubt reflecting changes in Heidegger's own thinking, the Analytic of Principles is said to be "the decisive step." With this change,

Heidegger's mature assessment of Kant takes shape. According to that assessment, Kant's critical philosophy is largely responsible for cementing the conception of beings, insofar as they can be experienced, as *objects*—precisely by virtue of moving beyond (transcending) them and making them subject to subjectivity (10: 114).

Kierkegaard, Søren (1813–55)

Søren Kierkegaard was a Danish philosopher whose writings on human existence from the standpoint of Christian faith helped spawn twentieth-century existentialism. While eschewing existentialism and the theological trappings of Kierkegaard's thought, Heidegger's existential analysis is deeply indebted to Kierkegaard's "nudgings" (63: 5). While not sharing Kierkegaard's "inclination and direction," Heidegger writes (in early letters to his student, Karl Löwith) of the need to reappropriate Kierkegaard in a strictly critical way, from out of "our own situation," for Kierkegaard achieves a level of methodological rigor "seldom reached" in philosophy or theology (9: 41). SZ rehearses numerous Kierkegaardian themes, three of which Heidegger explicitly identifies. (1) He touts Kierkegaard with having "explicitly seized and penetratingly thought through the problem of existence" (SZ 235n). (2) He observes that "no one has gone further than Kierkegaard in analyzing anxiety," and, indeed, much of Heidegger's analysis of anxiety in the face of nothing (in contrast to fear of something) can be traced to Kierkegaard's *Concept of Anxiety* (SZ 190n). (3) He notes that, of all the discernments of "the *existentiel* phenomenon of the moment," Kierkegaard's is likely "the most penetrating" (SZ, 338n).

Yet at practically every juncture in SZ where he mentions Kierkegaard's importance, Heidegger stresses that Kierkegaard's studies remain existentiel, i.e. theological and psychological, rather than existential. So, too, he later stresses the differences between his and Kierkegaard's conceptions of existence (35: 82ff; 49: 26–37). Nonetheless, the extent of Kierkegaard's influence on Heidegger's existential analysis exceeds the three themes noted above. As examples, consider: the concept of repetition or retrieval rehearses

Kierkegaard's *Repetition*, the centrality of care is prefigured in Kierkegaard's "The Cares of the Pagans" and "What We Learn from the Lilies of the Fields and the Birds of the Air," and the analysis of death bears striking resemblances to Kierkegaard's "At the Graveside." So, too, the inevitable fallenness and ultimate insignificance of the everyday world of empty talk and curiosity, together with the silent call of conscience and the authentic need to choose to die to that world and one's thoughtless conformity to it, present the reader of SZ with an *Either/Or* and *Sickness Unto Death* (the apt titles of Kierkegaard's books). Even as Heidegger moves beyond the confines of fundamental ontology, echoes of Kierkegaard's thought continue to resonate in Heidegger's rejection of any pretension to the primacy of an aesthetic dimension and in his stress on human fragility and its dependency on a giving beyond human control. Finally, like Kierkegaard, Heidegger is fond of deploying the metaphor of a leap—albeit a leap not of faith, but of thinking. "All thinking is a leap" (65: 237).

Knowing (*Erkennen, Wissen*)

In order to come to know something, we have to be in a relation to it already. We have to have some access to it, an access that in turn demands that it has made itself, and perhaps continues to make itself, present to us in keeping with the nature of our relation to it. In this manner Heidegger maintains that knowledge (*Erkennen*) is "a way of being of being-in-the-world," grounded on already being alongside a world, i.e. on being captivated by it. (That access is accordingly not the same as mere familiarity or knowledge by acquaintance.) Neither an internal property of a knower nor an external property of what is known, "knowledge is a mode of being-here, founded on being-in-the-world" (SZ 62).

The term *Erkennen* builds on *Kennen*, a word designating mere cognizance, familiarity, or acquaintance with something. The term *Wissen* means having seen, in the broad sense of seeing, i.e. perceiving or taking up something present as such (5: 46, 348f). In Heidegger's later work he often plays on these differences, contrasting philosophy as knowing (*Wissen*) with "technical-practical cognition" (*Erkennen*) and with merely accumulative acquaintances (*Kenntnisse*) with things (65: 62f, 122; 6.2: 428f). "Knowing is more primordial than any type of 'cognition' and any type of 'willing'" (66: 120; 51: 3). (This last phrase contrasts with a tendency, earlier in the 1930s, to conjoin knowing and willing; see 5: 54f; 40: 23f). Knowing also has "nothing to do with 'consciousness'" (66: 120). It is one thing to be cognizant of this or that, another thing to know the essence of something (51: 3–6, 12f). "Customary cognition" contrasts with "cognition as knowing," demonstrating that the difference between cognition and knowing is not rigid (51: 3). Philosophical knowing is characterized in various ways: "safeguarding the truth of what is true (the essence of truth in being-here)," "masterful knowing" that comes with thinking on the basis of the beginning, "knowing that withstands the distress of the abandonment of being," "the essential knowing that already stands in the other beginning," "steadfastness," and "the memory of being" (65: 59, 62f, 158; 66: 120; 70: 112; 5: 349). Knowing, under these descriptions, lies outside the capacity of modern science (65: 141f, 144, 149).

Külpe, Oswald (1862–1915)

Oswald Külpe, whose work is the subject of Heidegger's first scholarly article, proposed a critical realism, not as a system but as a method of knowing, dubbed "realization," i.e. the translation of the perceptible data of perceived reality into scientifically conceived actualities, relative to the respective domain of natural science. The reality to be grasped is presupposed, not produced; only the thoughts in which they are presented and understood are created. As with other Neo-Kantians, Külpe finds Kant's system of categories insufficient and even counterproductive for the purposes of science, since it leaves the impression that science's validating principles can be secured without inspection of the state of science. Hence, for Külpe, critical realism requires a new sort of metaphysics, namely, metaphysics as an inductive science, complementing individual, empirical sciences as the foundation of scientific knowledge. Despite a deep affinity for Külpe's realism that lasts well into the period of SZ, Heidegger embraces Rickert's argument that the actuality presupposed in all knowledge of the actual cannot be part of the content of the knowledge, but instead must be its form, namely, its givenness, articulated in judging by the subject. In Heidegger's habilitation, he notes the possibility of superseding (*aufheben*) these "two most significant and fruitful epistemological 'orientations' [critical realism and transcendental idealism] in a higher unity" (1: 404n3).

Language (*Sprache*)

When we choose and use words for emphasis or some other reason, they are tools, serving a purpose that we set for them (based on a history of such usage). By contrast, when linguists or philologists observe and compare one language with another or different terms within the same language, language is something on-hand in nature or culture. Yet language could not be handy or on-hand, were it not for language as an existential, i.e. the primordial discursive disclosure of Dasein. Discourse pertains only to Dasein *and vice versa*. Language as discourse constitutes being-in-the-world with others by making things apparent. We see, hear, and feel the things that discourse makes apparent to us. "We do not say what we see but rather we see what one says" (20: 75; SZ 163). Discourse articulates, that is to say, it sorts out in meaningful wholes the intelligibility of being-in-the-world but as a precondition rather than the result of any use of language for a purpose set by us. Discourse would not be what it is, were it not about something, said, shared (communicated), and made known. Along with this structure, keeping silent and listening (to others and to oneself) are also inherent in discourse. As such, "discourse is the existential-ontological foundation of language."

The Greeks focused on assertions to work out discourse's basic structures (including "categories of meaning"), an orientation that ushered in a grammar and logic based upon "the ontology of the on-hand." Since this orientation persists in the present, there is a pressing need to liberate grammar from logic and re-establish the science of language on a more primordial ontological basis, i.e. a positive understanding of the basic a priori structure of discourse (SZ 32f, 133, 160–6, 220, 335).

Heidegger returns to this topic in his 1934 lectures, *Logic as the*

Question of the Essence of Language. Traditional logic—and any "philosophy of language" oriented to logic—has "misconstrued" the essence of language by construing it as a particular object-domain, a mere means of expression, or secondary to thinking (38: 14–21, 169; 12: 89). Language is to be found, not in dictionaries and grammars, but in the give and take of conversation (38: 24f). The conversation entails that language is itself inherently historical, in keeping with how, and ultimately who, the respective human beings are. Moreover, "there *are* entities ... the world holds sway ... only by virtue of language" (38: 169; 4: 37f). While the world and, with it, both being *and* beings are thus beholden to language, it can by no means be traced to some "encapsulated subject." For language itself is "neither something subjective nor something objective." Instead, as respectively historical, it is nothing else than the way Dasein's exposedness to beings as a whole, by virtue of being handed over to being, "happens." How history happens, how we are exposed to beings, and the open possibilities to which we have been handed over and on which that exposure depends— all this is bound up with our relation to our respective, historical language. This essence of language, Heidegger adds in conclusion, unfolds not where language has been twisted into a tool or means of expression but "where it happens as a world-forming power, i.e. where it first prefigures the being of beings in advance ... The primordial language is the language of poetry" (38: 168ff; 39: 119).

On one level, language "plays with us," allowing us to become mired in the usual, superficial meanings of words, as though these were somehow intrinsically standard-setting and violated by any attempt to listen to what language might otherwise say. The ordinary use of language—the inevitable palaver (*Gerede*) of inauthentic discourse—is an abuse of it. It is one thing to use language, another to speak it. When we speak, it is the language itself that is speaking through us (8: 122f, 132f; 12: 17f, 150, 243, 254). Hence, in order to experience and listen to what language is saying, it is necessary to take leave of ordinary language—itself "a forgotten poem"—and prepare for language's transformation, a transformation from speaking exclusively of beings to saying what it is to be-historical (65: 78; 12: 28, 151, 255f). So, too, it is necessary to move beyond the usual attempts to conceive language as an instantiation of some universal, e.g. human activity, a means of information-transfer, a medium or field of expression (12: 238f). The poetic experience of language provides clues in this regard (12: 163, 171, 176f, 185, 190). George's poem "The Word," for example, relates the poetic experience of the dependency of things' being on words, a dependency that the poet can "sing" but not control (12: 214f).

Speaking is one thing, saying is another. For while we can speak without saying anything, saying always shows something to someone else, rendering it apparent. But every saying also entails what is not said, which includes not only what is not yet shown but also what cannot be shown, i.e. the mystery. Moreover, even when *we* are able to show something by saying something, letting something show itself precedes this showing—just as we can speak only after we have *listened* to what language says, i.e. shows (12: 243). The ways of saying things pervade the essence of language in which what is present and absent affords or refuses itself, shows or withholds itself. With a view to thinking how these various relations of saying (with diverse origins of their own) come together in language, Heidegger names the essence of language "the saga" or "the saying" (*die Sage*), understood not as a mere tale or legend, but in one of its original senses as showing and moving the world, revealing and sustaining the relations of its fourfold regions to one another, by keeping silently to itself (12: 184f, 188, 202f, 242f). Thus, the essence of language is the language of the essence, "the gathering that calls without a sound, the saga/the saying that moves the world-relation, the sound of stillness" (12: 204). The poet George *says* as much with his verse "Where the word breaks off no thing may be," since "an 'is' affords itself where the word breaks off" (12: 204).

Language is not merely the product of our activity of speaking. To the contrary, humans speak only by listening to what language says, something that great poets epitomize. At the same time, there is no language without human speakers. Language affords humans the ability to speak and show things, but it does so only to the extent that humans let it be heard (12: 243ff). Thus, language and being-human belong together. Yet the essence of language itself (the saga) holds them together insofar as it first affords the free opening of the clearing where whatever is can come into its own, i.e. where what is present can persist and what is absent can withdraw. Equivalently, language affords the sort of "there is" that "being" needs in order to come into its own as presence and, indeed, as a presence to mortals whereby they come into their own. The saga, the essence of language, animates this interconnected manner of coming-into-one's-own (*Ereignen*).

The *Ereignis*, the "appropriating event" that is the central theme of Heidegger's later philosophy, is the relation of all relations, because, far from being subsequent to its relata, it opens-and-appropriates historical being and Dasein to one another, thereby first bringing them into their own.

This appropriating event can be experienced—not produced or explained—in the way that the saga, the essence of language, affords being (the presence and absence of beings) to mortals. The saga thus allows human beings to come into their own so long as they are first silent in order to listen and answer to it (12: 249). In this relation of the saga to its speakers, the saga and the speakers (mortals) need each other, though the speakers are speakers only by virtue of first listening to the saga (what the language says). In this process, language appropriates speakers to it, those who respond appropriately to it. The distinctiveness of language thus resides in the appropriating event. Indeed, the appropriating event (*Ereignis*) itself is "telling" (*sagend*) even where, in the positionality of modern technology, language is reduced to formalizable, computable information (12: 251f). Clarifying a remark made over a decade earlier, Heidegger concludes that language is the house of being because language, as the saga, belongs to the appropriating event (12: 255; 9: 361; 79: 160–76).

Lask, Emil (1875–1915)

After studying with major figures in the southwest Neo-Kantian school (Rickert, Windelband), Emil Lask taught shortly in Heidelberg before dying on the eastern front in Galicia. Lask's *Logik der Philosophie und Kategorienlehre* (1910) and *Die Lehre vom Urteil* (1911) influenced the young Heidegger, particularly in his habilitation (1: 191). In Heidegger's second publication he observes that "Lask with this theory of predication tries to bring Aristotle and Kant as close to one another as possible" (1: 33). Lask's work builds on Hermann Lotze's distinction of the conception of validity from the concept of being (e.g. the difference between a proposition's truth and its being asserted *hic et nunc*) (1: 170). Lask contends that logic as the non-sensory domain of validity is "homeless" in a tradition that recognizes only the possibility of the sensory and the supersensory (metaphysics). Lask proposes a logic of philosophy, a theory of categories that corresponds to the two distinct spheres of validity and being (1: 24). This proposal thus extends Kant's doctrine of categories beyond the sensory domain to which Kant confined them. In addition to restricting categories to knowledge of nature, leaving the study of history in limbo, Kant lacks the categories for his own critique. As Heidegger puts it in his habilitation, "logic requires categories of its own. There must be a logic of logic" (1: 288). Lask further departs from Kant and moves closer to Aristotle by developing the categories without first assigning a foundational role to subjectivity. For Lask the category forms (i.e. it is valid for) material independent of knowledge, constituting a "sense" (1: 24f). Experience and judgments are based upon categorical validities, truths that are identical with the things themselves, rather than vice versa—a "relation of form" that lines up with the medieval doctrine of the transcendental character of *verum*, its convertibility with being (1: 265). Distinguishing the relation to the theoretical sense from the material grasped by it, Lask speaks of knowing as "living only in the truth, i.e. the theoretical sense," whereby the material is merely "meant." Echoing these themes, Heidegger observes that "whatever is known ... must enter into the world of sense" (1: 280). Yet for Heidegger this entry into the world of sense is only possible by judgment, and what distinguishes the logical domain is "intentionality" (1: 280f). Following Rickert, he contends that "remaining"—as Lask does—"within the logical sphere of sense and the structure of sense" is inadequate and that the relation to the subject must be taken into account. "One cannot view logic and its problems in their true light at all if the context, out of which they are interpreted, does not become a translogical context" (1: 405).

Last God, the (*der letzte Gott*)

Early and late, Heidegger makes no secret of his rejection of metaphysical approaches to the divinity. He dismisses "Christian

philosophy" as a "wooden iron" (40: 9) and, in the course
of demonstrating the onto-theological character of metaphysics,
observes that one can neither pray nor fall down on one's knees
before the God of philosophy (11: 77). In the *Contributions* he
goes even further, refusing to look for God among beings, decrying
the effort as destructive of anything divine (65: 400, 437). Nor
is God to be identified with historical being as the appropriating
event since God is in need of the latter no less than humans are.
Historical being is the "between" in which "Gods and humans
know each other, i.e. decide where they belong" (65: 409, 413,
428).

"The Last God"—Schelling's name for Jesus, the end of pagan
polytheism—is the title of the final movement of the *Contributions
to Philosophy*, the attempt to prepare for another beginning,
retrieving what was forgotten in the first beginning and its
metaphysical legacy, a legacy that includes a causal reduction of
being and beings to a supreme being. The last God accordingly
stands outside any theism or a-theism that presupposes metaphysics
(65: 411). At the same time, talk of "last" in this context does
not mean cessation but "the profoundest beginning," "the most
extreme and shortest decision about what is supreme," and "the
other beginning of immeasurable possibilities of our history" (65:
405ff, 411, 414). The last God unfolds in the hint (*Wink*) that
places beings in their uttermost abandonment by being and at the
same time radiates the truth of being—the self-concealing—at the
profoundest depths of that abandonment. At this point earth and
world meet again in the simplest struggle, taking place in the realms
and levels of sheltering the truth in beings, rescuing them from a
measureless yet distorted extinction (65: 410). This sheltering
is demanded by God Himself "and the way God needs us." His
passing-by demands that we stand fast in the midst of beings so
that they are maintained in the simplicity of the essences that they
have regained "as work, implement, thing, deed, look and word"
(65: 413). Thinking the truth of historical being succeeds "only if
in God's passing-by the empowerment of human beings becomes
apparent ..." (65: 414).

"How few know of this, that God waits for the grounding of the
truth of historical being and, with it, for the human being to make
the leap into being-here" (65: 417). The profoundest godlessness
lies in the illusion that the human being is waiting for God, as

though a site were not historically imparted to humans "standing in the furthest distance to the passing-by of the God," so as to refashion beings into their essential determination and liberate them "from the misuse of the machinations that, perverting everything, exhaust beings in exploitation" (65: 417).

Leap (*Sprung*)

"The Leap," the name of the third movement of the *Contributions to Philosophy*, designates what is most daring about originative thinking, "tossing everything customary behind and awaiting nothing immediately from beings, but instead, before anything else, jumping into the belongedness to historical being in its complete unfolding as the appropriating event." Though appearing as the height of recklessness, it is attuned by the awe (*Scheu*) in which the will, in the basic mood of reservedness, overcomes itself and steadfastly exposes itself to the nearness that is also most far away, namely, the nearness of the unhiddenness of beings that itself is hidden and grounded in Da-sein (65: 227). The leap is "the most extreme projection of the unfolding of historical being, such that we put ourselves into what is thus appropriated, become steadfast, and through the appropriating event first become ourselves." We are always already thrown and projecting, but what matters is whether, in projecting, we experience ourselves as thrown, "i.e. appropriated by historical being." The alternative is that what appears in the projection is reduced, as merely the emerging (*physis—idea*) in itself, to the process of being made present (65: 230f, 239). The beginning only happens in the leap, and beginning the other beginning requires the proper preparation or run-up. This preparation takes place by asking the basic question (What is being?), as a question springing from the distress of the *abandonment-of-being*, in order to "jump from it back into the primordial experience of thinking the truth of historical being" (65: 233; 69: 132).

The leap into that primordial experience leaps past talk of the "ontological difference," "conditions of the possibility," and "transcendence" into the appropriation of Dasein. That appropriation is the relation of Dasein and historical being (the happening of the concealed unhiddenness of beings), their mutual need for one another. So, too, leaping past metaphysical attempts to dismiss or overcome talk of "nothing" and the "not," the leap jumps into the "wholeheartedness of *the not in historical being*" and the fissure (*Zerklüftung*) that is the "unfolding" of that wholeheartedness (65: 244, 264, 278–82). This leap presents Dasein with the possibility of experiencing historical being in its hiddenness rather than simply leaving and forgetting it. While "the experience of historical being ... brings beings back into their limits and takes the apparent uniqueness of their primacy from them," they do not become anything less; to the contrary, "they are all the more, i.e. more essential in the essential unfolding of historical being" (65: 255, 262, 273). The leap thus presents the possibility of changing the relation, not only of historical being and Dasein, but also, in the process, of the relation of Dasein to beings—including the technological relation to the living, nature, and earth (65: 274–8).

Letting be (*Gelassenheit,* also "releasement")

In contrast to the unlikely prospects of simply abandoning or fully embracing technology, Heidegger proposes a stance of simultaneously saying yes and no to technological objects. Adopting an old word from Meister Eckhart, he calls this stance "equanimity towards things" (*Gelassenheit zu den Dingen*), i.e. letting them be. Genuine equanimity means that we have been released from our designs on things; here the translation "releasement" has the advantage of warding off the sense that letting be or not is something in our control, as though it were an exercise of our subjective will.

With this all-important proviso, however, letting be means letting technological objects into our daily world but also letting them be outside it, resting upon themselves "as things that are nothing absolute but remain instead dependent upon something higher." We view them no longer in a purely technical or technological way, but with a vigilant awareness that the sense of the technological world remains hidden from us. "Mystery" is the name for what in this way shows itself and at the same time withdraws. It is hidden in the technological world. Thus, hand-in-hand with the proposed equanimity is "openness to the mystery." In this way there is a chance of living in the world "in a completely different way," and there is the promise of a new basis, a new autochthony, one that calls back the old, quickly disappearing one into a new form. In the meantime, however, humanity on earth remains in danger of technology so beguiling that calculative thinking remains the only sort of thinking in use, the only sort of thinking that counts. The danger, in other words, is that we become indifferent to reflectiveness (*Nachdenken*) and thus throw away precisely what makes us human. What matters then is to save this essence of the human by keeping reflectiveness alive, since it is the lifeblood of the equanimity and openness described above (16: 527f).

Leibniz, Gottfried Wilhelm (1646–1716)

From his first extensive lectures on Leibniz in 1928 (GA 26) to his lectures in the mid–1950s on the principle of sufficient reason (GA 10), Heidegger repeatedly touts the importance of Leibniz, "the first to think clearly ... the volitional essence of the being of beings" (5: 245; 77: 53f). With his account of the unifying urge— the representing, perceptive will—as the defining feature of beings (monads) in general, Leibniz initiates the common theme of all major German thinkers from Kant to Nietzsche: a metaphysics of the will (7: 112; 8: 95; 10: 32, 96; 26: 103f, 112–16).

In addition to playing a pivotal role in the development of mathematical logic, computers, and the radical interpretation of subjectivity within German Idealism, "the thinking of Leibniz bears and stamps the chief tendency of what we can name the metaphysics of the modern age, thought broadly enough." His principle of sufficient reason first comes fully into its own in the current "techno-logical–scientific construction of the world." The self-proclaimed "atomic age" underwrites computational thinking to give "scientific thinking an axiomatic form." Modernity in this sense is only beginning, and it is the age of Leibniz, the age in which the principle of sufficient reason is the supreme principle (10: 31, 51f).

While Heidegger initially attempts to ground Leibniz's logic in Leibniz's metaphysics, he later casts doubt on the meaningfulness of the debate over the relative priority of Leibniz's logic or metaphysics.

However, in his mature treatment of Leibniz's philosophy, he criticizes it for failing to countenance the self-sameness and individuality, historicity and ungrounded character—not of beings—but of being. He also takes Leibniz to task for taking the principle of sufficient reason to be self-evident and for restricting the scope of its significance to beings.

Logic (*Logik*)

Heidegger describes logic as "the science of the forms of the basic configurations and basic rules of the assertion" (38: 5) and "the science of thinking, the doctrine of the rules of thinking and the forms of what is thought" (40: 128; 15: 278). Since the time of Aristotle, logic has consisted in analysis of assertions, their combination into the form of an inference, positing of rules (especially for inference), and consideration of formal structures (38: 2–5). While the Greeks understood language first as discourse, they focused on assertions to work out its basic structures (including "categories of meaning"), an orientation that ushered in a grammar and logic based upon "the ontology of the on-hand." Assertions, particularly once committed to writing, can be examined as something on-hand just as much as any natural object. Logic treats assertions in precisely this sense. It sprang from metaphysics and at the same time came to dominate the latter, contributing to the "fatal" view that being is "the emptiest and most universal concept" (5: 352; 65: 429). Far from being ontologically neutral, logic in this traditional sense solidifies metaphysics by subordinating all thinking and saying to the framework of what can be thought or said about beings. There is no justification of this subordination, and the presupposition that a logical interpretation of "being" is the only possible one is simply a "prejudice." The key to undermining this logical prejudice is to rethink language more fundamentally (SZ 32f, 133, 160–6, 220, 335; 65: 130). Mathematical or symbolic logic (*Logistik*) is unsuited for this purpose. "Symbolic logic has nothing to do with philosophy. It is pure calculation, higher-level mathematics, the mathematizing of all representing, applicable to anything possible. It is universally valid and thus presumes to be true." Taking symbolic logic to be philosophy goes hand-in-hand with European globalization, as the technological relation to being determines humanity in general (15: 437f).

Particularly in the 1920s, Heidegger does not invariably equate logic with traditional or formal logic of the sort criticized above. In keeping with his studies of Neo-Kantian forms of transcendental logic and Husserl's logical investigations, the early Heidegger endorses philosophical investigations of logic and its principles. Thus, he differentiates a "philosophical" logic as a science of truth as such from formal logic or logic as a theory of science (21: 5–19). In SZ he contrasts Plato and Aristotle's "productive logic" from the kind of logic that "limps behind them" (SZ 10). In the same spirit he affirms that logic can be "an essential path into philosophy, provided that it is philosophical" (26: 5f, 23–7). By 1929/30, however, he questions whether metaphysics' orientation to logic (the logic of assertions, to be sure) obstructs us from seeing the distinctive problem of the world ("the manifestation of beings as such and as a whole"). The truth or falsity of an assertion is founded upon a "pre-predicative manifestation or, better, a *pre-logical truth*" (29/30: 418–21, 494).

Logos

Logos stems from *legein*, a word that "of itself has nothing to do with saying and with language," describing instead "the original and fundamental relation to beings" (9: 280). Heidegger elaborates this relation by hearkening back to the original meaning of *legein* as "laying" something down in the sense of "bringing it to lie." Far from indiscriminately heaping things together, this bringing to lie is a "gathering for safekeeping," one that selects—literally, "reads out" (*Aus-lese*)—for that purpose. Such a lay of things is at work in the way that they lie sheltered together before us and concern us. This gathering safeguards them in their unhiddenness, allowing them to be present to us. The meaning of *logos* as saying, hearing, conversing (the essence of language) rests upon this gathering of things together, bringing them to lie and letting them be present to us, sheltered in their unhiddenness. "The *logos* of itself brings what appears, what comes forth to lie before us, to appear, to show itself, to luminous self-showing" (7: 218f; 40: 131–57).

Insofar as the *logos* lets things lie before us as such, "it discloses what is present in its presencing"—and since such dis-closing is *aletheia*, "it [*aletheia*] and *logos* are the same" (7: 225). Not the same as what is present or its presence, *logos*, like *aletheia*, is a name for "being" in the earliest era of Western philosophy. "Since the dawn of thinking 'being' names the presence of what is present, in the sense of the gathering that clears and shelters, which is thought and designated as the *logos*. The *logos* (*legein*, reading, gathering) is experienced on the basis of *aletheia*, the disclosing sheltering" (5: 352; 10: 161, 163; 40: 139ff). *Logos* as human language is rooted in this primordial sense of *logos* (9: 279).

Machination (*Machenschaft*)

In the age of machination, everything is taken to be something that can be made, as long as there is the will to do it. (*Machenschaft*—like the term for power, *Macht*—is related to the word for making or doing, *machen*). As far as machination is concerned, there are only beings, and they are exclusively what human beings can manipulate, calculate, and produce. Any resistance to it is mere material for its expansion. There may be problems and difficulties, but nothing is fundamentally questionable (herein lies the seeds of its nihilism) since what things fundamentally are has been decided. They are things made (products) with the power to make (produce) other such things. In other words, machination construes beings not simply as objects but as products, the outcome of *techne*. Since questioning cannot be fully eliminated, the age of machination compartmentalizes what persists as questionable in the innocuous form of lived experience (*Erlebnis*). Lived experience remains within the confines of machination by representing what is mysterious or enchanting, making it public and accessible to everyone, and thus making machination all the more necessary (65: 108f, 123f; 66: 17).

As the unconditional and exclusive dominance of making and the made, machination is the "mask of 'true actuality,'" devoid of limits or awe. Taking itself as eternal, machination insures and thus echoes the nullity of beings and the abandonment of being. Working under the schema of computing and thus explaining everything, it throws everything together in the same way, leaving them utterly alien to themselves (65: 151f; 66: 16–25).

While the Christian–biblical interpretation of beings as created sets the stage for the age of machination, the downfall of *aletheia* at the first beginning of Western thinking set it in motion. Nietzsche's conception of being as the will to power captures its essence. Machination is "the unconditional consummation of being as the will to power," and its devastation appears "in the form of the speediest and broadest sort of progress in all planning and calculation." It presents humanity with the opportunity to dominate the globe, completely reducing it to calculations of "commodities" and "values." Machination demands a kind of humanity that operates (*betreibt*) "an essentially rootless tradition of metaphysics." Establishing this aspect of machination is left to Americanism (66: 17f; 67: 148f, 150; 71: 93f, 101f, 111f).

Meaning (*Bedeutung*, MR & S: significance)

Meaning first takes shape in the use of implements, a use that is tied to Dasein's being-in-the-world and foregoing disclosure of its worldliness. Implements form a whole in which each refers to something else that it is for (*Wozu*). What is handy has, as such, this relevance to and involvement with something else. For example, a hammer is for hammering, hammering for attaching something, and so on. Yet there is no such relevance unless someone has let things that are handy "within an environment" be relevant, making it possible to use them as such. The relevance itself "as the being of the handy" is in each case uncovered only on the basis of a foregoing appreciation of an entire complex of relevance (*Bewandtnisganzheit*), a suitedness to the world that Dasein has already disclosed in allowing for that relevance. This disclosure is the understanding of world to which Dasein always already comports itself. This world is what, in the last analysis, the entire complex of relevance, the implements taken together, is for (*Worumwillen*).

This world is so familiar that the understanding lets itself be determined "in and by" the relations that designate the relevance of things, relations that refer them to one another by indicating what they are for. These relations, in just this sense, are their meaning (just as we might say, for example, the hammer is "meant" for hammering), and Dasein means something to itself precisely in virtue of its familiarity with those relations. In this way meaning extends across: (a) relations among implements (their *Wozu*, their relevance to one another), (b) the relation of an entire complex of implements to the world understood by Dasein (their *Worumwillen*, their relevance to Dasein as what they are for the sake of), and (c) the relation of Dasein to itself.

"Meaningfulness" (*Bedeutsamkeit*) is Heidegger's term for this entire, stratified complex, making up the structure (worldhood) of the world. "Meaningfulness is that on the basis of which the world as such is disclosed" (a world that becomes utterly meaningless in angst). Meaningfulness is the ontological condition of the possibility that Dasein, in interpreting, can disclose meanings "that for their part in turn found the possible being of word and language." When Dasein takes something *as* this or that, the interpretation lays out a relevance disclosed in the understanding of the world (SZ 83–8, 123, 143ff, 149f, 186f). In keeping with Heidegger's mature understanding of language as "the primordial essence of truth," he later rejects any implication that language rests upon more basic levels (SZ 442).

Whether this implication should be drawn from the analysis in SZ is complicated by the account of discourse as a basic existential. Discourse meaningfully articulates an intelligibility on the basis of some foregoing sense. That intelligibility—encompassing everything that falls within the active engagement of being-in-the-world and, equivalently, being-with—is "always already" sorted out in various ways. As a basic existential, discourse arguably shares in shaping that intelligibility, Dasein's foregoing engagement with the world. For example, it is easy to imagine a scenario where saying the phrase "You'll have to turn right at the light" can be a way of sorting out and shaping what is intelligible (what can be understood) about an approaching situation. Saying as much articulates a "whole of meaning," that can be broken down into meanings (turning, the light, right, etc.). In the discourse "the whole of meaning of intelligibility" comes to words. "The words accrue to the meanings. But lexical items [*Wörterdinge*] are not outfitted with meanings" (SZ 161). Against the backdrop of this account of the origin of meanings out of the meaningfulness, i.e. the worldhood of Dasein, Heidegger contends: "The doctrine of meaning is rooted in the ontology of Dasein" (SZ 166).

Metaphysics (*Metaphysik*)

Duns Scotus' commentary on Aristotle's *Metaphysics* begins with the question of "whether the subject matter of metaphysics is being qua being (as Avicenna supposes) or God and the intelligences (as the Commentator Averroes supposes)." This question encapsulates a long-standing debate over the content of Aristotle's metaphysics: is it basically ontology (a study of beings insofar as they exist) or theology (a study of the supreme or first being), or, if it is both, how are they related? Heidegger's own early metaphysical interests lie primarily with the ontological question. However, in SZ he complains that ontology is "naïve and opaque" if it has not first clarified sufficiently the sense of being that the question employs (SZ 11). In his maturer writings, Heidegger contends that "metaphysical thinking is always onto-logy or it is nothing at all" (5: 210). Since there is no being in general, but only the being of some entity or other, in SZ Heidegger investigates the question of the sense of being through the analysis of the entity whose being matters to it: Dasein. Posing the question of being is nothing other than a radical extension of a tendency inherent in Dasein itself, its pre-ontological understanding of being. "The ontological analysis of Dasein in general makes up the fundamental ontology," from which all other ontologies must spring (SZ 12–15).

No change in Heidegger's thinking expresses the difference between Heidegger I and Heidegger II as clearly as the change in his attitude toward metaphysics does. In a 1919 letter to the priest who married him and Elfriede, he writes that he finds himself forced to leave Catholicism "for reasons concerning the epistemology of history," but that he is committed to "Christianity and metaphysics," albeit in a new sense. For the following ten years he can be said to pursue this new sense of metaphysics, culminating in the fundamental ontology of SZ and the lectures and essays—notably "What is Metaphysics?"—that immediately follow it. In his 1928 lectures he introduces a "metaphysics of Dasein" or metontology, a turn back to Dasein in the wake of fundamental ontology (26: 199). In *Kant and the Problem of Metaphysics* he advances fundamental ontology as "merely the first step of the metaphysics of Dasein" (3: 232). During the early 1930s Heidegger begins to reconceive metaphysics. In 1929/30 he insists that, while metaphysics is a basic event in Dasein, it is no science and that we must leave open what it is (29/30: 12). In lectures in the summer of 1932 he begins to re-think in historical, non-metaphysical terms the first beginning of Western philosophy and the nearness yet hiddenness of what is originary in that beginning (35: 33–42). Nonetheless, he continues to employ "metaphysics" in a positive sense as late as his 1934/35 Hölderlin-lectures and the 1935 *Introduction to Metaphysics* (though in the latter he calls ontology into question).

However, by 1936 his break with metaphysics is complete. Appropriating a phrase in the title of a Carnap essay which is highly critical of him, Heidegger publishes an excerpt of his writings from this period under the title "Overturning of Metaphysics" (7: 67–98). Hegel's philosophy is said to be the beginning of the culmination of metaphysics that comes to an end, first in Nietzsche, then in technology. In asking its leading question "what are beings?" metaphysics recognizes only beings, not the sense of being, not historical being (the presence as such of beings to Dasein). It does not ask the basic question: "what is being?" "Meta-physics is the justification of the "physics" of beings through the constant flight in the face of historical being" (65: 423). Indeed, metaphysics does not countenance Dasein at all, taking its bearings instead from assertions about beings and the conception of beingness (*Seiendheit*) underlying those assertions. Thus, metaphysics makes being into a particular being, namely, an idea (65: 415, 426, 456, 472–92). Metaphysics purveys the illusion that being is given its due by affirming the vacuousness of nothing, namely, that beings are utterly devoid of nothing, that they provide the measure and basis for the determination of being, and that historical being does not have its own truth (70: 27). There are echoes of historical being in metaphysics but, in keeping with the first beginning of Western thinking, it never experiences the truth of historical being (71: 104f, 114). In the wake of his interpretation of Nietzsche's nihilism, Heidegger further associates metaphysics with a conception of beings in terms of a will to power, production, and machination. Whereas metaphysics thinks what is true of beings in terms of some epochal sense of being, it leaves unthought the truth of historical being (5: 209ff; 67: 40–51, 145ff). Not incidentally, world-views are a by-product of metaphysics, and the ends of art and metaphysics go hand-in-hand, respectively (67: 107–22).

In the 1950s Heidegger grounds the metaphysics of the will—dominating the German metaphysical tradition and underlying the hegemony of technology—in Leibniz's metaphysical principle of sufficient reason, where nothing is said *to be* that is not grounded in some expression or exercise of power. Also in the 1950s, rehearsing Scotus' query (see above), he characterizes metaphysics as onto-theology. The traditional debate over the subject matter of Aristotelian metaphysics is in fact integral to the history of metaphysics inasmuch as metaphysics takes some pre-eminent being or sense of being and generalizes to all beings. In this sense, Christian medieval thought identifies everything in terms of creation (creator and created), modernity identifies everything in terms of subjectivity (subjects and objects for subjects), positivism, like Nietzsche's will to power, takes there to be nothing that is not scientifically determinable and thus potentially useful.

Mineness (*Jemeinigkeit*)

In SZ Dasein's respective mineness signals that Dasein is in each case its own. The concept draws on the fact that in addressing Dasein, we are speaking of someone capable of saying "I am," "you are" (SZ 42). By citing both first and second person in this connection, Heidegger signals that this feature is recognizable in others, something that his analysis of "being-with" seems to suppose. However, he elaborates its significance mainly in terms of the first person. "Dasein is the entity that I respectively am myself" (SZ 53). The fact that each Dasein speaks in the first person indicates not only that it is related to itself (its being) but that it is capable of doing so in the form of self-possession or lack of self-possession. Mineness signifies that Dasein can choose itself, attain itself, lose itself, and that it may never attain itself but only appear to do so. Thus, the notions of authenticity and inauthenticity, of being and not being oneself, are grounded in the "respective mineness" of human existence.

Dasein's respective mineness is co-extensive with its existence. The two designations are synecdoches, in the sense that each designates the whole from a partial perspective. Together, Dasein's respective mineness and its factical existence (its facticity of having to be) distinguish it from anything on-hand within the world (SZ 41ff, 53, 191, 232, 240).

The ontological significance of Dasein's mineness is by no means the mere fact that Dasein is in each case someone capable of saying "I" or "my." In other words, its mineness does not consist simply in its capacity to use these indexicals (as opposed, for example, to mere demonstratives). The importance of mineness lies in the fact that Dasein's possession of itself can be illusory and, indeed, paradigmatically so when it identifies with an instantiation of the crowd, *das Man* (SZ 115f). The sense of authentically being one's own person requires that Dasein be capable of taking possession of itself from the vantage point of the first person. Hence, conscience—Dasein's call to itself to be who it authentically is—is also respectively mine or yours (SZ 278).

Modality (*Modalität*)

One way to approach the issue of modality is to start from a sense of actuality as the perceptibly given and define the other modalities (possibility and necessity) interchangeably by way of negation, as what is not perceptibly given but imaginary. On this view, the actual is what is the case, while possibility and necessity are what is not the case but may or must be respectively. More precisely, possibility (what may be) is not what is or what must be; necessity (what must be) is not what simply is or may be; actuality (what is) is not what merely may be or must be. In contrast to this approach, Heidegger takes a sense of possibility (rather than actuality) as primary and refuses to understand modalities by purely formal appeals to negation as a logical operator. Instead he not only contends that all three modalities are contained in being, but also questions the metaphysical view that together they exhaust the essence of being and that the actual is the primary modality of being (51: 23f; 67: 174). Insofar as the modalities concern beings, they have no bearing on the basic question of what being is (65: 287–82). In SZ Heidegger employs "modality" in the sense of an existential modification or mode (SZ 59, 305, 327).

Modernity (*Neuzeit*)

The origin of modernity is the transformation of the interpretation of beings and truth, prominently beginning with Descartes. To be a being is transformed from being created (*ens creatum*) to being perceived (*ens perceptum*), and truth is transformed into certainty, ultimately certainty as machination. Beings insofar as they are perceived by the ego (the subject of the cogito) replace the infinite being (*ens infinitum*) as the absolute being. Human liberation, conquest of the world, and the dominance of reason are all essential consequences of this transformation (88: 71f). "The will that sees an essential goal in the greatest possible duration of the greatest possible order of the greatest possible masses ... is the hidden metaphysical essence of modernity for three centuries." Heidegger credits Nietzsche with foreseeing that this will—in the form of technology—attains unconditional proportions in the twentieth century (51: 17). What characterizes modernity is the way that human beings assert themselves over everything through objectification. Having posited the world as the whole of producible objects, modern humanity sets itself up as the producer in relation to everything, including itself, and thereby emerges into a position of unconditioned dominance (5: 289). "The fundamental feature of modernity is the conquest of the world as a picture. The word 'picture' now means the image represented for producing." In modernity, the world becomes a world-picture, willfully fashioned and maintained by human beings in a process abetted by modern science (5: 88–96, 100ff, 106–11).

Moira

In characterizing thinking and being as the same, Parmenides names the unfolding duality of being and beings (presence and what is present) and the way that thinking unfolds within that duality. Heidegger glosses this "same" theme in both fragments as the revealing bestowal of the belonging-together of the duality and the thinking that comes about within it. Like the appropriating event, it cannot be described in terms solely of being or thinking or even their belonging-together. It is the unfolding of the twofold (being and beings) in the sense of their un-concealing (*aletheia*). Though thinking in a sense holds itself apart from the twofold, it does so only as required by unfolding, i.e. un-concealing the presence of what is present (7: 241f). Parmenides speaks of Moira—a goddess of fate—binding being to be a whole and immovable. Heidegger describes her as imparting the duality and yet fatefully concealing this unconcealment as such, so that only what is present comes to appear. This concealing opens the door to the privileged status of appearances and seeing, and eventually of the natural light of reason, a privileged status oblivious to the unconcealing of the twofold it presupposes. In this way Moira is the destiny of being, being in the sense of the twofold (7: 243f).

Mood (*Stimmung*)

Moods are different ways in which we are oriented to this or that, ways that disclose our situation holistically (albeit not completely). They affect how the world and entities within the world appear to us, e.g. as inviting or irritating, enthralling or threatening. Moods are pre-reflective, and they are matters neither of our choice nor our making. Instead they come over us as part of our thrownness into the world. If we try to adopt a certain attitude toward others, we may tap into or awaken latent moods, but the mere decision to adopt such an attitude cannot of itself produce a mood. Nor are we always clear about our moods' hold on us. Sometimes a friend or an event makes it clear that we have been acting out of fear or love, even while we have been blind to the fact. While some moods (e.g. fears) orient us to a specific being or beings, other moods (e.g. anxiety, kinds of boredom) orient us to our situation as a whole.

Moods have an existential significance. They tell us how we are, the disposition or state of mind we find ourselves in. Dasein always finds itself in a mood, always already attuned (*gestimmtes Sichbefinden*). "Mood represents the manner in which in each case I primarily am the thrown entity [that I am]" (SZ 340). It is far closer to the truth to say "I feel, therefore I am" than to say "I think, therefore I am," not only because moods precede knowing and willing, but also because they tell us, more fundamentally than anything else does, *that* we are. Yet they do not say where Dasein's existence comes from or where it is going. Instead they bring us face to face with the burdensomeness of existence as something handed over to us that we have to be—though they do so principally in flight from that burden. In all these ways, moods disclose to us our existence as something not to be confused with anything simply on-hand or handy (SZ 134–7, 265, 270, 276, 335, 339f; 71: 218).

Moods overcome us, but they come neither from without nor from within (as though they were mental states). Instead they emerge as a manner of being-in-the-world. *"The mood has in each case already disclosed being-in-the-world as a whole and first makes possible directing oneself to something"* (SZ 137). It also reveals Dasein's openness to the world, its capacity to be affected by the world and things within the world. At the same time there is no understanding that is not disposed and attuned, pervaded by a mood. A mood is a "medium" of thinking and acting (SZ 142, 148, 253, 335; 29/30: 101f).

In SZ Heidegger chiefly elaborates two moods, fear and angst, with the aim of showing that their basic existential character, consisting in "bringing" Dasein "back to" itself, is grounded in its temporality (SZ 340–5). However, he mentions several other moods that can be interpreted in this temporal way: hope, joy, enthusiasm, cheerfulness, disgust, sadness, melancholy, and despair (SZ 345).

The expression "basic mood" (*Grundstimmung*) only makes a single appearance in SZ, but becomes more important in Heidegger's writings after 1929. While these basic moods have a kinship with disposition as elaborated in SZ, Heidegger is later critical of that elaboration given its suggestion that a disposition is a condition (*Zustand*) (71: 221). As Heidegger's thinking moves from a transcendental to a more historical orientation, he examines several basic moods: boredom (GA 29/30), Hölderlin's holy mourning (39: 140, 182f), Greek wonder (GA 45), and the reserve, shock, and awe, characteristic of another beginning of thinking (GA 45, GA 65). He introduces the notion of mystery in terms of the mood that attunes us to the indeterminate manifestness of beings as a whole (9: 192ff). In his 1934 commentary on Hölderlin, he stresses that a mood is not something subjective, not a mere feeling, mental state, or epiphenomenon; nor can it be grasped by way of the traditional doctrine of the soul or mind. In fact, the character of basic moods compels us to give up the standard conception of human beings as rational animals or subjects, whose essence consists in representing and thinking objects. "The mood as mood allows the openness of beings to occur" (39: 82). Basic moods are not something in us; rather we find ourselves transported into them, and, as such, they first expose us, together with others, to entities (39: 89, 139, 223).

Taking Hölderlin's holy mourning as his model, Heidegger identifies four essential features of a basic mood. They *move* us *away* from one thing and *move* us *into* something else. Holy mourning, for example, moves us away from particular beings, placing us in a relation to the departed gods, and, at the same time, it moves us into relations to the earth, the landscape, and our homeland. In keeping with this dual movement and in a pre-representational way, a mood *opens up* the region or world within which things can first be explicitly represented. In its power to move us in both ways and open up a world, the mood "places Dasein on its grounds and before its abysses … determining for our Dasein the place open to it and the times of its being" (39: 141). The basic mood thus "hands our Dasein over to historical being in such a way that it must take over, shape, and bear the latter" (39: 222). Again, we do not simply represent things and objects and then have moods attaching to them; to the contrary, any representation is based upon a foregoing mood (39: 140). As exemplified by the joy that expresses itself in holy mourning, the wholeheartedness of a basic mood is such that it brings forth its opposite and swings within the resulting conflict (39: 148).

The first beginning of Western thinking sprung from the basic mood of astonishment in the face of the unhiddenness of things. The transition to another inception of thinking is necessitated by another basic mood, i.e. reserve (*Verhaltenheit*) (45: 1f; 65: 14ff). In the early 1930s, Heidegger depicts this mood in terms of Dasein's comportment (*Sich-verhalten*). Countering the tendency to lose ourselves in the entities toward which we comport ourselves, reserve is a matter of holding onto ourselves and thus comporting freely to entities, thanks to the understanding of being that transcends them (35: 87–90). By the second half of the 1930s, Heidegger jettisons the language of transcendence, but he retains reserve as the basic mood. The first step of another beginning for thinking begins with a transformation of human beings. The transformation consists in being moved to "be here" by *shock* and *awe*—shock at being's abandonment of beings, the casualness of the human pretension to be in complete control, and the supposed utility of everything; awe at the nearness and fecundity of being. This shock and awe characterize more explicitly what belongs primordially to the basic mood of *reserve*, the mood of preparedness for being's refusal (its hiddenness) but as a gift. As Dasein's "strongest and at the same time gentlest" preparation for the appropriating event, reserve grounds care, the decisive anticipation of the truth of historical being (65: 15, 33ff). These basic moods intimate and forebode, not in the sense of some predictive calculation, but in the sense of taking the measure of "the entire temporality: the time-space of the here [*Da*]" (65: 8, 12–23, 30–6, 46, 312–17, 374, 382, 395; 52: 171f; 70: 133ff). In another list of basic moods a few years later, however, reserve is missing and "thanks" is added (71: 222).

Mystery (*Geheimnis*)

Just as truth is not primarily the correctness of assertions, so untruth cannot be traced simply to an incorrect assertion. Insofar as we understand the openness of entities to us and, correlatively, our being-free-for that openness as essential to truth, the very opposite of truth in this sense, a hiddenness (a primordial "un-truth" in a way), is equally essential to truth. While not to be confused with falsity, this hiddenness is essential to truth since the unhiddenness of things supposes the clearing, the openness in the midst of beings that is itself hidden. The hiddenness or absence (*lethe*) that is entailed by experiencing truth as un-hiddenness (*aletheia*) is the hiddenness not simply of this or that entity but entities as a whole. "The hiddenness of entities as a whole, the genuine non-truth, is older than every manifestness of this or that entity." The hiding of the hidden (including the hiddenness of the hiding itself) is the mystery (*Geheimnis*). This mystery pervades our being-here, and our being-here preserves this mystery. This mystery is not simply what is enigmatic, unexplained, or questionable within the domain of what is manifest and accessible. As long as such enigmas are construed as no more than way-stations on the way to what is or can make them accessible, i.e. as long as "the hiddenness of entities as a whole" is indulged merely as a limit that occasionally announces itself, "the hiding as the basic happening has sunk in forgetfulness" (9: 194f).

Nearness (*Nähe*)

We are accustomed to calculating nearness and remoteness in terms of how near or far something is from our bodies. The near is what we can reach in some short segment of time where "reaching it" means being able to represent or produce it as something immediately present. The same holds, *mutatis mutandis*, for the remote. In both cases they have been "calculated away" (*verrechnet*) in terms of the available means of overcoming distances. We think of the near and far primarily as properties of things, properties that are theoretically determinable according to the same metric and that are practically manageable to an ever-increasing extent. Our technologies are dedicated to removing distances in order to make things available to us. To the extent that everything becomes near in this way, the near loses its character of nearness.

Nearness is that time-spatial remoteness that cannot be set aside by any overcoming of distances, for it is not a property of beings. It is rather the unfolding of the appropriating event, namely, the clearing for the hiddenness of the presence (being) of beings to Dasein. By no means static, nearness is the nearing of nearness and remoteness to one another. As the clearing, this nearing first lends the familiar space and the customary time their open character (*das Offene*). However, this open character is filled out and utterly distorted (or blocked: *verstellt*) by calculation in the service of an unbridled representation and production that look only to themselves when assessing things. "The vanishing of 'nearness' and 'remoteness' themselves in terms of distances, the reduction of both to numerical and set-like differences, is already the hidden *consequence* of the unconditional dominance of being in the sense of machination, the capacity to produce and represent beings." Nearness is the abyss of farness and vice versa; "both are the same, the abyss of the clearing of historical being." Hence, they are not subject to any measure. Conceivable only as abysses on the basis of the unfolding of historical being as the appropriating event, they spring from—and yet are retained by—historical being's refusal to show itself (66: 116).

As the hidden clearing of historical being, nearness opens being and beings to one another while concealing itself in the process. The essence of nearness coincides with the way things bring the fourfold near to one another. That is, the near brings the far near yet precisely as far. "Insofar as we preserve the thing, we inhabit the nearness. The nearing of the nearness is the authentic and the sole dimension of the mirror-play of the world." In this nearing, "the nearness itself conceals itself and remains in its way the closest" (7: 167f, 179, 182). So, too, nearness is the fourth dimension that brings the three dimensions of time near to one another by holding them all apart. "This nearing nearness has the character of refusal and withdrawal" (14: 20f). In keeping with this account, Heidegger also invokes the superlative "the nearest" to characterize being and the appropriating event. "Being is what is nearest" (9: 331, 336f). "The appropriating event is ... the nearest of the nearness and the remotest of the remote in which we mortals spend our lives" (12: 247; 11: 46). Similarly, he characterizes nearness as a way truth is illumined (5: 49) and connects it with the open region and "letting be" (77: 116, 149ff).

In SZ nearness characterizes the direction and distance of what is handy in our everyday dealings with implements. This nearness, regulated by the circumspective use of an implement, assigns it its place (*Platz*) in a region (*Gegend*). The embeddedness of nearness in circumspective practices reveals the distinctive spatiality of innerworldly beings, not afforded by scientific measurement and observation of space. Glasses on our noses, for example, are typically far less near to us than the wall-painting we are admiring (SZ 102ff, 107). Dasein's spatiality is characterized by a nearing in the sense of circumspectively bringing something into the nearness, removing the distance from it. After adding that this nearing also applies to specific ways of uncovering beings cognitively, Heidegger notes: "A specific tendency to nearness is inherent in Dasein" (SZ 105).

Negation (*Verneinung, Negation*)

Negation is a grammatical or logical operation performed by attaching a term like "not" to a word, clause, or sentence. Yet what "not" typically denotes is not simply the result of a human action of making distinctions, i.e. inserting negations into what is otherwise given. In order for us to negate something, its negatability and, thus, a sense of the "not" must be given in advance. This sense is given in the way that nothing is experienced in angst as the process of letting entities as a whole slip away (9: 116f; SZ 186f).

In SZ, Heidegger observes that the essence of the "not" remains obscure in logic and ontology (where it marks a lack or a transition), in part because they fail to investigate its ontological origin. His analysis of the existential (ontological) sense of guilt moves in this direction. In Dasein's primordial, existential guilt are two senses of "not," distinct from uses of "not" to indicate a privation of what is on-hand. Dasein is primordially guilty in the sense of *not* being the ground of its being and in the sense of being the ground for being one possibility and *not* another. These two nullities are constitutive of Dasein's thrownness and existence respectively. "Care is in its essence pervaded through and through by nullity [*Nichtigkeit*]. Care—the being of Dasein—accordingly means, as thrown projection: the (null) ground-being of a nullity" (SZ 285).

In his 1924 *Sophist* lectures, Heidegger glosses Plato's differentiation of empty, merely excluding negation (*enantiosis*) from a primordial, disclosing negation (*antithesis*). He observes that "here the problem of negation is posited for the first time and advanced in a first step" (19: 570, 558–74). Yet Plato's *me on* also signals the beginning of the decline from the pinnacle of Greek experience, where the nothing as the counterturning in being itself is not subordinated as something "negative" to the "positive." Neither the dialectic of German Idealism nor Nietzsche's work offset this subordination (53: 95f). "The negative retains its own essence and does not stand in the role of what could and should be set aside and overturned. Because it, as the counteressence, is an essence of its own, it must be born and esteemed with its counteressence on the basis of their unity" (53: 104).

Heidegger contrasts negating (*Verneinen*) that is fixed on the actual with "nihilating" (*Nichtung*). When we say "No, this is not the case," the negating is solely our doing, or so it would seem, since the negated is not part of what is actual. By contrast, nihilating comes with the recognition that nothing is as primordial as being. Such nihilating is the explicit self-restraint of the steadfastness in being-here, a kind of rigor by means of which—paradoxically—we engage in what is alien to that steadfastness (71: 133). So, too, Dasein "nihilates insofar as it ... itself belongs itself to the essence of being" (9: 360).

Nietzsche, Friedrich (1844–1900)

Nietzsche was nothing less than Heidegger's intellectual shadow for the most of two tumultuous decades. Between 1936 and 1940 he gives four lectures on Nietzsche's accounts of the will to power (as art and as knowledge), eternal recurrence, and nihilism. In 1941 he prepares lectures on Nietzsche's metaphysics and completes three related essays ("Metaphysics as History of Being," "Recollection of Metaphysics," "Sketches for a History of Being as Metaphysics"), followed by a fourth essay in 1944–6 ("Nihilism as Determined by the History of Being"). Heidegger publishes all of the foregoing as *Nietzsche I–II* in 1961 (GA 6.1, 6.2). He gives additional seminars and lectures on Nietzsche in 1937, 1938/39, and 1944 (GA 46, 87) and delivers the talk "The Word of Nietzsche: God is Dead" in 1943 (5: 209–67). Nietzschean themes abound in the *Contributions to Philosophy* and the subsequent volumes complementing it (GA 65–71). Heidegger's 1951/52 lectures, published in *What is Called Thinking?* (GA 8), are concerned with Nietzsche's thinking, and in 1953 he delivers the lecture "Who is Nietzsche's Zarathustra?" (7: 99–124).

This intense preoccupation stems from an appreciation of Nietzsche's accomplishments and limitations. As the culmination of Western metaphysics, Nietzsche's thought provides the most complete and compelling elaboration of what all previous thinkers had been striving to articulate. Nietzsche's greatness as a thinker consists then in unfolding in all its power what was first begun by the Greeks. Yet he is also a victim of that first beginning, and, sharing its obliviousness to being, he provides humanity in late modernity with a metaphysics (a conception of beings) that allows it free, technological reign over the earth. In the early 1930s, far from distancing himself from Nietzsche, Heidegger himself insists on the central philosophical importance of notions of willing, power, and violence. However, in his lectures he becomes increasingly critical of Nietzsche's thought, coming to the conclusion that nihilism is the consequence and not the ground of it. The remainder of this entry glosses Heidegger's reading of Nietzsche as a metaphysician in 1940, before turning to his somewhat more qualified assessment of Nietzsche in the 1950s.

Heidegger's interpretation of Nietzsche is controversial, not only because he makes free use of the posthumous work *Will to Power*, but more importantly because he regards Nietzsche's thinking as fundamentally metaphysical. Thinking is metaphysical if it contains conceptions of (1) what beings are as such (*Seiendheit, essentia*), (2) how they are as a whole (*existentia*), (3) truth, (4) truth's history, and (5) the humanity inhabiting and safeguarding those conceptions. By this measure, Nietzsche's thinking is metaphysical. The will to power is (1), the eternal recurrence is (2), justice is (3), nihilism is (4), and the overman is (5). Perspectival (calculating, value-positing) self-overcoming defines what beings are or, as Nietzsche would prefer, what life is. Since there is no goal and nothing more outside the will to power, its self-overpowering cannot be endlessly new but must turn eternally back to itself. Truth occurs as justice (as odd as that sounds to our ears) since whatever the consummate subjectivity of the will to power reveals and represents is, as such, justified. Because all old values (i.e. otherworldly values) amount to nothing from this perspective, the history of this truth is the history of the annihilation of old values and the transformation of values as values. Those who inhabit and safeguard the will to power overcome the subjectivity of unconditional rational representation, transforming the latter into the unconditional subjectivity of willing. Yet this transformation remains thoroughly modern; in Nietzsche's doctrine of the will to power, "Descartes celebrates his supreme triumph." The point of this demonstration of "the hidden unity" of Nietzsche's metaphysics is to demonstrate that it captures (but does not make) "the fundamental feature of the history of the age"—an age of unrestricted explanatory and productive capacity and "complete senselessness" (5: 239; 6.2: 13–19, 51, 231–300; 7: 85f; 55: 66ff, 90f, 104–7, 180; 67: 177–204).

In the early 1950s, when Heidegger returns to Nietzsche's thought, he credits him with appreciating the advancing technological devastation of the earth. Nietzsche understood how unprepared human beings are to take over the dominance of the earth (having murdered God) and, accordingly, how necessary their transformation is (their makeover into the overman: "Caesar with the soul of Christ"). In contrast to the lectures, Nietzsche appears more prominently as a transitional thinker (7: 113; 8: 31, 54f, 60f, 70).

Heidegger also focuses on Nietzsche's approach to the spirit of revenge, since it leads to the core of his metaphysics. "Zarathustra teaches the doctrine of the overman because he is the teacher of the eternal recurrence," i.e. the means of liberation from the spirit of revenge against time. Heidegger concurs, at least in part, with the motivation for Zarathustra's teaching, namely, to save the earth (the butt of human vengeance) by purging humanity of the spirit of revenge. Eternal recurrence frees the will from any revulsion against time's passing because the like (*das Gleiche*) constantly recurs (permitting the will, incidentally, to reverse itself). Hence, the doctrine of the eternal recurrence, as the supposed key to the will's complete liberation from revenge against time, is "the supreme triumph of the metaphysics of the will."

Yet revenge is not thereby overcome, and, indeed, Nietzsche says as much himself by noting (albeit in another context) the persistence of revenge even in "someone who takes life under his protection." Hence, the doctrines of the eternal recurrence and the overman present a riddle, the riddle of the relation between being and the human being. This relation (the appropriating event) thus flickers in Nietzsche's thinking. As the consummation of Western metaphysics, Nietzsche's thinking points to this unthought dimension "distinctly and confusedly at the same time." Nietzsche is philosophy's Moses; by taking metaphysics to its extreme limits, limits that explain the entire course of the history of metaphysics, he is able to point to, but not enter, the promised land (7: 113–23; 8: 97f, 106–10). In the history of Western metaphysics, the being of beings has been thought, but the truth of being as being—i.e. the appropriating event, the presence of beings to Dasein—has remained unthought. Nietzsche's metaphysics is no exception. Taking a cue from Nietzsche's own remark that the battle for power over the earth is conducted in the name of basic philo-sophical doctrines, Heidegger characterizes the battle, not as a battle for mastery of beings, but as a confrontation of the power of beings (metaphysics) and the truth of being (thinking historical being as the appropriating event) (6.2: 234f).

Nihilism (*Nihilismus*)

Nihilism consists in forgetting being or thinking of it as nothing (*nihil* in Latin). A nihilist relates exclusively to beings and rejects the experience and question of being. Metaphysics, in its concerns for beings as a whole (ontology) and/or for the supreme being (theology), is oblivious to being itself. Thus, metaphysics is not only constitutionally incapable of overcoming nihilism; it is "the authentic nihilism." So, too, the inquiry into being is "the first and only fruitful step towards genuinely overturning nihilism" (40: 155; 67: 216).

Heidegger credits Nietzsche's philosophy with being the first to think and experience nihilism, what Nietzsche understands as the death of God and any otherworldly, supersensible values or order of being, i.e. the historical event when all previous values are devalued. Nietzsche attempts to overcome nihilism with his conception of the will to power as the fundamental principle of beings in general and his conception of the overman, the human being who re-values all previous values on the basis of this principle (6.2: 22–9; 67: 200, 206). In this connection Heidegger glosses the forms of nihilism identified by Nietzsche: pessimism as its preliminary form, the incomplete nihilism in which we live (attempts to elude nihilism without re-valuing previous values), the extreme nihilism (entailing first the passive nihilism that recognizes no truth and then the active nihilism that recognizes truth as a form of the will to power), and, finally, the transformation of extreme nihilism as active into "ecstatic-classical" nihilism (6.2: 77–83). Only this "ecstatic-classical" nihilism—"a divine way of thinking"—genuinely recognizes previous values to be (worth) nothing.

However, Nietzsche's attempt to overcome nihilism indicates that he does not experience how "the genuine essence of nihilism presents itself," namely, its history of having nothing to do with being. Nietzsche understands his classical nihilism ironically, i.e. as nihilism to such an extreme that it is no longer nihilism. But precisely nihilism of this variety, Heidegger contends, is "authentic nihilism"; it cannot be an overturning of nihilism since it has nothing to do with being as such. Nietzsche is dismissive of talk of "being" (he prefers "life" and "becoming"), but a more telltale sign of his obliviousness to being is his failure to take the question of nothing itself seriously. On the assumption that everything is either an entity or nothing at all, Nietzsche regards "nothing" as the latter, something utterly null and void (*das nur Nichtige*). His classical nihilism is the consummate nihilism because it exempts itself from any need to think the nothing itself (6.2: 33, 43f; 67: 205–10).

Nothing (*Nichts*)

Rather than locate the origin of the concept of nothing in acts of negation, Heidegger locates negation in nothing, the nothing that, in the sense of the slipping away of beings as a whole (including ourselves), is revealed in the basic mood of angst. The nothing encountered in angst is neither an entity nor object; nor is it grasped or somehow detached from beings as a whole, e.g. as though it annihilated or negated them. Instead it is encountered with beings as a whole, as they slip away from it. The essence of nothing, the way entities slip away, is the nihilation of them (again, not to be confused with their annihilation) that also first brings Dasein face to face with the primordial openness of beings as such—that they are and are not nothing. Dasein is "held-out-into the nothing" and thus over beings as a whole, allowing it to experience that nihilation. By being held out over beings as a whole into the nothing, Dasein transcends them and, without this transcending, it could not relate to beings as such. Transcendence, freedom, and being a self all presuppose "the primordial openness of the nothing," and, as such, the nothing belongs to the essential unfolding of being. While purely logical negation (the use of "not") is grounded in nothing's process of nihilating, it is not the only, or even the most prominent, way in which Dasein experiences it, particularly when one considers such experiences as being bitterly deprived or painfully rejected. The question of nothing, Heidegger contends in 1929, is a metaphysical question because, by transcending beings as a whole, it both encompasses the whole of metaphysics and puts the questioner herself in question. This account of the nothing (as inherent, qua nihilating, in the being of beings) puts science in question to the extent that science, oblivious to its metaphysical roots, attends solely to what is and nothing else (9: 105–22; SZ 186–9).

Later Heidegger contends that metaphysics is incapable of thinking the nothing (71: 132). Yet he carries over much of his earlier account of nothing. "What is absolutely not nothing are entities. Nothing itself, however, is being" (71: 121). The notion that the nothing, as the "denial" of being, is dependent upon and relative to being is precipitous. Not only does it problematically presume that nothing can be reduced to a denial, but it fails to consider that nothing could be equiprimordial with being. "The originary nothing is the purely affording clearing as the opening-up of the turn. In this nothing the refusal as the basic feature of the abyss unfolds. On the basis of this nothing and its nihilating, i.e. refusing, i.e. beginning, the not and the negative [Nein-hafte] in the difference determines itself. Insofar, however, as the nothing is historical being, historical being is essentially the difference as the originary, hidden, and refused parting" (71: 124). As the "in-between" in the differentiation of historical being and beings, the nothing belongs to the beginning (70: 26).

The source of the "not" of negation and "saying no" is to be found neither among objects (beings and their properties) nor in the subjectivity of thinking. Instead the "nihilating" unfolds in being itself, and this nihilating is the essence of "nothing" (9: 359f). Human beings can become shepherds of being only by being place-holders of the nothing, thinking its essential unfolding as different from everything present and absent, a thinking that is the very opposite of nihilism (12: 103).

Objectivity (*Gegenständigkeit, Objektivität*)

Objectivity is a modern way of construing beings, namely, precisely insofar as they are represented to, by, and for a subject. The subject here is not any contingent, individual subject but a rational subjectivity that countenances only what can be the object of inference and calculation (10: 118) "Neither the medieval nor Greek thinking represented what is present as an object" (7: 45). Though Descartes and Leibniz set the modern stage for objectivity, Kant is the central figure who, working from the basic presupposition of the subject–object relation, equates experience with the experience of the objectivity of objects and being with being the object of a possible experience. "Beings are beings as objects for consciousness" (10: 113). Though springing from the hegemony of the experience of objectivity, modern techno-science increasingly displays a capacity to dispense with objects in favor of forces and a standing reserve. Things are not objects. That is to say, in no way is their thinghood tied, like objectivity is, to representing (*vorstellen*) or producing (*herstellen*) them (79: 5ff).

Ontic (*ontisch*)

Ontic is an adjective that Heidegger uses to designate a specific entity (or specific entities) as well as the description, interpretation or investigation of it (or them). Heidegger contrasts an ontic investigation with an ontological investigation that is directed at disclosing an entity's manner of being as such. What distinguishes Dasein ontically is that being matters to it, that it is ontological or, more precisely, that it has a preontological understanding of being. Hence, Dasein enjoys an "ontic-ontological" prerogative among beings as the first being to be investigated. "Fundamental ontology must be sought in the existential analysis of Dasein" (SZ 11f, 16f). The same phenomenon or conception (e.g. world, assertion, relevance, *substantia*, being towards death, conscience, the They) can be interpreted ontically or ontologically, i.e. as one being among others or with a view to its manner or sense of being (SZ 57, 64f, 76, 82ff, 94, 196, 199, 260, 279, 309). What is ontic can be pre-scientific or scientific. Ontic sciences are positive sciences (e.g. mathematics, chemistry, theology, psychology) (9: 48f; SZ 50). The distinction between ontic and ontological investigations corresponds to the ontological difference between beings (entities) and being as well as to the cognate difference between ontic and ontological truth (9: 134). Heidegger's use of the term "ontic" wanes with his subsequent criticism of ontology and the ontological difference (67: 62f; 77: 139).

Ontology (*Ontologie*)

Ontology is the science of beings insofar as they exist or, equivalently, the science of being qua being. In early Freiburg lectures Heidegger complains of the inadequacy of traditional ontology's equation of "being" with "being an object," an equation that obstructs access to Dasein (both because Dasein is not itself *prima facie* an object and because it does not *prima facie* comport itself to objects). In those lectures "ontology" accordingly signifies not a specific academic discipline, but "any inquiry directed at being as such" (63: 1ff). While iterating this usage in SZ (SZ 11), Heidegger also identifies various traditional ontologies, e.g. ancient, medieval, and Cartesian. Any ontology, he insists, is naïve if it does not first clarify sufficiently the sense of being. Moreover, every ontology is founded on the ontic structure of Dasein as the sole entity with a pre-ontological understanding of being. Heidegger accordingly insists on the necessity of undertaking the *fundamental ontology* from which all other ontologies must spring: namely, an inquiry into the foundational sense of being that an existential analysis of Dasein yields (SZ 11–14, 17, 27, 37, 183). This project also contrasts with traditional ontology which, oblivious to that foundational sense, takes its bearings from being on-hand (SZ 159, 165). Because this project demands differentiating being from beings (something traditional ontology forgoes), it also entails the destruction of the history of traditional ontology and the adoption of a phenomenological method (SZ 27, 35, 37f). By 1935, however, Heidegger gives up on the term, not least because his project was rejected by academic philosophers who treated ontology in the traditional sense of "the composition and exposition of a branch within its system" (see 40: 31f, 133, 142; 67: 62, 125, 148; 67: 148).

Onto-theo-logy (*Onto-theo-logie*)

In a manner that remains unthought by it, metaphysics corresponds to being as *logos*, namely, the way beings are gathered together and already lying before us. In this sense, being as *logos* is the unifying ground of beings that, however, manifests itself (and thus is concealed) as a thought. Inasmuch as metaphysics is based upon thinking this thought, i.e. being as the ground of beings, it is fundamentally a kind of "logic" (as Hegel, whose metaphysics is a science of logic, preeminently appreciated). More precisely, it thinks being as what grounds beings both by virtue of being common to them all (ontology) and by virtue of being their ultimate ground, the supreme being (theology). Given that these two metaphysical senses of grounding, onto-logical and theo-logical, are forms of logic (i.e. attempts to think the being of beings as beings' ground), metaphysics is essentially an "onto-theo-logic." Ontology and theology entail one another. Only if something exists, is it created (caused), and, only if there is a creator (cause), does something exist. According to onto-theology, there is nothing more fundamental to say about being than this (11: 63–8, 75ff).

In order to explain the origin of the onto-theo-logical constitution of metaphysics, it is necessary to "step back" from metaphysics to what it leaves unthought and forgets: the difference between being and beings. The difference can be thought but not pictured, in part because any attempt to represent it misconstrues the difference as a relation supplied by us or as something unessential to what are misleadingly taken to be relata. Being differs from beings by virtue of passing over into them, coming over them, obviously not in the sense that they are already, but rather in the sense that they first arrive by this means, unhidden, of themselves. So differentiated, *being* (coming over, revealing beings) and *beings* (arriving in a way that remains hidden) unfold from the same (*Selbe*). The difference, so conceived, is "the carrying out" (*Austrag*) of both, unconcealing and concealing, at once. In this process, being and beings reciprocally ground one another. They "essentially unfold as thus differentiated from the same, the difference [*Unter-schied*]." The fatal step of metaphysics occurs when the grounding itself appears and/or is taken to be a particular being (*Seiendes*) that demands a grounding by another particular being, the supreme cause. In this way, metaphysics is forgetful of being. It thinks of what differs in the difference (being and beings) as beings without attending to the difference as such or, as Heidegger also puts it, to being as the difference (11: 69ff, 74f).

Open (*das Offene*)

The open is the place of being. As such, its importance in Heidegger's mature thinking can scarcely be underestimated. In the context of Western metaphysics, as being is equated with beings as a whole and/or relegated to an empty concept, being itself (the dynamic presence of beings) withdraws from view, while it is in fact "the open" (*das öffnende Offene*) that opens human beings and beings to one another (54: 225).

The open is not the same as a horizon. Insofar as we experience horizons as extending beyond (transcending) objects, referring back to the representing of them, we do not experience what allows the horizons to be what they are. Our field of vision is an open region that we look out into, but its openness is not due to our looking into it. In fact, we see only a certain limit of it, namely, a horizon. As the open space surrounding us, the horizon of objects and the representation of them is, as it were, only one side of that space, the side turned towards us. This open region itself, whether forming the latter sort of horizon or not, is what affords everything shelter and a place to stay (*Unterkunft*), but also and more basically, far from being some inert space, it is what actively gathers everything together to abide, while resting on itself. This open region (*Gegnet*) is the region of regions, "the abiding expanse that, gathering everything together, opens itself so that in it the open is sustained and brought to let each [thing] to emerge in its resting" (77: 114). This abiding expanse (*verweilende Weite*) withdraws rather than coming to meet us. What appears in it are not objects standing opposite us but things that rest on returning to the abiding expanse as what they belong to. The open region lets things be things, not objects (77: 138f). "The historical rests upon the open region and ... dispatching itself to the human being, it regionalizes [*vergegnet*] human beings, bringing them into their essence" (77: 142). In its literal, etymological sense as "un-closedness" (*Ent-schlossenheit*), resoluteness is "explicitly having taken over the self-opening of Dasein *for* the open" (77: 143). *Steadfastness* is the reserved and persevering comportment of letting-be, receptive to the open-region. Heidegger plainly exploits metaphors throughout this account, noting that, while the abiding expanse of the open region cannot be objectively described or represented, it can be named and thought (77: 114–23, 144f).

The account of the open region glossed in the preceding paragraph stems from 1944/45. While the account exposes limitations of his earlier transcendental–horizonal approach, it also hearkens back to his frequent references to the open, often as a synonym for the clearing, where care and then ecstatic–horizonal temporality determine that openness (SZ 350, 386, 393, 408, 421). In SZ Heidegger also speaks of Dasein's openness to the world, to others, and to itself (SZ 137, 163, 177, 188). In the spring of 1930 he also contrasts the way an animal is in its open space with a human being's "pre-logical openness for beings," an openness that underlies understanding beings as being (29/30: 388–92, 402ff, 416ff, 483, 492–506).

The new accent that Heidegger gives to openness (culminating in the 1944/45 account) begins to take shape in the early 1930s with his shift from transcendental philosophy to thinking being historically. A work of art, for example, holds open the openness of the world, while bringing the earth (everything which closes itself off) into the open (5: 31ff; 65: 388; 71: 17). Beings are first able to be distinguished from one another in the openness of the "between" constituting Dasein's thrown projection (65: 304, 325, 454). "The here [Da] means the appropriated open—the appropriated clearing of being" (71: 211). There must also be the open space [das Offene] into which whatever is unhidden, removed from hiding, steps forth. By the same token, correctness, representation, and the subject–object relation in general presuppose that opening—as does errancy itself (65: 316, 339, 360; 66: 259).

The open is what is closest (Nächste) and whenever we attend to something in its unhiddenness, we also mean the open yet without explicitly considering, let alone looking in advance to, its essence such that it could guide "all experiencing of entities" (54: 212; 66: 116). Unhiddenness points to "the open and the openness," not as something that is the outcome of a disclosing, but instead as "the ground and the essential beginning of unhiddenness" (54: 213). "Freedom" is a synonym for "the open" as what in an originary manner opens itself. Only by coming into the open—the clearing as "the open of being itself"—are human beings able to let beings be what they are. The human eye could never become what it is without the open, nor could theoria, the Greek experience of being. At the same time it is the play-space (Spielraum) for what is still undetermined and undecided, and thus the occasion for erring and losing one's way (54: 213–20). "The open, into which each entity is freed into its free space ... *is being itself*. Everything unhidden is as such sheltered in the openness of being, i.e. the ground-less." Although human beings alone see into the open, this does not entitle them to bring being itself explicitly into the open, "i.e. to think and to say being." To the contrary, because human beings are fixated largely on beings alone (i.e. what appears unhidden in the open), they learn how to overlook being and become alienated from the open (54: 224f).

Overturning metaphysics (*Überwindung der Metaphysik*)

Overturning metaphysics is a pervasive concern in Heidegger's writings after 1935. The concern stems in part from his appreciation of just how entrenched metaphysical habits are, i.e. the habits of thinking only of beings. Attempts to reduce being to something constantly on-hand and, in the process, to pretend to transcend historical existence, are natural and naturally errant extensions of the human pursuit of well-being. Yet, in their forgottenness of being, these attempts are also fatal, leading to the monolithic equation of being with the useful and computable (70: 19–25). Those metaphysical habits of thinking are traceable not only to the fact that Aristotle's metaphysics is at bottom physics—an attempt to think the essence of the beings of *physis*—but also to the fact that *physis* (the original Greek term for being) itself withdraws, leaving the field as it were to the presence of beings alone (67: 10, 38f, 56). The history of purported attempts to overthrow or move beyond traditional metaphysics demonstrates its staying power. Kant's transcendental philosophy, Nietzsche's inversion of Platonism in the form of the will to power, positivism and naturalism, and the computational thinking that informs (modern) technology each reconstitute metaphysics in different ways (67: 38). In each case, being has been reduced to some paradigmatic manner of being (objective, powerful, measurable and observable, useful) and/or to the set of all such beings. Overturning metaphysics cannot be a matter of replacing historical being (the presence of beings to Dasein) with something else (e.g. "becoming" or "life"), since either approach amounts to construing it as an entity. (Heidegger criticizes his own work from SZ to the essay "On the Essence of Ground" for being too close to metaphysics in this way; see 67: 99ff, 125, 132f).

While the overturning is a turn to Dasein, it stems from historical being itself or, more precisely, from the way its truth unfolds *against* the failure of its grounding in the first beginning of Western thinking. Historical being wrests itself free (*entwindet*) from the supremacy of beings and the metaphysics grounded on that supremacy. Historical being wrests itself free by attuning human beings to its abandonment, an abandonment reflected in the hegemony of machination where there are only beings and the only question is how they are made. The abandonment of being reflected in machination completely upsets and terrifies (*ent-setzt*) human beings but also transports them to the truth of that abandonment (67: 7–12, 17f, 20, 36)

Between the being of metaphysics and historical being, there are no bridges; only a leap attains the other beginning. The overturning is not a metaphysics of metaphysics, not a change of views or doctrines, but "the historical transformation of the essence of historical being," a transformation that entails an essential transformation of human beings (67: 13, 33, 39). Whereas metaphysics is a thoroughgoing evasion of the groundlessness of being, overturning metaphysics grounds metaphysics' essence and its determination of history in the experience of the truth of historical being as an abyss. In this regard, the overturning is the first historical revelation of the essence of history, coinciding with the overturning of nihilism as the culmination of metaphysics (66: 111f; 67: 16ff, 36, 38f; 71: 86).

Instead of "overturning" metaphysics, Heidegger sometimes speaks of "winding back" or "coming to terms with" (*verwinden*) it. The term has the advantage of canceling any suggestion of overthrowing or abolishing metaphysics. *Verwinden* can mean "getting over," but in the sense of getting over getting old rather than in the sense of getting over a cold. The experience of historical being allows us to get over metaphysics, by winding it back to what was ignored from its inception. Overturning, conceived in this sense, thus has nothing to do with superseding. Heidegger accordingly employs the term to set it off "against *any* human and especially modern subjective and, above all, Hegelian misinterpretation" (7: 69–98; 67: 35).

In the early 1940s Heideger also speaks of *Dasein* winding historical being back into the appropriating event (71: 135, 141). Winding historical being back into the appropriating event is the process of letting it swing freely and not be marshaled into the forward march of the absolute or a will to power. Insofar as human beings come to be here (*da zu sein*) and find themselves to be appropriated, they do not supersede or overtake historical being. Instead they come to terms with being appropriated by it (71: 141). Metaphysics is the progression from the first "unwinding" (*Entwindung*) that can only be recalled in the experience of the other beginning, "in the pain of the difference and winding-back" (71: 137).

Historical being is the unique, bountiful beginning of the descent (*Anfang als Untergang*) into its departure (*Abschied*), a hiddenness that makes possible the gift of unhiddenness. Precisely in this departure, historical being preserves its "originary dignity"; winding it back to its beginning (i.e. the descent into its departure) is the ultimate way of dignifying it. Since Plato, the question of being is decisively equated with the question of what beings are, not what being is. Historical being "saves itself" in its own truth, a truth that does not correspond to any beings, in a stark departure from the unhiddenness of them at its inception. Hence, "on the basis of the beginning [the first beginning of Western thinking], winding historical being back into the departure becomes a necessity." Yet talk of historical being is transitional and hardly the last word. Indeed, in the saying of historical being, "what is explicitly said is not historical being, but the appropriating event of the beginning, that can no more be addressed as historical being" (70: 19–27, 83f, 92f, 100).

Parmenides

Parmenides is one of the three thinkers of the first beginning who understand being as *physis* in the sense of what emerges and holds sway over whatever is, the constant presence and manifest appearance of beings (40: 77, 96). What distinguishes these thinkers from their successors is their understanding of *physis* in the light of *aletheia*, as a manner of becoming unhidden, and in the light of *logos*, as the primordial gathering of being and beings in that process. Yet while clearly appreciating the primordial senses of *physis*, *aletheia*, and *logos*, they do not think through the full implications of these senses. Thus, the first beginning falls short of articulating the originary beginning and sets the stage for another beginning.

Parmenides' fragment—"thinking and being are the same"—is the guiding principle of Western philosophy (40: 111; 7: 223). On Heidegger's reading, the fragment means that appearing (*einai*) and taking up (*noein*) what appears belong together, vying with one another, as is true of being qua *physis* generally (40: 105f). In other words, in and with the appearing of being (*genitivus appositivus*) is the perceiving of it (40: 106; 6.1: 475; 7: 245; 11: 36–9; 5: 90; 8: 244f). That this co-belonging takes the form of a struggle is one reason for inferring that Parmenides and Heraclitus say the same (40: 74, 104). Though there is no explicit word about humans in the fragment, what matters is determining "the essence of the human being on the basis of the happening of the essential belongedness of being and taking-up" (40: 107, 111). The fragment—the co-belonging of being's appearance and the way of taking it up—provides a standpoint for such a determination, but only if anachronistic conceptions of humanity are held at bay.

Sophocles' characterization of the uncanniness of human beings elucidates this way (Parmenides' way) of understanding humanity. What is uncanny is that, in the human exercise of technical violence against nature, nature discloses its overwhelming fittingness. This uncanniness "happens" in the interplay of *techne* and *dike*. The co-belonging of taking-up and being is "nothing other than this interplay" (40: 126). For "taking up" is a *de-cision for* being *against* nothing and, thereby, a confrontation *with* mere appearance—in keeping with the three possible paths of philosophy (being, nothing, and seeming) indicated in Parmenides' Fragment 6 (40: 84ff). This deciding "must use violence in holding out against the constantly pressing ensnarement in the everyday" (40: 128). Parmenides' saying thus refers to a struggle in which *logos* plays a role, together with *noein*. Taking-up (*noein*) and gathering (*logos* in the primordial, pre-discursive sense) co-belong to being. So, too, taking-up by *discursively* gathering discloses being—at least until the conceptions of *logos* and *noein* degenerate into something possessed by human beings rather than vice versa (40: 129–33; 7:

235). This degeneration, commencing shortly after Parmenides, led to complete misunderstandings (Plotinus, Hegel) of his famous fragment (40: 104f, 108, 111; 7: 226–30; for further discussion of Parmenides, see 11: 36ff; 15: 75, 394–407; 35: 103–95; 62: 209–31; GA 7; GA 8; GA 54).

Pass (*Zuspiel*)

"The Pass" (or "Playing Forth") is the title of the second "movement" of the *Contributions*, and it is necessitated by the first movement, i.e. the *resonance* of the distress at being abandoned by being. Rather than running counter to the first beginning (since all counterings are essentially co-determined by what they counter), the pass passes the first beginning on to the truth of its history and thus to what is utterly other than it. "Philosophy is not finished with metaphysics;" to the contrary, metaphysics' essential impossibility must be "played out" (*zugespielt*) so that "philosophy itself is passed over into its other beginning" (65: 173, 183–7). The question of truth (*aletheia*) remains unasked in the first beginning, and this non-event propels Western thinking in the direction of metaphysics. Knowledge of this fact *passes* on *to* us the necessity of preparing for the other beginning and experiencing the distressing abandonment-of-being that corresponds to that non-event (65: 82, 169, 186). The pass is the *transition* from the first to the other beginning, i.e. from metaphysics' leading question of what beings are to the fundamental question of what being is. It is also the *overturning* of metaphysics since metaphysics' practice of rising above beings (construed as on-hand and as objects) to some conception of their being (beingness) becomes impossible as soon as it is clear that "the essential unfolding of historical being requires the grounding of the *truth* of historical being and [that] this grounding must be carried out as *Da-sein* ..." (65: 172, 176).

"The Pass" in the *Contributions* accordingly focuses on the experience of beings as a constantly emerging presence (*physis*, *aletheia*) in the first beginning, Plato's decisive interpretation of that presence as *idea* (with a view to *techne*), and the subsequent development of Platonism and idealism, culminating in Nietzsche's metaphysics (65: 176, 190f, 195f, 202–4). Returning in this way to the first beginning is not to be confused with transporting ourselves into the past or making it actual again. Instead it is a means of experiencing what began in that beginning as a means of preparing for another beginning. What began in the first beginning is an obliviousness to the presence (the being) of beings, thanks to being's own concealment of itself (65: 185).

People (*Volk*)

A passing mention of "the people" in SZ (as the community in which destiny unfolds) gives way to repeated rhetorical reference to the will and mission of the German people in 1933/34 (SZ 384f; 16: 150f, 188–93, 232f). In Heidegger's first lectures after resigning as rector, he acknowledges the polyvalent uses of the term "people," but nonetheless looks to whether there is a distinctive unity underlying these uses. Attempts to determine that unity on the basis of geography, timeline, biology, or race are of no help since they only yield a collection of individuals. Nor are conceptions of the people as a body, soul, or spirit, since these determinations substitute a conception of *what* a people is for *who* we are as a people. Saying "who we are as a people" entails deciding to be who we are, a decision that co-determines history. Being a people is thus not primarily a matter of nature or human nature, but of the historical character of its being-here (*Da-sein*) and its specific way of being-with-others—attuned to and working with, for, and against others within a tradition. While underlying individual experience, a people stands in stark contrast to a collection of isolated subjects or egos. "The being of the people is neither the mere occurring of a population nor an animal being." As a necessary means of securing that the people endures, "the state is the historical being of the people" (38: 60–70, 97, 109, 125, 157, 165).

Two years later, in the *Contributions*, Heidegger outlines a people that is yet-to-come and again does so in terms of its historical character as something that is a matter of authentic decision (65: 50, 97). However, its coming-into-its-own depends on its philosophy and, indeed, a philosophy that comes *over* the people just as much as it comes "out" of the people. Rather than being something that can be calculated and prescribed on the basis of any sort of endowments, the philosophy of a people succeeds "only when philosophy continues to adhere to its first essential beginning." "Only in this way can it move the 'people' into the truth of historical being instead of being violated-and-inseminated [*genotzüchtigt*] by an alleged people into something without an essence" (65: 42f). Nor is the people or its preservation the goal of all history; it is not even the people's goal, not least because making its preservation the goal confuses a condition for setting a goal with the goal itself (65: 24f, 98f, 102f). When it comes to the question of the people, the Platonic manner of thinking in terms of ideas or values fails, as do Romantic reactionary attempts to extol culture's supposed roots in a "people" (65: 42f, 139, 496). In keeping with Heidegger's earlier rejections of conceiving a people in biological terms, he shows his disdain for reductions of types of inquiry, politics, and history to biological stereotypes or "populist" designs (65: 54, 163, 493).

Phenomenology (*Phänomenologie*)

"The fundamental problem of phenomenology" is, in Heidegger's 1919 lectures, the question of the scientific disclosure of the sphere of lived experience. The basic stance of living as such, in which that sphere is disclosed, is pre-theoretical. Though it is the basis for theoretical disciplines, it is "something that no conceptual system, however so broadly constructed, but only the phenomenological life … attains" (56/57: 109f). Phenomenology is an empowering, reflexive way of experiencing living, "an understanding intuition, the *hermeneutical intuition* … from which all theoretically-objectifying, even transcendent positing falls out" (56/57: 117). The following semester, phenomenology's basic problem is described as "the accessibility of the domain-of-origin of factical life." Life is worldly—a *Lebenswelt*—yet neither an object nor anchored in subjectivity. Phenomenology seeks to grasp its genuine origin, not in some ultimate universal, but in concrete forms, via an intuitive understanding that is at once destructive, interpretive, and reconstructive (58: 33, 80, 138, 145, 147f, 185). In lectures a few years later (1923) Heidegger makes it clear that he has no use for contemporary appropriations of phenomenology. Contrary to these betrayals of its promise, he describes phenomenology as a way of doing research that steps away from the subject matter initially given and back to that on which it is based, in part through "historical critique," through dismantling tradition's ways of covering up the subject matter (63: 67–77). Indeed, his first Marburg lectures, "Introduction to Phenomenological Research," take the form of a historical critique of the Cartesian (and, via Descartes, Thomistic) roots of Husserlian phenomenology (17: 109–22).

By the mid–1920s, existence replaces life as the object of an analysis that continues to be a self-styled phenomenology of the pre-thematic and factical (SZ 13, 37). In a purely formal sense, phenomenology consists in describing phenomena on their own terms, letting what shows itself (the phenomenon) be seen of itself, just as it shows itself of itself. However, in contrast to the purely formal concept of phenomenon as what shows itself initially and for the most part, the strictly "phenomenological" concept of phenomenon refers to "what initially and for the most part just does *not* show itself, what is *hidden* but is at the same time something that essentially pertains to what is initially and mostly apparent, such that it makes up its sense and ground." What in a special sense is hidden or shows itself only in a distorted way is the being of beings. Being is thus the phenomenon that phenomenology has to grasp. Because phenomenology is the way of accessing and determining what is supposed to be the theme of ontology, "*ontology is only possible as phenomenology*"—and fundamental ontology is only possible as phenomenology of Dasein. The methodical sense of this phenomenology is "hermeneutical" in the original meaning of the word, namely, as the way the authentic sense of being is made known to Dasein (SZ 27, 34–8, 58, 67; 12: 90f; 65: 188).

In lectures delivered shortly after the completion of SZ, Heidegger iterates that phenomenology is the method of ontology, but also adds how it is specifically reductive (leading the multifaceted apprehensions of beings back to the understanding of their being), constructive (freely projecting being in order to bring it into view since it is not accessible as beings are), and destructive (dismantling and tracing traditional concepts down to their historical sources with a view to determining the concepts' genuine character) (24: 25–32, 466f).

Heidegger later clearly distances himself from transcendental phenomenology, as the center of gravity of his thinking shifts from Dasein to the mutual appropriation of being and Dasein. Since, however, that appropriating event is the hidden presence of beings to Dasein, and since the other beginning is its retrieval through a hermeneutical dismantling (destruction) of the history of metaphysics, phenomenological aspects of Heidegger's early thinking persist in his mature thinking. Heidegger acknowledges as much. In 1963, after noting that the time of phenomenological philosophy might seem to be over as philosophy moves in other directions, he protests that phenomenology is not a direction. Instead it is "thinking's possibility of corresponding to the claim of what needs to be thought" (14: 101; 11: 148f). A decade later he affirms that thinking of being is an exercise in phenomenological seeing, a phenomenology of what is not apparent (15: 374ff, 399, 417).

Philosophical anthropology
(*philosophische Anthropologie*)

Because the analysis of Dasein is oriented to the question of being, it does not provide an ontology of Dasein, of the sort required to erect a "philosophical anthropology" on an adequate foundation. Instead the interpretation yields "only a few, not inessential pieces" for such a project (SZ 17). The analysis of Dasein, as "a kind of ontology," is distinct from the ontic discipline of anthropology as well as from movements to develop a philosophical anthropology. Such tendencies are misguided because they fail to make the requisite analysis of Dasein's way of being (SZ 47–50). Yet this differentiation does not rule out an "existential" anthropology or an "ontic" anthropology, based upon the ontological analysis of Dasein. The former presents factual existentiel possibilities and interprets them according to their existential structure (SZ 131, 183, 194, 200, 301), while the latter has the task of presenting (in a way that bears the stamp of the analysis of Dasein) the demonstrable, existentiel possibilities of social–historical and individual Dasein (89: 163f).

Shortly after the publication of SZ, Max Scheler's and Helmut Plessner's philosophical anthropologies appear. With their works

in mind, Heidegger criticizes the very idea of philosophical anthropology, both for its indeterminacy and its inherent limitation.
Philosophical anthropology ("Descartes' supreme triumph")
attempts to encompass the results of all the sciences that consider
human beings. Not only is it impossible to survey the empirical
results of all these disciplines, but their approaches are fundamentally diverse. As a result, anthropology becomes so all-encompassing
that it is utterly indeterminate. The inherent limitation of philosophical anthropology consists in its failure to explain why all
central philosophical problems are to be traced to the human
being. No age knows as much about human beings as the present,
but no age knows as little about what a human being is (3: 208–14;
5: 99f; 31: 122).

Philosophy (*Philosophie*)

Heidegger's relation to philosophy was never an easy one. As early
as his first Marburg lectures (1923), he announces that philosophy
is at end (17: 1), and in a 1964 lecture, after equating philosophy
with metaphysics, he asks what task remains for thinking, now
that philosophy has come to an end (14: 74). Yet in the inter-
vening years, he understands what he is doing as philosophy, albeit
under differing descriptions. In SZ, after designating ontology and
phenomenology as two names for philosophy, differentiated in
terms of its object and manner of treatment, Heidegger asserts:
"Philosophy is universal hermeneutical ontology, proceeding from
the hermeneutics of Dasein," as the point from which all philosophical questioning springs and to which it recurs (SZ 38, 50n.
1, 436). Philosophy is not a way of forming a world-view, but it is
a science, albeit a "transcendental or temporal science," ontology
as opposed to positive, ontic sciences (24: 455–66). At the same
time, the differentiation of philosophy from a world-view is not
unqualified. In the spring of 1929, he observes that philosophizing
happens only on the basis of a world-view as the hold or stance
(*Haltung*) of being-in-the-world (27: 396f).

By late 1929, however, adamantly rejecting the notion that
philosophy is either a science or a proclamation of a world-view,
he identifies its basic task with metaphysics, albeit in a way that

departs from tradition by placing both in question. In philosophizing (what Novalis rightly calls "homesickness, the urge to be at home everywhere"), human beings chase themselves away from everyday normalcy and back to "the ground of things" (29/30: 1ff, 31–6, 85ff; 31: 35f; 9: 199f). Philosophical thinking is metaphysical precisely because of its comprehensiveness, at once "going after the whole and gripping [human] existence through and through" (29/30: 13). By contrast, sciences are always concerned with some particular segment of reality. Once the realm of beings is divided up into conscious and non-conscious, living and non-living, cellular and intra-cellular, atomic and sub-atomic, etc., there is no place left for philosophy—nor should there be (31: 4). Nor is it theoretical knowledge bound up with practical application. Instead it is more primordial than theory or practice (31: 18f). So, too, philosophical thinking is not to be confused with laying the foundation for knowledge (a Kantian pursuit of the logic of science's basic concepts), absolute knowledge (Hegel), concern for the isolated existence of the individual human being as such (Kierkegaard, Nietzsche) or the establishment of a world-view. Not to be confused with science, a world-view, a foundation for knowledge, absolute knowledge, or a concern with existence, philosophy is the ceaselessly questioning, historical "struggle over the being of beings" (31: 36f; 36/37: 9–12).

By the mid–1930s, Heidegger gives up any pretense of philosophy as metaphysics. The *Contributions to Philosophy* venture the transition from metaphysics altogether to another, more originary beginning of philosophical thinking (65: 3f, 36–54, 435f). Philosophy is not centered in propositions since neither propositions nor what they assert are what is "the true" in philosophy. Philosophical thinking always appears alien because it dislocates everything from its familiar terrain by putting human beings into their relation to historical being and thereby rendering impossible any exclusively representational, calculative thinking about things on-hand, i.e. the sort of thinking centered on propositions and proofs (65: 13f). As the mindfulness of historical being, philosophy is necessarily mindful of who is mindful, i.e. the human being's selfhood (not to be confused with the "I") grounded in the steadfastness of Dasein (65: 48–54). As the thinking of historical being, philosophy can never be confirmed by facts, by beings; it breaks ties with its entanglement in justifying science, interpreting culture, serving a world-view, and metaphysics ("its own first essence that degenerates into something unessential") (65: 45, 422, 435). While philosophy must be overturned insofar as its essence is metaphysics, there is thus an "originary philosophy, the essential thinking" that thinks neither humans nor God, neither the world nor the earth, neither beings as such nor beings as a whole but historical being (69: 168f).

The moniker "philosophy" thus remains while the identification of it as metaphysics goes—at least in the *Contributions*. Yet even as he was writing the latter, he elsewhere identifies philosophy with onto-theology (42: 88). Since he equates onto-theology with metaphysics, we can see in this identification the seeds of his later assessment of philosophy. For when he claims in 1964, as noted above, that philosophy has come to an end, he equates it with metaphysics or, more precisely, with its consummation in the form of the hegemony of sciences whose basic feature is technological (14: 72).

Nevertheless, in the 1955 address "*Qu'est-ce que la philosophie?*" Heidegger continues to uphold philosophy in a certain sense. On the one hand, he explains how philosophy became metaphysics, principally through Aristotle's coinage of Western philosophy's leading question: what are beings? The answer lies in *ousia* in the sense of their beingness. Aristotle also specifies that philosophy is the science (*episteme*) of the "first principles and causes" of beings, as though those principles and causes constituted their being. With all its subsequent variations, philosophy, so construed, remains the same from Aristotle through Nietzsche. Elsewhere, as noted, Heidegger equates this tradition of philosophy with metaphysics (onto-theology) and pleas for thinking past it. In the 1955 address, however, he strikes a more positive note, suggesting that to learn what philosophy is, we must learn to converse with philosophers by corresponding (*entsprechen*) to what speaks to them and, indeed, constantly to us. Equivalently, we must learn to correspond in an attuned way (*gestimmt*) to what philosophy is "on the way to": the being of beings. Thus, the being of beings—the very fact that beings are—opened itself up to the Greeks in their astonishment at the fact. Cartesian doubt is a very different sort of attunement but, like astonishment for the Greeks, it gives rise to a pathos that is the *arche* of modern philosophy. Since this corresponding (*Ent-sprechen*) is a form of speaking that takes its bearings from language, the answer to the question of what philosophy is cannot be answered without an adequate consideration of language and the relation between thinking and poetry (11: 7–26). While the label "philosophy" falls in Heidegger's later thinking on both sides of the fault-lines between representational–justificatory thinking and mindful, poetic thinking, what matters—the difference between those fault-lines themselves—is unambiguous.

Plato

Plato's thinking is the standard for the entire history of philosophy, since "all metaphysics, together with its opponent, positivism, speaks the language of Plato" (14: 71, 82). Particularly at the beginning of metaphysics, his thought plays a central role, commencing a "continual decline," where "the truth of the interpretation of 'being' is never questioned" and "thinking is determined from the standpoint of a suitably purified way of representing beings" (55: 56ff, 113; 65: 134, 188, 458). "Since Plato," the primordial significance of *aletheia* as the conflict of unhiddenness with hiddenness gives way to an interpretation of it exclusively as the light of the idea that enables what is seen and seeing it. In the process of reinterpreting being as the unhiddenness (presence) of beings and thus yoking them to perceivers, Plato transforms truth (*aletheia*) into a matter of correctness (6.2: 196; 34: 34f, 99n. 2; 40: 190–3; 65: 333ff, 453, 457, 480; 70: 45; GA 19). Reinterpreting his predecessors' account of *physis* as the constant emergence of things, Plato presupposes that to be is by nature to be unhidden and, indeed, that the *idea* is "the really real" precisely as what is more unhidden than what it illuminates, indeed, the most unhidden (*alethinon*) and ever so.

Underlying Plato's identification of being with the unhiddenness of beings is his insight into the powerful role that the looks of things play in our lives. As we walk through a forest, we see trees, not so much this or that individual tree but what has the look (*eidos*) of a tree, i.e. the way the trees present themselves and are present. So, too, the idea of the tree lets us see what it *is*, lets it come to us. Similarly, a bed is based upon the way it looks in the carpenter's image or draft of it. Thus, across the natural/artificial divide, things have looks, and these looks constitute what they are. Plato's conception of being in terms of *eidos* is thus tied to a reinterpretation of *physis* to make it conform to *techne* (given the productiveness of the look, i.e. its role in production) and to a reinterpretation of being as something constant and common (given the commonness of the look) (6.1: 173–7; 52: 91; 65: 63, 75f, 126, 184, 206, 209; 71: 71f). An idea makes it possible to see things only because it is seen in some way itself, thus entailing "a primordial binding unity of viewing and being viewed." While acknowledging that this remark moves beyond what Plato literally says, Heidegger also takes pains to distinguish Plato from latter-day Platonists who, as idealists, confuse the looks of a thing with its representation (6.1: 152f; 34: 51, 57, 70f, 73, 106; 65: 208, 214f).

The first Greek thinkers experience *aletheia* as a conflict of hiddenness and unhiddenness. There are two signs that this experience begins to fade in Plato's thinking: first, his construal of *aletheia* as "pertaining to *beings*,—in such a way that beings *themselves* are addressed as unhidden, that beings and [being] unhidden are *lumped together*" and, second, his obliviousness to the question of unhiddenness as such (34: 93, 123f). If we do not understand hiddenness, then we can scarcely understand unhiddenness. Examining illusion or falsity (*pseudos*)—Plato's tactic in the *Theaetetus*—to clarify the meaning of *aletheia* (un-hiddenness) already betrays an obliviousness to its privative character (34: 125). Plato's tendency to construe *aletheia* in terms of light (*fos*) is also part and parcel of this obliviousness to the hiddenness supposed by it (65: 332). His crucial misstep (and departure from his predecessors) consists in taking unhiddenness (*aletheia*) for granted as the illuminating look (*idea, eidos*) of beings rather than as the unhiddenness of the self-concealing *physis*. Neither the unhiddenness as such nor the hiddenness that it presupposes is questioned. Also going unasked in Plato's construal of *aletheia* in terms of the accessibility and manifestness of beings is the openness that renders them accessible, encompassing far more than the relation (the yoke) of the perceivable and the perceiving of it (65: 333).

Plato's separation of art from the realm of truth is tied to his conception of being as the *eidos*. Whereas art, like a mirror, lets things show themselves through something else (e.g. a canvas), the *idea* lets things show themselves of themselves. Since Plato speaks of a God as the original producer here (in contrast to the carpenter or painter), Heidegger concludes that "the essence of the idea and thereby of being is grounded in the supposition of a creator." Art is furthest removed from truth in the first instance, the self-showing of the *idea*, because it is a subordinate form of producing, presenting the look of things from fewer sides (6.1: 184–9).

Following this gloss of *Republic* X, Heidegger turns to the relation of truth and beauty in Plato's *Phaedrus*, his "most accomplished" dialogue. While human beings tend to forget that they are mostly engaged with mere appearances, the beautiful draws them back to being as what is most remote and hidden yet essential to being human. By affording us a glimpse of being, a glimpse that enchants and enraptures us, beauty accomplishes the same thing that truth does. To be sure, art and truth remain at odds inasmuch as the latter is supposedly a non-sensuous illumination. Nonetheless, overcoming obliviousness to being must take place in the realm of appearances, "the site of beauty." Insofar as art brings forth the beautiful, it remains at a distance from the truth, but the distance is, for Plato, a felicitous one, since "the beautiful elevates us beyond the sensuous and carries us back to the true." Nonetheless, in a strict sense a fundamental discordance between art and truth remains, one that Platonism evades by supposing being in such a way that the evasion is not apparent (6.1: 198–202).

Despite Heidegger's largely critical stance toward Plato, Plato's account of the good as the highest idea foreshadows a central theme of Heidegger's mature thinking. Just as the sun makes the visible and seeing possible, so the highest idea, the idea of the good, is what empowers knower and known. In this sense the good is the "first and final power," the *dunamis* higher than actuality, enabling but beyond the unhiddenness (being, ideas) of beings. Despite the basic differences between Plato's idea of the good and Nietzsche's concept of value, the course of Western *metaphysics* takes its course from Plato's idea to the interpretation of being as the will to power, precisely because the good as the highest idea is what enables beings to be (6.2: 198–210). At the same time, in flagging what grounds unhiddenness as the presence of being to human beings, this highest idea also points to Heidegger's central, *non-metaphysical* theme of the appropriating event (34: 105, 108–13; 9: 160f).

Poetry (*Dichtung*)

There is a standard conception of poetry as an "expression of the soul, of lived experience," individual or collective (39: 26f). On this conception, so much in vogue in German thought (not least through Dilthey's 1905 "Lived Experience and Poetry"), the poem is above all else the external product of an inner human experience, whether that of its creator or interpreter. It owes its essence to human subjectivity. Departing from this widespread conception, Heidegger understands poetry as "the fundamental event of historical being," the way that "historical being brings itself to itself in words" (39: 257). The word for poetry in this connection is *Dichtung*, a noun that corresponds to the verb, *dichten*, that can mean "to compose," but also "to create, to make up." Exploiting both Teutonic and Greek roots of *dichten*, Heidegger characterizes it as "saying in the manner of making apparent by pointing" (39: 30). What poetry points to and makes apparent is not something on-hand, but the mystery of historical being (39: 237). By not flinching from it, the poet brings it to words and thus "establishes" it. Historical being is precisely the appropriating event that opens entities up to human beings (it is the presence of beings to us), concealing itself in the process. Poetry points historical being out to human beings but not as something that is fully formed or determinate, independent of the poetic creation itself. "Where words break off," not only things, but also historical being sinks into oblivion (12: 214). While "poetry finds being by saying it," poetry is anything but arbitrary. For what makes poetry's finding so pre-eminent is not that what is to be found is completely hidden but that "it is always already disclosed to human beings and the nearest of all that is most near" (53: 149). Poetry is nothing less than the steadfast "exposedness to historical being and, as this, the basic happening of the historical being-here of the human being" (39: 36).

Heidegger glosses five remarks by Hölderlin, "the poet of poets," to clarify the essence of poetry. Poetry is

(1) "the most innocent of all occupations,"

and yet it exposes itself to the all-exceeding power of historical being in the form of the play of language, which is

(2) "of all goods, the most dangerous, given to human beings ... to produce what they are."

Language is the most dangerous because it has the power to reveal but also to dissemble, to hide, and to degenerate into palaver (*Gerede*). Yet inasmuch as there is no history without a world and no world without language, language secures the historicity and the supreme possibility of being human, thanks to the fact that

(3) "we are a conversation and can listen to one another."

There is *one* conversation, where we can listen to one another, because, in words that are essential, what is "one and the same" is apparent to us, and on its basis "we are one and thus authentically ourselves. The conversation and its unity bear our being-here" (4: 39). At the same time what is "one and the same" can be manifest only in the light of something that remains.

(4) "Yet what remains, the poets found,"

namely, the gods and the earth, humans and their history as a people. In this sense, "poetry is the verbal founding of being," and yet a founding that is a gift since, as Hölderlin puts it,

(5) "human beings nonetheless dwell poetically on this earth."

For common sense, what is real is what is on-hand everyday, while poetry is mere fabrication and fiction. Yet for those in the know and those who genuinely act, the reverse is the case (39: 217; 4: 38). It is hopeless to try to understand our earthly existence ("dwelling") in terms of things that are on-hand or accessible and what we can do with them. Instead poetry articulates the gift of dwelling that, far from being any particular entity, is nothing less than our historical being itself.

The essence of poetry is the founding (*Stiftung*) of truth, its bestowing, grounding, and inception "at a specific time" (4: 47; 5: 50, 63). Poetry founds the truth by bestowing on us something in excess of all that went before, something incapable of being gauged by anything on-hand or accessible. At the same time poetry grounds an historical humanity, not out of nothing, but by opening up what is hidden from it, what it has already been thrown into and what it rests upon: the earth. In bestowing and grounding in these ways, poetry is also the inception of a conflict, the fundamental conflict of hiddenness and unhiddenness that is the essence of truth.

In advance of any capsulation of truth as the property of a judgment, truth essentially unfolds as the "opposition of clearing and a twofold concealment"—refusal and dissembling (5: 48). Truth occurs in this sense in art as the struggle of earth and world, because art is composed or created (*gedichtet*), and this poetic character is inherent in all art (5: 24f, 59, 62f). "Poetry is the saying of the world and earth, the saying of the play-space of their struggle and, with that, of the sight of all nearness and remoteness of the gods" (5: 61; 54: 20, 23, 25f). Yet, if there is a poetry to painting, music, sculpture, it is not because they are reducible to poetry in the narrow sense (*Poesie*) but because they all have their own linguistic character, and they all have that character because the truth occurring in them, the manifestness of particular beings, is not possible without language (5: 61). Poetry epitomizes the fact that "we do not have language but rather language has us" (39: 23, 38, 67, 74; 4: 38). Nonetheless, given that language is poetry in the broader sense, i.e. as the "illuminating projecting of the truth," poetry in the narrower sense (poesy) as a work of language (*Sprachwerk*) enjoys a privileged position among the arts. Poesy is the most primordial poetry because "language preserves the primordial essence of poetry," poetry in the broader sense (5: 61f).

Four important points about poetry are corollaries to its founding character. First, poetry is grounded in basic moods. "A poet speaks from a mood that determines the ground and basis and resounds through the space on which and in which the poetic saying founds a being. We call this mood the basic mood of poetry" (39: 79). Hölderlin writes from the experience of the holy mourning at the departure of the gods, a mourning that continues to hold them near without denying a remoteness that is their doing and not ours. Second, the essence of poetry, by first naming and thus establishing the essence of things, enables language. Language is not something on-hand without poetry or a tool that poetry takes up. Accordingly, the essence of language is to be understood on the basis of the essence of poetry and not vice versa (4: 43). Third, poets are "half-gods," they have to be able to attend to divine hints and at the same time intimate them to humanity, to a people. Thus, the poet is cast into the "realm-between" divinities and humans, where it is decided who the human being is and where he settles in his Dasein (4: 47). Historical being is an abyss, hidden from beings, and its hiddenness has created what is essentially dangerous in the present time, namely, human obliviousness to it. "This danger is *the* danger ... In order to see and show the danger, there must be the sort of mortals who first reach into the abyss" (5: 295f). Those mortals are the poets in this needy time. Fourth, the significance of poetry is necessarily indirect, polyvalent, and partially hidden. So, too, it is in an important sense beyond the reach of any interpretation and report. These characteristics of poetry are traceable to the fact that the truth that it discloses is the very conflict of hiddenness and unhiddenness. It discloses by leaving what is unsayable unsaid. "What essentially unfolds as being and is never an entity and something actual and, hence, thus constantly appears as nothing, that can only be said in poetry or thought in thinking" (53: 150).

Heidegger's conception of poetry heavily influences his efforts to rethink being historically and its appropriation of human beings. At times his remarks about the need for the transformation of human beings into *Dasein* appear as an attempt to reinterpret them in his image of the poet, disabusing them of the pretense of mastering being, with a view to transforming them into its shepherds. Heidegger characterizes his *Contributions to Philosophy* as an attempt to think what Hölderlin's poetry says. Yet, while intimately connected, poetry and philosophy "live on the most separate mountains" (11: 26; 12: 184f, 203f; 40: 174).

Positionality (*Gestell*)

In the modern technological age, everything is represented (*vor-gestellt*) and/or produced (*her-gestellt*) in a calculated way, coercively placed (*gestellt*) and able to be ordered (*be-stellbar*) as a uniform, replicable piece of a standing reserve (*Bestand*). Together these ways of pre-positioning how entities are present in modern technology constitute *positionality*, the essence of modern technology (79: 32, 40). One ordinary meaning of

Gestell is a shelf. The essence of modern technology shelves whatever is into the standing reserve. "Positionality is as it were the photographic negative of the appropriating event" (15: 366). The appropriating event (the presence of beings to Dasein) is discernible in its modern destiny as positionality but precisely as not yet developed.

The standing reserve is a self-enclosed circuit of ordering, with a "violence that overtakes everything." Nothing has any standing outside it, and whatever is present is so only by virtue of its standing in the standing reserve. Human beings are no exception. What is particularly dangerous about positionality is the illusion that it is solely a matter of human exploitation and machination (79: 29ff). The forces of nature also do not elude positionality, for the forces of nature placed in the service of technology are represented by physics in the same way that positionality positions whatever is present. Hence, "nature is for physics the standing-reserve of energy and matter." "Modern technology is not applied natural science but rather modern natural science is the application of the essence of modern technology," where nature is already secured as the "basic standing-reserve," capable of being calculated in advance (79: 41ff).

The way things once affected us, thanks to their proximity or remoteness, wanes as they become objects of our calculations and representations. This objectification opens the way to positionality where everything is equally near and far, where things no longer really matter to us, and where everything is subject to the same, indifferent accounting. Indeed, in the standing reserve there are no longer even objects (79: 23ff, 42, 44).

Positionality unfolds as the danger, but the danger remains "covered over and distorted/obstructed [*verstellt*]." "This distortion/blockage is what is most dangerous in the danger." What distorts it is, once again, the appearance of technology as a tool in human hands (79: 68). Positionality, the essence of technology, can never be mastered or undone by anything humans do. For it is the destiny of how beings present themselves to human beings (the destiny of being) that this essence remains concealed. Nonetheless, it also remains true that without humanity there is no unconcealing. While technology is not *overturned* (*überwunden*) by humans, they can play a necessary, *corresponding* role in turning it back (*verwunden*) into its still-hidden truth. For this to happen, for an essential relationship between technology (being) and human beings to establish itself, "modern humanity must first find its way back into the breadth of its essential space." This space's dimensions come solely from the co-hold (*Ver-hältnis*) of being and human beings on one another, i.e. the way the safeguarding of being (the presence of beings) is handed over (*vereignet*) to the essence of the human being. If human beings do not first cultivate this essential space and learn to dwell in it, they are incapable of anything within the destiny now holding sway (79: 20, 69f).

Positionality's Greek roots are discernible in the connection between *physis* and *thesis*. Indeed, positionality determines an epoch because its essential character of co-positioning everything as a product, stocking everything in the standing reserve, rests on the destiny of historical being at the beginning, namely, the understanding of *physis*. *Physis* is what allows things to come about and be present. To be sure, the Greeks recognized the difference between the natural and the artificial (the technical). Nevertheless, the understanding of *physis* sets the stage for conflating them, for conceiving nature's way of bringing things forth as itself a way of positioning (*Stellen*) and producing them out of itself and, indeed, for human representing (*Vor-stellen*) and producing (*Her-stellen*). "The genealogy of positionality's essence as the essence of technology points and reaches into the essential derivation of the Western-European and currently planetary destiny of being from *physis* in which the unhiddenness of presence lays its claim as the hidden originary essence of being" (79: 65).

Possibility (*Möglichkeit*)

"Higher than actuality stands *possibility*." This statement follows from the fact that, while what is actual surfaces only in the context of Dasein's being-in-the-world, being-in-the-world is itself inherently a possibility, indeed, a possibility of possibilities. "Dasein comports itself to its being as its ownmost possibility," and, because it is respectively its possibility, "it *can* lose and find itself," not as something actually on-hand but as a possibility (SZ 38, 42). "Dasein is in each instance what it can be and how it is its possibility." The way Dasein is its possibility existentially (preeminently in manners of concern, solicitude, and its capability-of-being in relation to itself) is distinct from "empty, logical possibility" just as it is from "the contingency of something on-hand." Whereas "possibility," as a modal category of on-handness is ontologically subordinate to actuality and necessity (i.e. it signifies the "*not yet* actual and the *not ever* necessary"), possibility as an existential is "the most primordial and ultimately positive ontological determinacy of Dasein." Dasein is the "*thrown possibility* through and through," a capability-of-being that has been handed over to itself and has always already projected itself onto possibilities. "The understanding, as projecting, is the type of being of Dasein, in which it *is* its possibilities as possibilities" (SZ 143ff, 181). In this projective understanding, entities in general (not only Dasein) are disclosed in terms of their possibilities (SZ 151). Angst, however, discloses the possibility distinctive to Dasein, bringing it face to face with "its *being-free for* ... the authenticity of its being as a possibility that it always already is" (SZ 188, 191, 265f). The basic possibilities of Dasein, authenticity and inauthenticity, entail corresponding existentiel, factical possibilities (SZ 188, 191, 193, 295, 298f). "The authentic being towards death is an existentiel possibility of Dasein" (SZ 260). Death is neither an on-hand nor handy possibility but a possibility of being of Dasein, its ownmost possibility, an exceptional possibility that Dasein has to take over. So, too, dying is an ontological possibility grounded in Dasein's care (SZ 250ff, 261). "The disclosedness of the possibility is grounded in the anticipating enabling [*Ermöglichung*]" (SZ 264, 324). Conscience, existentially conceived, testifies to the possibility that Dasein is and the resoluteness that, hearkening to conscience, anticipates death, bringing Dasein back to this possibility (SZ 270, 274, 287f, 307). The possibility that Dasein is, authentically or inauthentically, is grounded in its temporality (SZ 337f).

In Heidegger's later work he continues to insist that the possible is, at least at times, "more in being" (*seiender*) than the actual. Far from being consigned to sheer non-being, the possible is the process of being present (*Anwesung*) of the vanishing and the oncoming. At the same time he is wary of the hidden metaphysical agenda behind questions of possibility (52: 117ff; 65: 475; 67: 23–9, 174).

Presence (*Anwesenheit, Anwesen*)

Since Plato, there has been a tendency to equate an entity's being with its presence (*Anwesenheit*), understanding it thereby in terms of a specific temporal mode, namely, the present (*Gegenwart*) (SZ 25). The more present something is, the more it is said to be, such that the supreme beings (Plato's ideas, Aristotle's unmoved mover) are constantly present. Their presence entails that they are constantly in place and accessible. For subsequent thinking, presence becomes problematical, at once giving way to—while also underlying—the conception of being as the objectivity of objects, the reality of the real (7: 45; 8: 241; 65: 31).

By contrast, in keeping with the root sense of *aletheia* as un-hiddenness, early Greek thinkers (Anaximander, Heraclitus, and Parmenides) appreciate how every presence is interwined in multiple ways with absence. The same can be said for Hölderlin's poetry. "Every process of coming to be present [*Anwesung*] is at once in itself a process of being absent. What is present extends as such, not somehow merely after the fact and by the way, but in accordance with its essence, into what is absent" (52: 101, 117). The movements and happening of history have this sort of presence, presence in the sense of the appropriating event that lets what is present come to be present (14: 45).

There are accordingly two senses of presence at work in Heidegger's work. "Presence" can stand for the metaphysical conception of the present-ness of beings in the sense of their accessibility to someone here and now. The attempt in SZ to demonstrate that time is the sense of Dasein's being lays the groundwork for dismantling this conception. "Presence" can also stand for the robust, historical sense of the appropriating event that grounds and affords the coming to presence. While critical of the metaphysical conception of presence, Heidegger embraces the robust sense. Not reducible to the now, presence in this robust sense encompasses the handy and on-hand, the having been and the future, since all of the latter affect us, i.e. they are in a way present to us—even in or because of the ways they are absent (12: 116; 14: 11, 16f). There is presence only by virtue of the clearing, "the open space for everything that comes to be present and to be absent." Philosophy as metaphysics fails to inquire into being as

being, i.e. to inquire how there can be presence or "the open" as
such (14: 80f, 86f).

Primordiality (*Ursprünglichkeit*)

The term *ursprünglich* typically stands for original. In SZ it
occasionally signifies what is original or initial in a temporal sense,
e.g. "the original meaning of the word" or "expressions" (SZ 37,
54, 119). However, it predominantly designates a fundamental
or basic character. In order to differentiate this designation from
a temporal one, *ursprünglich* is translated primordial. Thus the
fundamental structure of the existential analysis, i.e. being-in-the-
world, is "a priori" and "primordial" (SZ 41, 54, 130, 180). What
is primordial is not necessarily simple or exclusive. Basic existentials, for example, are "equiprimordial." Understanding is not
reducible to discourse or vice versa. Instead, each is equally basic
and existentially constitutive of being-here (SZ 131).

Psychologism (*Psychologismus*)

The most concentrated attack on psychologism, the attempt to
reduce logical principles to empirical descriptions of mental states
or contents, is to be found in the Prolegomena to Husserl's
Logical Investigations. In his dissertation, building upon Husserl's
arguments, Heidegger critically investigates four psychologistic
theories of judgment (those of Wilhelm Wundt, Heinrich Meier,
Franz Brentano with Anton Marty, and Theodor Lipps) with the
aim of establishing the essence of judgment as the "cell" of logic and
thus the most effective way to distinguish between psychology and
logic. Because psychologistic theories are "genuinely unfamiliar"
with the logical form of actuality, namely, the sense and validity
(*Geltung*) of a judgment, they look in vain for the essence of
judgment in the behavior of the psychological subject. What is
logically distinctive of judgment is a "sense, a 'static' phenomenon
that stands outside of any development and alteration, that thus
does not *become*, does not emerge, but instead is valid; something
that can in every case be 'grasped' by the judging subject but

never be altered by this grasping" (1: 179). In Heidegger's 1925 lectures on logic, he returns to the debate, using the dubiousness of Neo-Kantian arguments against psychologism and the "naturalization of consciousness" as a springboard to demonstrating the superiority of Husserl's approach (21: 92, 35–53, 89–109).

Questioning (*Fragen*)

Every question asks about something (*das Gefragte*), interrogates someone or something (*das Befragte*), and asks for something (*das Erfragte*). Corresponding to this threefold structure, SZ asks about being by interrogating Dasein (who Dasein *is*) in order to determine the sense of being (SZ 5ff). In 1932 Heidegger redeploys this threefold structure, with the significant difference that "beings" replaces "Dasein" and "ground" replaces "sense" (35: 49f; see also 46–76).

In 1923, attempting to clarify Husserl's problem-oriented project, Heidegger distinguishes twelve components of questioning, the first three of which coincide roughly with the structure indicated above. The additional components include a question's connection with a problem, how a question is encountered, and above all the interpretation of the question as a manner of seeking, i.e. not a "theoretical" phenomenon but instead "a *specific care* of Dasein." In the same context Heidegger distinguishes answering in the form of valid propositions—aimed ultimately at "an ideal possible connection of all valid propositions altogether"—and answering oriented toward bringing the inquirer into "a specific *fundamental relation*" to the entity inquired about, in the face of the inherent danger of being pushed away from it. Instead of moving beyond questions to an objective structure, answering in the latter sense prompts ever renewed questioning. Problems are questions that have been explicitly made part of a research program and thus tend to take for granted as already settled—without further questioning—what is interrogated. Neo-Kantian examinations of history as a "history of problems," where problems are objectified from "a specific philosophical standpoint," contrast with research that is genuinely free of such a standpoint (17: 73–9).

As early as 1930, Heidegger distinguishes the leading question (*Leitfrage*) from the fundamental question (*Grundfrage*) of metaphysics (31: 113–38). The leading question is the question posed by metaphysics: what are beings? (Or equivalently, what are beings insofar as they exist?) In the history of metaphysics, answers to this question are variations on a common theme, an extension of physics (hence, *meta ta physika*), whether in the form of the *constant presence* of things (Plato's *idea* and Aristotle's *physis*), creation (Aquinas), objectivity (Kant), spirit (Hegel), or will to power (Nietzsche). These answers (to the question of what beings are) are made from the standpoint of beings and, indeed, in a way always tied to some pre-eminent being. Hence, metaphysics is inevitably onto-theology. Modern philosophy attempts to raise these answers to the level of theory or science (an absolute science or speculative knowledge), keeping the inquiry at arm's length from the inquirer herself, with the result that philosophy is not "the first and ultimate possibility of human existence" (31: 35).

The fundamental question (*Grundfrage*) is, by contrast, the question of being itself, i.e. what is being? (alternatively, what is the sense, the truth, the essence of being itself?). It is vain to attempt to determine being from the standpoint of this or that particular being, since any particular being already *is* and so would yield a circular definition of what being is. And in addition, the fundamental question differs from the leading question by questioning its very ground. For the fundamental question asks how it happens that being is understood the way it is (e.g. as constant presence in the history of metaphysics). Since being is only in relation to human beings, the fundamental question addresses this relation, the way that being appropriates us and vice versa (SZ 200, 212; 9: 114; 16: 704). Rather than keeping the inquirer at a safe theoretical distance, this question puts the inquirer himself in question. Given the temporal orientation of the Greek and, subsequently, self-evident understanding of being as presence, the question of being *and* time is a first attempt to raise the fundamental question as a question more primordial than the leading question. The question of the connection of being and time "compels" us to put in question the human being as the being who understands being and does so in terms of time (31: 118–31).

Heidegger also glosses the difference between the leading and the fundamental questions in terms of the question of the difference between being and beings. In posing the leading question and thus presupposing this difference, metaphysics cannot put that difference in question, cannot question its ground. By contrast, the fundamental question of the truth of being itself asks what being is such that it yields this difference. The answer is historical being as the appropriating event that opens being and Dasein up to one another, where each needs the other. While the leading question asks what makes a being a being, the fundamental question asks how it happens that beings are present to Dasein.

The transition from the leading question to the fundamental question coincides with the transition from the first beginning to the second beginning (65: 75ff, 428ff, 456ff, 465ff). In this connection, the question of why there are beings and not rather nothing is a transitional question. Since a supreme being already *is* and thus cannot be the answer to this question, the question is a springboard for the leap into historical being (65: 421, 509).

Heidegger's mature thinking continues to take the form of questioning, e.g. questions of poets, the thing, technology, Zarathustra. Echoing his comments about authentic questioning twenty-five years earlier, he remarks that "questioning is the piety of thinking" (7: 36). However, he subsequently criticizes the remark. Referring to the poetic experience of language as one of thinking, he notes that the authentic gesture of thinking is not questioning but listening to what language already bestows. Because questioning is always related to the search for grounds, it is necessary to move beyond questioning to listening, to letting language and things speak for themselves (9: 169a; 12: 13, 164ff, 170).

Reality (*Realität*)

"Reality," an ontological designation, refers to inner-worldly entities. It may refer to being-handy as well as being-on-hand. Historically, however, it designates the sheer on-handness of things. But all modes of being of what is inner-worldly are ontologically founded upon being-in-the-world. If "reality" is taken, in its traditional sense, to designate what is on-hand, it enjoys no privileged status among the modes of being of inner-worldly beings and cannot characterize the world and Dasein in an ontologically adequate manner (SZ 211).

Questioning, believing, presupposing, or attempting to prove the reality of the external world is senseless since any sense of reality presupposes being-in-the-world. Adopting any of these postures toward the external world confuses the world-phenomenon (characteristic of Dasein's "being-in") with the being of inner-worldly entities (SZ 202, 206f). Strictly epistemological orientations fall short, as do phenomenological improvements of the concept of subject or consciousness, because they omit existential analysis. "Inner-worldly entities are respectively already disclosed with being-here as being-in-the-world." This claim might speak for realism if realism were not committed to (a) the possibility and need for proving the world's reality and (b) the attempt "to explain reality ontically through real causal connections" (SZ 207). By denying the latter, idealism has the better of realism. Yet idealism forfeits this advantage as long it fails to provide an ontological analysis of consciousness itself.

Appreciative (like Dilthey) that reality is never primarily given in thinking and conceiving, Scheler locates the source of the sense of reality in the experience of resistance. However, resistance does not occur in a vacuum. Meeting resistance from something within-the-world presupposes already "being out for" something in a context of relevance. In other words, the discovery of resistance is only possible on the basis of the disclosure of the world. "Resistance characterizes the 'external world' in the sense of inner-worldly beings but never in the sense of the world" (SZ 211). The fact that reality is ontologically grounded in Dasein's being does not mean that what is real could only be what it is if Dasein exists. Just as there is being only as long as Dasein ("the ontic possibility of understanding being") is, so, too, reality but not the real depends upon the existence of Dasein. If Dasein does not exist, then it can be said neither that an entity is nor that it is not.

Reason (*Vernunft*)

"Reason" (*Vernunft*, the Latin *ratio*) traditionally stands for the capacity to infer a proposition from one or more other propositions, where the latter provide the reason for the inference. According to the principle of sufficient reason (hereafter "psr") something can be said to exist "only if it is asserted in a proposition that satisfies the basic psr" (10: 36, 42). The psr's "enormous power consists in the fact that it pervades, guides, and carries all knowing that expresses itself in propositions" (10: 35). In this way the psr holds of being (what *is* in that sense), where *being* is identified with *being an object*, and being an object is identical to having a sufficient reason for being. Being an object in this way demands supplying finite knowing subjects with a sufficient reason (10: 118). In the modern era, rationality, as this demand, has "interposed itself between the thinking human being and his world, in order to take control of human representing in a new way" (10: 37). The powerfulness of the psr—what exerts power in it—is irreducible to what human subjects do or what happens within the world. Nevertheless, its power is precisely its seemingly empowering demand that the human subject provide herself with the reasons for whatever is (10: 42). Herein lies "the aspect of the unconditional and thorough-going claim of supplying the mathematically-technical, computable grounds, the total 'rationalization'" (10: 155).

Since the grounds required by a rational explanation are external to the things themselves, it tends to look past them, failing to consider them on their own terms. Instead it looks for causes or conditions as reasons for some privileged aspects of things, e.g. their utility or power. Not coincidentally, the more doggedly we pursue and penetrate such grounds and reasons, the more uprooted we seem to be (10: 47, 118). Moreover, despite the beholdenness of modern science, modern technology, and the modern university to the psr, consideration of it is not to be found in the sciences or the university (10: 37f, 44). Nor is it possible for the sciences, answering the demands placed upon them, to consider the psr that is their very element (10: 46f). Rationality is taken for granted, a rationality that is both underdetermined and overdetermined—underdetermined by virtue of seizing upon only certain aspects of things and overdetermined by virtue of subjecting everything to its explanatory ambitions (10: 119). It is not only "the usual scientific-technical way of presenting things" that fails here; the philosophical doctrine that the principle of sufficient reason is an immediately illuminating principle "evades the decisive questions of thinking" (10: 52). In the wholesale pursuit of explanatory inference, there is no place for the utter self-sameness and uniqueness, the historicity and non-dependence of being (10: 161–9). Paradoxically, exclusive pursuit of the sufficient reason of beings loses sight of the way beings are grounded in their presence to Dasein.

Rectoral Address (*Rektoratsrede*)

Upon becoming rector of Freiburg University and joining the Nazi Party in the spring of 1933, Heidegger gave the address "The Self-assertion of the German University." "Self-assertion" here means the primordial, common will to realize the university's essence, i.e. science. Since science educates the leaders (*Führer*) and guardians of the German people's fate, this will is at once the will to realize the spiritual mission of the people (*Volk*) as a people who know themselves in their state (*Staat*). Knowledge of the spiritual mission combines with pro-active knowledge of the people and knowledge of the state's destiny to create "the full and primordial science." This science truly obtains (becoming the innermost necessity of existence) only if "we submit to the power of the *beginning* of our historical-spiritual existence": Greek philosophy. For the Greeks, science, while impotent in the face of fate, is the supreme praxis, the power encompassing existence as a whole and keeping it focused. Nor is this beginning *passé*. To the contrary, "the beginning still *is* ... it stands before us." Yet it stands before us with a difference, namely, with our experience of the death of God, as Nietzsche identifies that difference, and the abandonment that difference entails. With this experience, the Greek wonder, once overcome by knowing, is transformed into questioning as the supreme form of knowledge, capable of disclosing what is essential. Such questioning breaks down the fragmentary character of the sciences and brings them back to the fruitfulness of the world-forming powers of human, historical existence. In a university committed to such questioning, professional or technical education takes a backseat, and there is no place for career-seekers.

If the will is there for the essence of science in this sense, it creates for the people "a truly *spiritual* world," where "spirit" signifies "the primordially attuned, knowing resoluteness for the essence of being," but also "the power of preserving at the deepest level the forces, rooted in the earth and blood, of the people." This remark exemplifies how Heidegger combines National Socialist rhetoric with his vision of the leadership role of the university. The will to realize the essence of science requires the university's instructors to sustain inquiry in the face of the danger of the world's constant uncertainty. If they do, they are fortified for "leadership." The student body also resolutely wills the essence of the university by placing themselves under the law of what is essential to being students. In contrast to the negative freedom that goes by the name of "academic freedom," the supreme freedom is self-legislation. Exercising this freedom, students bind themselves to work-service, military-service, and the service of knowledge. While all three forms of service are equiprimordial (echoing the National Socialist policy of *Gleichschaltung*), Heidegger stresses that knowing is not in the service of professions but vice versa.

Heidegger concludes the address with the charge to teachers and students to form a community of battle, the battle of their opposing wills that "alone keeps the opposition open and plants ... the basic mood out of which the self-limiting self-assertion empowers the resolute self-examination to genuine self-administration." Whether this happens or not depends on what each decides. Yet, referring to the recent National Socialist seizure of power as the "greatness of this outbreak," he adds that "the most youthful force of the people has already *decided*" (16: 107–17).

In 1945 Heidegger pens a defense of his Rectoral Address, along with his ill-fated and short-lived rectorate, as an attempt to save what he could from the destructive policies of the ministry (16: 372–94). He noted the disapproval that he immediately experienced from party officials, accusing him of a "private National Socialism that circumvents the perspectives of the party program" (16: 381).

Representing (*Vorstellen*)

Not to be confused with genuine thinking, representing something or, equivalently, placing it before oneself is "the fundamental feature of previous thinking" and the "metaphysical ground of modernity." It serves as the basis for what Nietzsche calls the last man's "blinking," where only what is placed before him has any standing (8: 59, 87).

The modern equation of beings with objects is carried out in a "placing-before [or representing] that aims at bringing each entity before it in such a way that the calculating human can become sure and thus certain of it." Though seventeenth- and eighteenth-century German philosophers use the term *Vorstellung* to translate the Latin *representatio*, it does not necessarily signify replicas or pictures in the mind. It can signify the presentation or placement of something before a subject—as in Brentano's claim that all consciousness is or rests upon a presentation (*Vorstellung*). Heidegger suggests that, in order to grasp the modern notion fully, attention should be paid to the original force of the term: "placing before oneself and relative to oneself. By this means, the entity comes to stand, as an object, and thus first receives the seal of being." Descartes in particular equates thinking with representing, where to represent means "to place something before oneself and to secure it as such" by way of calculating it. Instead of merely perceiving or taking up what is present, placing-before (representing) attacks it so as to take hold of it, with the result that the entity is no longer what is present but an object, something positioned, standing opposite (*Gegenstand*) the subject. "Placing-before is a fore-going, dominating objectification." As beings become objects in this Cartesian representational thinking, human beings become subjects (5: 87, 92, 108ff). In this way, representing is inherently, even if for the most part tacitly, willful, a point raised to metaphysical stature by Leibniz and Nietzsche (77: 53f; 6.2: 266ff). While reducing entities to objects, the juggernaut of modern representational thinking also precludes thought of being as something other than entities or objects. "For representing, everything becomes a being" (7: 232). In representing, a "trace of Dasein" shows itself, namely, its "standing out into the open," but this trace is obscured in the representing itself, as "it remains back in the soul as an occurrence and act that ultimately as 'I' itself forms what is opposite it into an object" (65: 306, 316).

Reserve (*Verhaltenheit*)

The basic mood motivating Greek thinking (and understanding of *aletheia*) is astonishment (*thaumazein*) at the simple fact that things exist at all, i.e. that they are unhidden rather than hidden.

Thanks to this wonder, something simple and quite ordinary becomes something quite extraordinary (45: 171). This wonder at "the being of beings" first attunes human beings to truth as unhiddenness and inaugurates Western thinking. Yet despite being originally so taken by things' unhiddenness, this thinking finds nothing in that unhiddenness (*aletheia*) to question. Instead, Greek thinkers (notably Plato and Aristotle) relate to the prevailing unhiddenness of things (their *physis*) by actively cultivating it in a mode of knowing called *techne*.

This "technical" way of relating to things, necessitated by wonder, provides fertile soil for developing *aletheia* as unhiddenness into mere correctness. The more the recognition of the entities in their unhiddenness develops into *techne*, the more unavoidable it becomes that the looks of entities (the "ideas") alone provide the measure of them, leading to the correspondence theory of truth. The original essence of *aletheia* is ineluctably lost and, with it, the basic mood necessitating it. Beings become objects, truth becomes the correctness of representing them, and astonishment at the sheer existence (unhiddenness) of things gives way to indifference to being as simply the most commonplace of commonplaces. Along the way, a desire for ever-increasing familiarity with ever more things and facility in reckoning with them gradually takes hold (45: 180–4; 66: 109f, 177). "The entities *are* and yet remain abandoned by historical being and left over to themselves in order thus to become only the object of machination" (45: 185).

Yet the ensuing nihilism might be "the concealed ground of a still concealed, basic mood that would compel [*nötigte*] us to a different necessity, [that] of a *different* primordial questioning and beginning" (45: 186). That basic mood combines both shock (*Erschrecken*) at the abandonment of being, bringing us back to the fact that beings are and that historical being has withdrawn, and awe (*Scheu*) at this historical, appropriating event. Reserve is the basic mood combining this shock and awe. Why "reserve"? Because it is the knowledge that we are not in control (hence, the shock at the pretension to the contrary, i.e. the self-deceptive will-to-power-trip induced by historical being's hiddenness and by the metaphysical assumption that there are only beings) and the knowledge, too, that we are nonetheless appropriated by historical being (hence, the awe at the fact that the historical being of beings is their *presence* to us, that it needs us). With the knowledge that historical being is not something to be explained in the way that beings are explained (namely, by relating them to other beings), reserve is the basic mood in which questioning turns to what deserves to be questioned above all else: the hiddenness of historical being. Reserve attunes us to the appropriating event and, in the process, demands that we begin to think anew. It demands, that is, that we think "from out of this appropriating event," as it were, steadfastly and decisively yet humbly about the truth of the historical being of beings—as the appropriating event that grounds their unhiddenness to us and our openness to them. Although we are no longer preservers of the astonishing unhiddenness of beings (as the Greeks putatively were), reserve transforms us into vigilant guardians of the clearing for the self-concealing of historical being. Reserve is anything but a retreat or recoil from beings. To the contrary, by not trying to turn them into objects or master them, it lets them be. Reserve is the ground of care, sheltering the truth and its unfolding into concerns and transactions with beings (65: 14ff, 35, 251, 261, 407; 45: 189f).

Resoluteness (*Entschlossenheit*)

Dasein's disclosedness is the "primordial truth," and resoluteness is the eminent mode of that disclosedness, "the most primordial because *authentic* truth of Dasein." Resoluteness means "allowing oneself to be called up" from a forlorn, mindless conformity to the group (the They). Because being resolute means "being authentically oneself," it is not to be confused with mere independence from social conventions. A resolute Dasein does not detach itself from its world but instead thrusts itself directly into its concerns and ways of solicitously being-with others. Indeed, being-with-one-another authentically—even being the conscience of others—springs from resoluteness. "In resoluteness what matters to Dasein is that capability-of-being [*Seinkönnen*] that is most its own, a capability that, as thrown, can project itself only onto definite factical possibilities." Precisely in this way, being resolute first provides Dasein "the authentic transparency," disclosing the situation that it finds itself in—situated in a place as well as in circumstances, involvements, and relationships—with a view to disclosing and choosing the factical possibilities therein. Resolute Dasein discloses these possibilities from a heritage (*Erbe*) that it takes over as thrown. In one sense, then, nothing changes; in another sense, everything does when Dasein's care is authentic, when its disclosedness of its being-in-the-world—and all that entails—is authentic, i.e. resolute (SZ 270, 297–301, 307ff, 383f).

Resoluteness consists, too, in authentically *understanding* the call of conscience which amounts to "wanting-to-have-conscience" in the existential sense, i.e. letting its ownmost self act on it, while embracing the existential guilt most proper to it, i.e. the responsibility of existing. To be resolute is to hear Dasein's silent call to itself to be itself as the entity responsible for the choices it makes—not in the abstract, but in terms of the factical possibilities that it projects. Thus, resoluteness is "the existentiel choosing of the choice to be oneself" (SZ 270). But it is also inherent in resoluteness that it project itself upon this guilt "which Dasein is, *as long as it is*," i.e. constantly, "to the very end." "Resoluteness becomes authentically what it can be, *as understanding and being to the end*, i.e. as anticipating death ... *It contains the authentic being towards death in itself as the possible existentiel modality of its own authenticity*" (SZ 305). Only in anticipating death, i.e. projecting the possibility most proper to Dasein, the possibility of its impossibility, and doing so with a constant resolve, is Dasein authentically resolute; "it is authentically and entirely what it can be only as *anticipatory resoluteness*" (SZ 309).

In SZ the account of resoluteness holds special importance for insuring that the anticipation of death is "an existentiel possibility to which Dasein in itself attests." The account justifies the ontological projection of Dasein as a whole (being unto death) by grounding it in "an ontical possibility of Dasein." The account of resoluteness is thus "a definite ontical way of taking authentic existence, a factical ideal" that serves as a necessary presupposition of the ontological interpretation of Dasein (SZ 309f).

The phenomenon of resoluteness is also central to analyses of freedom, time, and historicity in SZ. Resolute Dasein renders itself free for its world, on the basis of the aim—more precisely, the for-the-sake-of which (*Worumwillen*)—that Dasein has itself chosen (SZ 298). In being resolute, Dasein keeps its resolve free for the respective factical possibilities, including that of taking back a decision (SZ 307f). In resoluteness, the present is fetched back from its dispersal in immediate concerns and maintained in terms of the future and what has been. This authentic present is the moment (*Augenblick*), the way that Dasein resolutely focuses on the situational possibilities and circumstances to be taken care of. In a sense Dasein is thus enraptured by the situation, and the moment is that rapture "*maintained* in resoluteness" (SZ 338). Dasein's primordial happening (*Geschehen*)—what determines its existence as historical (*geschichtlich*)—lies in the authentic resoluteness in which Dasein hands itself down to itself, free for death, in a possibility it has both inherited and chosen (SZ 382ff).

Heidegger also plays on the etymology of the word (*ent-schlossen* as "not closed off") (9: 194), declaring that what was thought by 'resoluteness' in SZ is "the self-opening for the open." It consists "not [in] the decided action of a subject but instead [in] opening Dasein up from its captivity among beings to the openness of being" (5: 55; 13: 63; 65: 87; 77: 143).

Resonance (*Anklang*)

Resonance is the echo of historical being that reverberates in the obliviousness to it, i.e. the total ascendancy of particular beings over it. This ascendancy coincides with the development of metaphysics that the first beginning of Western thinking sets in motion. In the current era, this ascendancy takes the form of machination, the consummation of the metaphysics of presence where what it means to be is exhausted by categories of production, manipulation, and power. Historical being, from the first beginning of Western thinking, refuses to be so categorized, and instead it shelters and conceals itself in the manifestness of beings, which amounts to abandoning them. Historical being's refusal resounds in its abandonment of beings, allowing them to become objects of machination. Corresponding to this resonance is the recognition of the distressfulness of the obliviousness to historical being.

The resonance is also the first and closest sign of the other beginning, indicating the transition from the first to the other beginning. The resonance is the reverberation of the originary experience of being at the inception (*Anfängnis*) of Western thinking, an experience that was forgotten, as it descended into metaphysics. By resonating and thus letting the truth of historical being prevail, the resonance makes possible the transition of history into its truth. History does not simply pass into another age within the time-space of metaphysics. Instead time-space itself becomes something else insofar as it first comes into its own as Da-sein. For the resonance to resound, it must be possible to detect, at least in a preparatory fashion, how a hint of historical being is experienced in the way that particular beings have been conceived (65: 107–114; 71: 75–9, 86).

Rickert, Heinrich (1863–1936)

In SS 1912 Heidegger first attended Heinrich Rickert's lectures "Introduction to Epistemology and Metaphysics." Heidegger would later write his habilitation under Rickert's direction and even considered following Rickert to Heidelberg, when he transferred there in 1916. From Rickert, Heidegger writes in 1915, he received his first glimpse into the essence of logic, "the discipline that interests me most" (16: 38). Logic in this case is transcendental logic, aimed at determining the conditions of the possibility of science, natural and historical. Rickert pursued the general question of *The Object of Knowledge* (1892, 1904), the title of his first major work. Since the question concerned the subject-independent, i.e. transcendent object, the question is a transcendental question. What conveys objectivity to knowledge is not something real, but ideal; it is a matter, not of the content, but of the form of knowledge, expressed in judgment. Part of Rickert's strategy for establishing transcendental idealism is to refashion the conception of knowledge, by debunking conceptions of it as consisting of representations that picture or reproduce actualities. Instead knowledge consists in the sense of a true sentence, i.e. a value (*Wert*). "Only the value that rests perfectly in itself, that as such is completely independent of any relation to a being and utterly to any subject, towards which it turns, is the transcendent object: the essence of transcendence completely merges in its unconditioned validity" ("Zwei Wege der Erkenntnistheorie," *Kant-Studien* 14 [1909]: 210). Attempted solutions to the problem of a *Weltanschauung* ("what the world means … whether our life has value") falter, Rickert contends, on the failed conception of the world, which in reality consists of values and the actuality of both subjects and objects. Philosophy's task is to provide a world-view by establishing values and relating them to actuality, via a third realm, that of sense. In this way he distinguishes the three realms of actuality, value, and sense along with "the three ways of mastering them: explaining, understanding, and interpreting." While the influence of Rickert's transcendental idealism on Heidegger is patent in his habilitation and beyond, Heidegger subjects Rickert's philosophy of value to harsh criticism in his first Freiburg lectures. He criticizes Rickert for, among other things: construing givenness as a category, transporting the entire set of problems into a sphere completely alien to "factical experience of the surrounding world," confounding the immanent and the transcendent, reducing everything objective to an object of knowledge, and reducing knowledge and evidence to feelings. He also takes Rickert to task for failing to account for the status of sense, and for appealing, all too simply and ambiguously, to negation to distinguish beings and values (56/57: 169–203; 58: 133ff, 226).

Rilke, Rainer Maria (1875-1926)

Best known for his *Duino Elegies* (1912–22) and *Sonnets to Orpheus* (1922), Rilke is taken seriously by Heidegger, if only because his thinking is "thoughtlessly thrown together" with Rilke's. Heidegger's interpretation of Rilke helps him clarify how his thinking departs from modern metaphysical conceptions of being and subjectivity. Heidegger and Rilke share a similar critical attitude toward the manifestations of that conception and the role of poetry in reversing it. In his 1927 lectures he cites Rilke's *The Notebooks of Malte Laurids Brigge* as a testimony to how poetry is nothing but the elementary emergence of existence as being-in-the-world into words (27: 244ff). Various Rilkean themes find their way into Heidegger's work: a sense of not being at home juxtaposed with the counter-pull of custom; an appreciation of the devastating effects of willful self-advancement, reducing things to objects and commodities; the violence of modern technological domination of the earth (in collusion with market forces); the hegemony of image-less, calculating forms of representation and production; the image of the moon as the site of the strife between the hidden and the open. Yet in the early 1940s, Heidegger takes pains to distinguish his and Rilke's conceptions of the open. A few years later he expands his discussion of Rilke from before while muting its critical tones in a lecture "What are Poets For?" (*Wozu Dichter?*), commemorating the twentieth anniversary of Rilke's death.

"While the human being technologically builds up the world as object, he tears down, willfully and completely, the way into the open, a way that has in any case already been blocked" (5: 293). Cognizant that Rilke recognizes the need for a transition from this sort of objectifying subjectivity, Heidegger nonetheless argues that Rilke's conception of this transition fails for two complementary reasons. First, Rilke works under a modern metaphysical conception of nature as a nexus of pure forces, in keeping with the modern metaphysical conception of being as a form of self-willing. Second, he conceives the transition as turning inward, within consciousness. The attempt to save things by transforming them poetically into the inner realm (*Duino Elegies*) operates under the fundamental metaphysical supposition of what it opposes, i.e. the supposition that to be is to be present and thus available to a subject. Thus, the inwardizing (*Er-innerung*) that Rilke calls for not only leaves the world of objects in place but also finds a place, a presence for everything—including the absences of death, the past, and the future—inside (5: 292ff, 305ff). Rilke's failure to make a clean break with the modern, willful metaphysics (epitomized by Nietzsche) is exemplified in the turn inward, the turn to the very sort of subjectivity that objectifies entities, and by the assumption that, inwardly, everything can be recovered without loss.

Rilke's conception of the open further exemplifies "the modern biologistic metaphysics" underlying his poetry. The open is, for Rilke, not being but the endless progression of beings (like the open water of high seas), something that non-rational animals alone see. Rilke's view is that the open is always "outside" human beings and that animals "see" more than humans do, because humans objectify everything. Hence, a chasm separates what Rilke means by the 'open' and "the open in the sense of *aletheia*," i.e. "the open space of the clearing of being, distinct from all beings," that human beings alone see (53: 113n; 54: 226, 231–9; 71: 18, 211; 5: 284–319).

Scheler, Max (1874–1928)

A leading phenomenologist and developer of philosophical anthropology, Max Scheler was an important interlocutor, in person and in print, for the early Heidegger. In SZ Heidegger touts Scheler's insight into the fundamentally constitutive character of others and of dispositions in human existence, and he draws on Scheler's discussion of conscience and critique of Kant's concept of the I. But he also takes Scheler to task for not entering into the question of the being of Dasein (SZ 47f, 116, 139, 208, 210, 291, 321). Heidegger also appropriates Scheler's concept of un-curbing (*Enthemmung*) to characterize the way something brings itself into action—a drive or urge, Leibniz's *appetitus*—without need of an external cause (26: 102f). In the fall of 1927 Heidegger visits Scheler who raises several major criticisms of SZ. Upon hearing of Scheler's death the following spring, Heidegger tells his students that Scheler was "the mightiest philosophical force ... in contemporary philosophy" (26: 62).

Two years later Heidegger criticizes Scheler's philosophical anthropology for approaching the human being as unifying physical, plant and animal, and spiritual stages of being. In addition to its misleading implication of a hierarchy, the basic error of this approach is its attempt to understand these stages, not on the basis of Dasein and its understanding of being, but from a psychological perspective that is subordinate to nature, thereby precluding the possibility of understanding the essence of nature itself. At the same time, Heidegger praises Scheler and draws on his insight into the openness-to-the-world, free from the environment, that characterizes the spiritual essence of a human being (29/30: 283, 287).

Schelling, Friedrich Wilhelm Joseph (1775–1854)

Along with Fichte and Hegel, Schelling is a key figure in the development of German idealism, a movement that Heidegger touts for its fearless, speculative recognition of the absoluteness of the subjectivity dominating the metaphysics of modernity. Yet Heidegger concentrates on Schelling's 1809 *Freedom-Treatise*, a work that in some respects begins to break the mold of German idealism. Heidegger's reading is, by his own account, one-sidedly interested in Schelling's differentiation of ground and existence, as it bears on the question of being and the history of metaphysics (42: 181, 253). In 1936 he touts the *Treatise* for its unfulfilled promise, as it deliberately moves beyond the onto-theological confines of German idealism to a "higher realism," one that appreciates the existential significance of freedom and its import for the question of being (42: 157f, 166ff). By contrast, in 1941 he is content to emphasize the *Treatise*'s place at the "summit" of German idealism, revealing the essential core of Western metaphysics while preparing the way for Nietzsche's insight into the will to power as the ever-operative destiny of Western thinking from its beginning (46: 1f, 118–22; 9: 360). Whereas in 1936 the affinity of Schelling's conception of existence with ek-sistence is suggested, in 1941 Heidegger disavows any connection between Schelling's conception and the conception in SZ (42: 187; 46: 75).

Science (*Wissenschaft*)

In Heidegger's earliest lectures he conceives philosophy as a primal science, and phenomenology as a science of origins—in both cases inherently reflexive investigations of pre-theoretical experience or factical life (56/57: 16; 58: 2f). In SZ Heidegger distinguishes ontology as the science of being from ontic ("positive") sciences, i.e. sciences of beings, where the former (a phenomenological analysis of existence) makes explicit the sense of being that is presupposed by the latter. Through its interpretation of beings with respect to the basic constitution of their being, ontological investigation yields the basic concepts of the positive sciences. These sciences are ways in which Dasein relates to beings. Genuine movement in a science consists in revising its basic concepts, where the science's niveau is determined by its capacity for a crisis in regard to those concepts. The common feature of the two types of science is the objectification or thematization of their subject matter (SZ 10–13, 45, 50ff, 152f; 24: 465f).

According to SZ ontic sciences of beings become purely theoretical via the shift from relating to things as handy to relating to them as simply on-hand, though both ways of relating to things are dependent upon the timely transcendence, characteristic of being-in-the-world. Heidegger thus distinguishes a "logical" concept of science (concerned with justification in the form of the connection of valid propositions) from an "existential" concept (concerned with the manner of being-in-the-world that discovers beings or discloses being). Theoretical comportment comes about existentially when the handiness of what is encountered is overlooked and its surroundings become unconfined, i.e. its place becomes a position in space-time. "The universe of what is on-hand becomes the theme." What is decisive in modern physics, "the classic example for the historical development of a science," consists in the "mathematical projection of nature itself," an a priori projection of the constitution of its being. Thanks to this projection, modern physics uncovers what is on-hand and opens the horizon for further quantitative determination of the features of it. Science in general is thematization, aiming at freeing-up something encountered within-the-world so that it can become an object and objectively determinable. This thematization of beings within-the-world has, as its basic presupposition, Dasein's transcendence, its foregoing disclosedness of the world by virtue of being-in-the-world (SZ 27, 34–7, 50, 262f, 324, 351, 357f).

By 1930 Heidegger no longer conceives philosophy as science (29/39: 3f). By the mid–1930s his earlier assessment of the purely theoretical prospects of ontic science changes, as he revisits its distinctively modern form. Much like Feyerabend a few decades later, he stresses science's historically unprecedented power, cutting into "all the forms of organization of modern life," but he characteristically rejects the notion that modern science is "more correct" than Greek science (5: 77; 7: 40). Indeed, science is not knowing (65: 145, 149, 144–66). Reprising remarks in SZ, he also rejects the notion that the basic feature of modern science is a concern for concrete facts over abstraction, experimentation, or reliance upon measurement and calculation. In none of these respects does it differ essentially from ancient *episteme* and medieval *scientia* (41: 66ff). Heidegger locates its essence instead in the mathematical, methodical, and operational character of its research.

By "mathematical," however, Heidegger does not have first in mind the development of analytic geometry and calculus. Their importance granted, there is a more basic understanding of the mathematical, stemming from the Greek term, signifying some foregoing, access-enabling familiarity, e.g. the bodily character of bodies, the vegetative character of plants, etc., that makes learning possible. Because numbers make up what is most familiar about things, the term "mathematical" becomes reserved for the numerical, when in fact the latter is determined by the former. There are accordingly pre-thematic and thematic senses of "the mathematical." Thanks to the pre-thematic sense, i.e. the familiar ways that things manifest themselves to us, there is the thematic sense, i.e. the determination to take them up explicitly in terms of some aspect of how they are already given to us. In the latter sense, "the mathematical is the basic presupposition of knowing things" (5: 78; 41: 68–77).

Modern physics is paradigmatically *mathematical* in this latter, broad sense because it opens up a region of nature by projecting the region's specific, basic outline and designating in advance the constraints under which research stands in relation to that region. Newton's First Law and its anticipation by Galileo demonstrate this projected character. Thanks to their pre-designated constraints, physical sciences possess their distinctive rigor and exactness. Yet what makes up nature (and what subsequently qualifies as nature) is something with which the researcher is already familiar from the outset, namely, the self-enclosed connection of movement of space-time related points of mass (albeit where no movement or direction, no place or time has precedence over any other). Other sciences— not only historical, humanistic sciences (*Geisteswissenschaften*), but also sciences of the living—lack this exactness, not because they are less difficult (they are just as difficult), but because their rigor is of another order (5: 77f; 41: 86–95).

The mathematical (projective) character of modern natural science comes into its own as a *method* whereby facts are rendered objective by being fixed in terms of explanatory laws. The search for explanation entails experiment but, unlike pre-modern experimentation, the experiments presuppose the representation of a law to be confirmed or not, a law that is in turn based upon the science's mathematical-projection of the basic outline of nature (41: 93f). Modern science inevitably specializes because it is research, grounded upon the projection of a circumscribed region of objects. What keeps it from diffusing into random investigations is its third distinctive character: its *operational* make-up.

By referring to modern science as an "operation" (*Betrieb*), Heidegger flags how it advances by adapting and orienting itself to its own results, thus necessitating its institutional character. The operation includes planning research, reciprocally checking and communicating results, and regulating the exchange of talents. All of this contributes to the expansion of science and the priority of the scientific method over whatever is (in nature and history). Along the way, the researcher displaces the scholar and takes on the shape of a technician.

Underlying modern science is a conception of beings as objects of some explanatory representation, by way of calculating either their future or past course (nature or history, respectively). "Only what becomes an object of this sort *is*, counts as being." Modern science seeks "the being of beings in such objectivity." Identifying Descartes as the source of the metaphysical underpinnings of modern science, Heidegger adds that this objectification is accomplished by way of representing beings to the subject in such a way that, in the course of computing and calculating, he can be certain of them. The human being becomes "the middle" of things, the being "on which every being is grounded in terms of its being and its truth" (5: 87f; 7: 41: 97f, 105f; 65: 158).

In effect, modern science goes hand-in-hand with the twin facts that mark modernity: the world becomes a picture, and modern humanity becomes the subject (making, selling, and consuming the picture). Science plays an integral role in establishing the world-picture, peculiar to modernity, in which everything is by virtue of being an object, i.e. pictured, represented, and placed before human subjects. With this world-picture, "willfully" produced and maintained by human beings, a way of being human ensues that occupies the realm of human capabilities for "taking control of beings as a whole" (5: 92). Science is "an indispensable form" of this human "self-executing" (*Sichrichtens*), "setting in play the unrestricted violence of the calculation, planning, and breeding of all things" (5: 94).

In a 1954 lecture Heidegger iterates many of these aspects of science but with a different accent. Science tracks down what is actual and works it over in a calculating manner—whether it be nature, the human being, history, or language—so that it can be represented and pursued as a secure domain of objects (or, in the case of nuclear and quantum physics, as a constancy that, encompassing subjects and objects, represents the complete dominance of this relation). Theory is a way of purposefully securing a region of actuality as a domain of objects for which the theory sets the standards. Yet, as the theory of the actual, modern science is not a mere fabrication of human beings. Nature, human existence, history, and language are respectively presupposed by physics, psychiatry, historical disciplines, and philology as something that cannot be traversed ("gotten around") by those sciences. They cannot be traversed because sciences always attend to only one type of presence of things, i.e. their objectivity and, indeed, only insofar as they can appear that way. For the same reason, the sciences effectively block any access to what underlies what they respectively objectify. Given their method, sciences are inherently irreflexive (there can be no physics of physics, philology of philology, mathematics of mathematics, etc.), prompting Heidegger to make the provocative remark: "Science does not think" (7: 49–62; 8: 9).

Self (*Selbst*)

"The self is never 'I'" (65: 322). Consciousness of oneself as an "I" goes hand-in-hand with modern subjectivity, the conception of the subject that represents things. While there is a trace of being-here ("a standing out into the open") in representing things as objects, this trace is so obscured by the representing itself that the process of standing out "remains in the *soul* as a process and act of the soul that as 'I' itself ultimately forms what stands over against it into an object." In modernity these trappings of ego-consciousness become "the guiding thread and point of orientation for the determination of other beings" (65: 316, 313, 52f, 236, 306, 319ff, 355, 425, 440, 444, 448f, 488f). This subjectivity is responsible for the domination of machination with its "ahistorical gigantic enterprises" in the present world (65: 135f, 441ff, 450). In Heidegger's list of decisions standing before us, the first is the decision "whether the human being wants to remain 'subject' *or* whether he grounds being-here" (65: 90).

The ego of consciousness is worlds apart from the self of being-here. For consciousness of the ego as the center of the representation of things obstructs what distinguishes being-here: "to *be* the clearing for the concealing, in the steadfastness of the selfhood that is the grounding of the truth in beings" (65: 316). Heidegger accordingly characterizes being-here as "being-a-self," as "ground of the self," determining what it is in terms of "selfhood" (65: 300, 302, 303). "*Selfhood* is more primordial than any I and You and We" (65: 320).

This selfhood is not something already on-hand or given, even tacitly (e.g. something that can reveal itself upon reflection as necessarily accompanying all clear, i.e. conscious representations). Selfhood has nothing at all to do with the complex of a subject representing an object or with clarifying "'self'-consciousness" (65: 67; SZ 319). Instead selfhood coincides with the appropriating event in which Dasein becomes itself because, thanks to that event, beings are present to it. "To the extent that being-here is appropriated to *itself* as belonging to the appropriating event, it *itself* comes to itself but never as though the self were an already on-hand condition, only one that previously had not been reached" (65: 320). By the same token, Heidegger's account of the self is not directed at human beings as they now are but at the transformation of them into being-here. Selfhood requires "a new determination of the human being." The crucial question is "how the *self* is to be grounded, in the realm of which 'we,' you and I, respectively come to our *selves*" (65: 11f, 32, 67, 84f, 230, 297, 300, 439–43, 455, 458, 488ff).

Already in Heidegger's early lectures he criticizes psychological analyses that take the I as something immediately given (58: 247) or as constituting and constituted forms of consciousness, i.e. Natorp's theory-driven conception of the I at the expense of the world of the self (*Selbstwelt*) (59: 122–8, 132–7, 142f, 164). The world of the self is reflexive, i.e. we experience ourselves in what we are doing and our shared experiences. In the process, no "I" figures as the way that the experiencing itself becomes accessible. "And the *lifeworld*—the surrounding world, the shared world, the world of the self—is lived in a situation of the self"—not the I (58: 62, 97, 221).

By taking seriously Dasein's everyday identification with the They-self, the existential analysis in SZ directly challenges suppositions that the "I" and the "self" necessarily refer to a substance or subject as the unity of experiences that we call our own. For the They-self, what is typically expressed in talk of the "I," is precisely not the authentic self. More generally, the notions of substance (Descartes' *cogito*) and subject (Kant's "I think") refer "not to the selfhood of the I qua self, but to the sameness and constancy of something always already on-hand." Kant appreciated the inapplicability of the metaphysical conceptions of rational psychology to the conception of the self. However, by conceiving the "I think" as an "isolated subject [somehow] accompanying representations," he continues to understand "the being of the I as the reality of the *res cogitans*," i.e. in categories suited not to existence but to things on-hand within the world.

There is a constancy to the authentic self, not a constancy already on-hand but a constancy that has been attained in anticipatory resoluteness. Care is not founded in a self, but the ontological structure of this resoluteness as authentic care reveals "the existentiality of the selfhood of the self." The authentic self is the primordial phenomenal basis for the question of the being of the "I" (SZ 319–23).

Sense (*Sinn*, MR & S: meaning)

To be here is from the outset and constantly to be projecting possibilities. Sense is what the respective projection is projected at (*das Woraufhin*), without necessarily coming into view "explicitly and thematically" itself. So construed, the sense's importance to the projection is patent. Something projected can only be adequately conceived, in view of that towards which the projection projects it (SZ 324). Hence, far from being necessary but indifferent or incidental to the projection, i.e. to existence in the case of Dasein, sense is constitutive of the projection, grounding it and making it possible and intelligible (SZ 151). For this reason, unearthing a projection's sense is also equivalent to describing the projection itself more basically. Heidegger depicts temporality as the sense of existence in just this way. With this conception of sense in hand, Heidegger can insist that the sense of Dasein's being is not something outside it but instead "the self-understanding Dasein itself" (SZ 325), an insistence in keeping with the immanence he demands of his analysis at every level.

Sense is not only the tacit target and necessary condition of a projection, rendering it intelligible, but also a way of describing it more fundamentally. While elusive, this way of understanding sense is consistent with certain ordinary uses of the term. For example, we may ask a driver who just made a turn: "Why did you do this? What is the sense of turning here?" When he responds that he has to go to a store, we not only understand the sense of the turn, and, indeed, understand it to be something grounding the turn, but also can use that sense to describe the turn more precisely ("he's not simply making a turn, he's going to the store").

Heidegger's construal of the relation between sense and existence has ramifications, too, for understanding beings other than Dasein. By virtue of the way Dasein is *in* its world, it understands, however inchoately, both its own being (existence) and the manner of being of entities uncovered within the world (reality). Indeed, every ontic experience of an entity presupposes a "more or less transparent" projection of its sort of being (when we use the hammer, we project it as handy). But along with the projection of these other sorts of being, there is something towards which they are projected, "from which, as it were, the understanding of being nourishes itself" (SZ 324).

In Heidegger's early lectures, he works with a "context of sense," encompassing different senses of comportment: the *content* of what one comports oneself to, the manner of one's *relation* or access to it, the *performance* (how one comports oneself to the object), and the *timeliness* of the performance in a situation (*Gehaltssinn Bezugssinn, Vollzugssinn, Zeitigungssinn*) (59: 49–86; 61: 52f).

Heidegger conceives "sense" in SZ, as noted above, in terms of Dasein's projection, its understanding. However, since this conception lends to sense's being construed as a human accomplishment, talk of the "sense" of being gives way to that of the "truth" of being (15: 334f; 65: 43).

Sign (*Zeichen*)

In SZ Heidegger highlights how signs and their function of showing (*zeigen*) are embedded in a system of serviceable references constituting what is handy in general, e.g. the hammer refers to nails, hammer and nails to boards, etc., within an entire complex of implements. Precisely because a complex of implements is inconspicuous, circumspective dealing in the environment needs an implement that takes over the job of rendering conspicuous what the complex or sub-complexes are for (*Wozu*). Herein lies the function of signs. They are themselves implements but implements for showing. Heidegger discusses a car's turn signal (an arrow), which signals turns to pedestrians and other drivers. As the example suggests, signs have to be conspicuous. They need to stand out from among the complex of otherwise inconspicuous tools and their environment in order to show the way in a commonly discernible fashion (think of a crossroads with and without a stop or yield sign) (SZ 78ff). Once established, signs can obviously become so interwoven into our concerns (*Besorgen*) that we barely take note of them. For example, when driving, we typically do not think about the red stop light at all while holding a foot on the break in response to the conspicuous red light.

In Heidegger's later discussions of language, he bemoans the loss of saying resulting from approaches to language that, taking their bearings from the perceivable shape of oral and written words as such, treat it as a system of signifying (*Bezeichnen*) and meaning, a system of information. This purely semiotic approach destroys and renders unattainable the primordial sense of saying and logos (7: 237, 244).

Spatiality (*Räumlichkeit*)

Spatiality is not the space of extension (the defining character of non-thinking substances), as Descartes would have it. Neither the way implements are within-the-world nor the way Dasein is being-in-the-world is a matter of being inside a space the way an extended entity is enclosed within extended boundaries (where both the entity and the enclosure are on-hand in space). What is handy within-the-world has a certain nearness and a certain direction (providing access to it) that are based upon a specific circumspective use of the implement. That circumspective use assigns what is handy its handy place within a handy region (while there are no places without regions or vice versa). The region is the *Wohin*, a word that, combining the "where to" and the "what for," points to the specific horizon of the world's meaningfulness. For example, the road before me has a nearness and a direction, i.e. a place that takes me to other places within a region that allows me to work, to pick up my son, etc. The region is not a set of positions within an observed space of three dimensions but the orientation of a manifold of places of the handy, i.e. the entities in our environment that we encounter as closest to us. This orientation, the environmental space of these entities, makes up the way they are "around us."

In order to be able to encounter what is handy in its environmental space, Dasein must be itself spatial in its distinctive manner of being, i.e. as being-in-the-world (rather than on-hand or handy). Its spatiality consists in bringing things into its proximity, i.e. bringing them near it, in a way that also orients it and them. Dasein does so for the most part circumspectively, procuring them in order to have them at hand ready for this or that task. But it can also bring things near in the sense of a purely cognitive discovery. "The tendency to nearness is inherent in Dasein." The remoteness and nearness that are uncovered in Dasein's circumspection are not objective distances of things on-hand. Thus, while I cannot say in any exact measurement how far my computer mouse is from my wrist, I do know that it is a hand's reach away. "The circumspective de-distancing of Dasein's everydayness uncovers the being-in-itself of the 'true world,' of the entities that Dasein is respectively already alongside." An exclusive orientation to distances as measured quantities covers over "the primordial spatiality of being-in." The glasses on our noses are much farther from us than the words we read on the computer screen.

In bringing something near it in its concern, Dasein orients itself, not to the "I-thing outfitted with a body," but to the sphere of what is circumspectively first at hand. Dasein's spatiality is thus not to be determined by the place where the body is on-hand. The way it brings what is handy near is always oriented to a region in which they have their place. I am much closer to my collaborator calling from Santa Fe than the stranger I pass on the street in Boston. The two main characteristics of Dasein's spatiality, its bringing near and its orienting what is handy, are "modes of being of being-in-the-world, that are led in advance *by the circumspection* of concern." Left and right, for example, are not subjective feelings but "orientations into an already handy world respectively."

The handiness of implements can be encountered spatially only because Dasein, in its spatiality, brings them near it and orients them. Opening up a complex of relevance is at the same time allowing for this relevance in a region. "In the meaningfulness with which Dasein is familiar in its concerns lies the essential co-disclosedness of space." Space is uncovered in view of a region towards which (*wohin*) a handy complex of implements can be oriented. The orientation is determined on the basis of the meaningfulness constitutive for the world, allowing for designating the here and the there. Hence, what is encountered as handy has in each case a relevance in a region. "Inherent in the totality of relevance that makes up the being of the handy is a regional, spatial relevance."

Yet neither the region respectively uncovered nor the respective spatiality is explicitly in view. While they remain inconspicuous, being-in-the-world uncovers space in this spatiality, rendering it accessible for knowing. Insofar as Dasein is spatial as described above, space is a priori, though it is not in a subject any more than the world is in space. Heidegger's analysis in SZ, glossed above, argues for the distinctively spatial make-up of what is handy and the distinctive spatiality of being-in-the-world—in contrast to the homogeneous space of nature devoid of a world. Nonetheless, he refrains from venturing to say what sort of being space is, though he does indicate that it need not have the being of the handy, the on-hand, or Da-sein (SZ 101–13).

In SZ Heidegger attempts to ground Dasein's spatiality in its temporality. This grounding is not a derivation that reduces space to time, but rather a demonstration of "the temporal conditions of the possibility of the spatiality characteristic of Dasein." Dasein's self-orienting discovery of a region is grounded in the *ecstatic* character of expectancy of a possible here and there (where "expectancy" designates the inauthentic future). The way that Dasein makes room for itself (*Sicheinräumen*), by bringing what is handy near it, is an expectancy of a region as a specific *horizon*, from which, by removing distance, it comes back to what is nearest.

"Only on the basis of ecstatic-horizonal temporality is it possible for Dasein to break into space." This attempt to trace Dasein's spatiality back to temporality is truncated to a fault, and Heidegger later remarks that the attempt is untenable (SZ 367ff; 14: 29; 65: 387).

Steadfastness (*Inständigkeit*)

Particularly in the *Contributions* sequence (GA 65–71), Heidegger cites the necessity of steadfastness in being-here and being human, i.e. steadfastness in recognizing and safeguarding the gift of the presence of beings to us. Steadfastness embodies the strength, decisiveness, mildness, and simplicity required to endure and carry on the hiddenness and withdrawal of being as the presence of beings to Dasein (the appropriating event) (9: 196ff; 65: 298ff). Upsetting and relieving (*entsetzend*) the human pretense of being sufficiently competent to deal with beings, Dasein determines human beings to steadfastness (70: 14f, 52). This steadfastness is the claim made by historical being as the appropriating event on the essence of the human being. Responding to this claim, steadfastness unfolds into its own freedom as knowing, grounding the previously hidden Dasein in the process. After characterizing freedom as the liberation of the essence of the human being, Heidegger adds: "Liberation is the steadfastness of Dasein" (70: 112f). Steadfastness safeguards *the* property to which the human being is historically handed over as his own, "in which he has the authentic dimension of his being," namely, Dasein as "the place of the clearing of the appropriating event." Knowing is this steadfastness, but it is knowing, not in the sense of being familiar with lots of things, but in the sense of being cautious (*Behutsamkeit*) and being obedient (*Folgsamkeit*) (71: 212f). "The supreme property of humankind that in the wake of the overturning of metaphysics becomes ready for steadfastness in Da-sein (and so takes over the grounding of the truth of historical being and enters into its history) is, as a consequence of thus entering into the appropriating event, *poverty*. Poverty means here not deficiency but the steadfastness (the mentality, the attunement) in the simple and unique—but this is the unfolding of historical being" (70: 132; 71: 24, 109, 211–17). Steadfastly releasing oneself to the open region is "the genuine essence of the spontaneity of thinking" (77: 145). (For instructive, earlier uses of 'steadfastness,' see 16: 71; 38: 167; 39: 264ff).

Step-back (*Schritt zurück*)

The step back from the difference between being and beings to the forgotten concealment of difference itself at the beginning of Western thinking is a step back from "metaphysics into the essence of metaphysics." Far from being an empty universal, being is epochal. By holding itself back, it opens up beings to human beings for a particular epoch. The step back today must be prepared by considering how beings as a whole now are, i.e. dominated by "the essence of modern techniques." "The presentation and development of entities dominated by the essence of techniques is called 'technology,'" a term that designates "the metaphysics of the atomic age." So the step back from metaphysics into its essence is the step back from technology into the essence of modern techniques, an essence that is what first needs to be thought (11: 59ff).

Stepping back in this way contrasts with Hegel's treatment of the history of philosophy. Heidegger agrees with Hegel about the need to engage "the force of earlier thinking." Yet while Hegel does so in order to relate what was previously thought to an ever-higher system that surpasses it, Heidegger looks for what was un-thought but provides the essential space for what was thought. The measuring-stick of what is un-thought demands "the freeing up of traditional thinking into what it has been [*Gewesenes*] but remains saved-up and stored." This *Gewesenes* "pervades the tradition from the beginning, constantly prevails ahead of it, yet without being thought explicitly and as what is beginning [*das Anfangende*]." In contrast to a Hegelian superseding (*Aufhebung*) leading to the region of the absolutely posited truth, the dialogue with the history in the sense of stepping back points to "the realm previously skipped over" (11: 57f).

Subjectivity (*Subjektivität*)

Though Heidegger's thinking from its inception takes aim at modern conceptions of subjectivity, his existential analysis, by his own account, attempts to give an ontological account of subjectivity. Though the references to subjectivity in SZ are sparse, they demonstrate that he takes his existential analysis to yield "the A priori of 'actual' subjectivity," in contrast to ideas of a pure ego and of consciousness in general (SZ 24, 106, 229, 382). Dasein transcends beings (and thus can use and know them) by virtue of projecting a world. This world is "subjective," and yet, "as temporally-transcendent," it "is more 'objective' than any 'object'" (SZ 366). He takes pains to distinguish "genuine subjectivity" from any subject–object relation, typically mis-construed as a cognitive relation where subject and object are both on-hand, and where the problem is how the subject steps out of its inner sphere into the outer sphere of the object. The problem is a pseudo-problem since "transcendence is the primordial constitution of the subjectivity of the subject" (26: 160ff, 190, 205f, 211). Similarly, in 1929, after rejecting traditional attempts to understand transcendence as a flight into the objective (e.g. the Platonic ideas), Heidegger observes that transcendence can only be grasped "through a constantly renewed ontological interpretation of the subjectivity of the subject" (9: 162).

In Heidegger's later writings he reserves the term "subjectivity" for the modern conception of a subject, instituted by Descartes and variously amplified by Kant (transcendental subject), Hegel (absolute subject), and Nietzsche (subjectivity as unrestricted will to power). Crucial to the emergence of modern subjectivity is Descartes' transference of the "subject" of traditional ontology (the fundamental character of being as *substantia* or *hypokeimenon* and condition of everything else that might be said of beings) to the *cogito*, the thinking human subject. What else there is depends upon what the subject represents as an object with certainty, and nothing can escape this objectification. Inherent in this subjectivity is "the unconditional removal of all barriers to the realm of possible objectification and to the right to decide about them" (5: 109f). "Subjectivity and only it brings about [*zeitigt*] the supreme objectivity (in the form of technology)" (69: 44). The objectification of all beings and the nihilism it spawns form the essence of the event "through which the human being establishes his essence in subjectivity" (6.2: 342). Heidegger sometimes distinguishes subjectification (*Subjectität*) from subjectivity: "*The name subjectification is supposed to stress that being is determined, to be sure, from the standpoint of the* subjectum, *but not necessarily through an I*" (6.2: 410, 411ff). "Modern metaphysics, as the metaphysics of subjectification, thinks the being of beings in the sense of the will" (5: 243f, 133; 69: 72).

The subjectivity of humankind characterizes modernity because it is the consummation of metaphysics, and this consummation is the empowering of the machination. "The essential consequence of *subjectivity* is the nationalism of peoples and the socialism of the people ... The essential consequence of the history of subjectivity is the unrestricted battle for power and thus unlimited wars ..." (69: 44; see, too, 5: 105–11, 133; 6.2: 268–75, 410–13; 41: 105f; 49: 90; 67: 98; 69: 44).

Technology (*Technik*)

A technology is a way of bringing something into the open. "It reveals what does not itself bring itself forth and is not yet at hand" (7: 14). As such, it is not simply a means, an instrument, or human activity, but belongs to the realm of knowing, the realm where truth in the sense of *aletheia*—dis-closing—occurs. Since disclosing as such is not our doing but far more something upon which we are dependent, purely instrumental, i.e. anthropological views of technology do not get at this essence of technology.

What distinguishes modern technology is the way it reveals by challenging nature to deliver energy that can be extracted, stored up, and ordered up at will. Modern technology reveals energies concealed in nature, by placing, ordering, hunting—all senses of *stellen*—them into the open and then reforming, storing, distributing, and re-distributing them. What is stored and able to be on order in this way is a standing reserve (*Bestand*)—and it is seemingly everything. In the modern age this aggressive way of disclosing "first begins to unfold as a destiny of the truth of beings as a whole" (5: 289). While the disclosing is never something man-made, human beings operate the technologies and in this way take part in them. "Positionality" (*Ge-stell*) designates the essence of modern technology, "positioning, i.e. challenging human beings to disclose the actual as standing-reserve in the manner of ordering" (7: 21). Human beings are challenged by "the unconditioned dominance of the essence of modern technology together with this technology itself" to order the entirety of the world as a "uniform standing reserve, secured by an ultimate world-formula and accordingly computable" (4: 178). An early indication that humanity rose to this challenge is the rise of modern mathematical physics, which already "positions nature to exhibit itself as a complex of forces capable of being calculated in advance" (7: 23). In addition to modern science, other necessary consequences of the essence of technology include "the total state," the means and forms of the organization of world opinion and everyday notions, the technological objectification of life and the living, as well as the development of human beings into subjects and the world into an object (5: 290).

Positionality is part of our destiny, though it is largely unheeded, thanks to repeated, hopeless attempts to master technology "with one's mortal will" (4: 178). Yet this destiny is never a fate that coerces. To be sure, by challenging us to reveal everything only as a standing-reserve, the positionality—not the machinery of technology itself—presents "the supreme danger," blocking other forms of revealing and closing off access to whatever else things are, to who we are, and to the very disclosing on which it depends. Yet, as Hölderlin puts it, "where danger is, grows / also the saving power." What is potentially redeeming in positionality is what affords it, i.e. the appropriating event that also needs human beings and thereby appropriates them to the truth ("the supreme dignity of their essence"). Yet it is redeeming only if we begin to pay attention to the essence of technology rather than continuing to represent it as an instrument and attempting to master it. To this end, art (as a non-aesthetic, poetic *techne* of the beautiful) may well be capable of making this redemptive character apparent through a decisive confrontation with technology.

Theology (*Theologie*)

A positive, i.e. ontic science, theology is "absolutely different" from philosophy. Yet it is part of the development of belief, by virtue of participating expressly in the historical happening of revelation. Theology is a historical science in this sense. Revelation reveals and thereby reverses Dasein's obliviousness to God. Belief is "rebirth as a mode of historically existing, on the part of the Dasein factically believing, in *the* history that begins with the happening of revelation; in *the* history to which, in accordance with the meaning of revelation, a specific outermost end has already been posited." By virtue of overturning pre-Christian existence, this rebirth entails an "existential–ontological" understanding of human Dasein, the elaboration of which is the task of ontology. "Ontology accordingly functions merely as a corrective of the ontic and, to be sure, pre-Christian content of theological grounding concepts." By no means a matter of deducing theological content, ontology "formally indicates" the ontological character of shared concepts (e.g. guilt) as a means of freeing up the specific origin of theological concepts in belief (9: 53, 64f; 40: 8f).

They (*das Man*, S: the One)

In German *man* is a pronoun that sometimes refers to an indefinite subject. For example, in directions on assembling a bike: "first one counts the pieces" (*erst zählt man die Stücke*), "one" translates *man* and stands for anybody attempting to assemble the bike. *Man* can also refer to a group or to society insofar as its practices and beliefs shape or even constrain individual behavior. For example, a mother may say to a child mis-behaving in public: "One does not do that" (*Das tut man nicht*). In the verse from the Gershwins' song, "They all laughed at Christopher Columbus [*Man hat Christopher Columbus ausgelacht*] when he said the world was round," *man* translates "they" as the source of public opinion, the views and voices of the crowd.

Leaning on this range of meanings, Heidegger erects this pronoun into the noun, *das Man*, to designate Dasein in its average everyday way of being-with others where, figuratively and literally, it exists by following the crowd. The They "prescribes" and "maps out in advance the interpretation of the world and being-in-the-world that lies closest [to us]." In its everyday existence, Dasein exists for the sake of the They. Yet, like any existential, the They is a way of disclosing, enacted by nothing else but Dasein itself. This existential embodies several characteristics of the constancy of everyday Dasein, all exhibiting "inauthenticity and a failure to stand on one's own." In our everyday existence, everything— artifacts, tools, nature, others, our own respective selves—is given to us initially in the terms that are familiar to us, by virtue of our immersion in the They (SZ 127ff). So powerful is its hold on Dasein that only anxiety, an experience of utter meaningless (nothingness), can free Dasein to other, *authentic* possibilities.

Thing (*Ding*)

Heidegger first considers the thinghood of things in the mid–1930s, as he notes the deficiencies of traditional conceptions of a thing: namely, as a substance with accidents (the bearer of features), as the unity of a sensory manifold, and as a formed matter. The first conception is so wide that it fails to distinguish things from non-things (e.g. tools or works), the second conception mistakenly supposes that sensations are closer to us than things, and the third conception confuses things with products and tools. The reason for thinking's difficulty here is the resistance of things—withholding themselves belongs to their very essence (5: 16f).

In lectures published as "What is a Thing?" Heidegger notes that the first conception mentioned above is the "natural" one, while the third one enjoys a certain priority. The first conception is natural because of the correspondence of propositions' subject–predicate structure to the structure of things as bearers of properties (41: 33–7). Yet what is natural is always a historical matter, and, in this case, the integrated conception of things, propositions, and truth has roots in Plato and Aristotle. Hence, one task is to show the history of this conception as a means of demonstrating that it is not inevitable and initiating a transformation of our stance towards things (41: 49). For everyday experience of things is not trumped by scientific accounts of them and, indeed, contemporary science "genuinely lacks a primordial relation to things" (41: 39f). Not incidentally, the priority enjoyed by the third conception is connected to the formation of modern science that determines things as material points of mass in motion in a pure spatio-temporal order, forming the substratum for all other things and their juxtapositions. Kant's conception of things as objects of mathematical experience allegedly shows that this priority is historical (41: 187).

In contrast to these largely critical discussions, Heidegger's first Bremen lecture "The Thing" attempts to say what things are as something close to us. Science is of no help since it "annihilates" things as things, not least because things are not objects that can be represented for the simple reason that, in order to be represented, they first have to show themselves. But things in themselves do not show themselves. For a cognate reason, a thing such as a jug is not so much a thing because it is produced as it is produced because of the thing it is. What makes a jug a jug, however, is that it takes up and holds what is poured into it in order to dispense that water or wine in turn. The thingness of this thing—the jug as jug—essentially unfolds (*west*) as a gift of earth and sky, and a libation of mortals offered to the divine. Earth and sky, mortals and divinities are all unfolded together into a single foursome in this gift. The way that these four are gathered together and come into their own in the gift, transpiring in it, is the way the jug as jug is a thing or, alternatively, the way the "thing things" (79: 13). It is also why things matter to us, for in the experience of them, we are closer to the foursome, in keeping with each of the four's respective distance from us. In the single unfolding of the four, each illuminates and mirrors the other in the play of a mutual opening up and appropriating. This mirroring play is the way the world unfolds, the way it "worlds" and that things matter to us. If we let things unfold from the world in this mirroring play, in this unfolding of the world, we think of them as they are, i.e. as things, and, if we think of things as things, we are affected by them as such and they matter to us (79: 5–23; 7: 165–84).

Thinking (*Denken*)

There is a form of thinking that consists in representing and calculating, epitomized by reliance upon computers. This form of thinking coincides with "dissolving philosophy into technologized sciences" (14: 73). Yet this form of thinking is quite unsuited to thinking being itself (the presence of beings). The word translated "representation" here (*Vorstellung*) can be taken as something internal to the mind (a Kantian *representatio*, equivalent to the Cartesian *idée*) or as what is most basically present to consciousness (as in Brentano's maxim: "All consciousness is either a presentation [*Vorstellung*] or founded upon one"). Yet, in either case, what is paradigmatically represented or presented is a particular being, so that attempting to think being in this way tends to reduce it to a particular being and, indeed, typically to an object. So, too, while numbers are beings of a sort, being itself is not a number, as attempts to think being by means of calculating would have to suppose. Even inference, if not regarded as reducible to calculation, is based upon assertions, referring to states of affairs and relations, but being itself is reducible to none of the latter. Hence, traditionally logical thinking or even dialectical thinking, taking its bearings from logic, can be a barrier to genuinely thinking being—and not merely beings (40: 124–31, 194–7).

Moreover, while computational thinking is a kind of willing, genuine thinking is contemplative, corresponding to a "not willing," letting things be rather than seeing what we can do with them, how we can willfully use them. While this letting-be is an act higher than all worldly deeds, it also lies, strictly speaking, outside the distinction between activity and passivity insofar as the distinction pertains to willing and insofar as the letting-be is not something we awaken of ourselves. Thinking is letting-be in the sense of being released *into* the abiding expanse in which things are present and absent. Yet it is the open region itself that, by letting us into it, lets us genuinely think things, lets us let them be. Just as the open region is an abiding expanse, so genuine thinking, thinking that is not the stepchild of willing is, like the open region itself, a movement as much as it is a path (6.2: 264; 77: 106–24, 146).

Since science does not think, genuine thinking is not to be confused with science. Thinking does not solve cosmic riddles, produce usable, practical wisdom, or even endow us with the capacity to act. Far from being presupposition-less, thinking goes straight to its presuppositions and engages them (8: 164). So, too, it is more intent on saying being than drawing out the implications of assertions about beings (14: 28). Its path is not some well-traveled street or, for that matter, anything that exists in advance of its questioning. At the same time, while erecting its path by questioning in advance, thinking does not leave the cleared path behind but projects it forward (8: 174). Thinking is never absolute, and, hence, an abyss separates its problematic character from faith (8: 181). While computational thinking focuses on entities or kinds of entities and their relations under some forgone presumption of what it means for them to be, genuine thinking attempts to think the presence (being) of beings, i.e. historical being as the appropriating event.

Thinking is a form of commemorating (*Andenken*) and thanking (*Danken*). It commemorates and greets what, once begun, still comes toward us, the otherwise forgotten, historical destiny of being (4: 96f, 100, 131f, 142–51; 8: 155f; 13: 82; 71: 313ff, 322f, 328f; 77: 145). Thinking is a way of expressing gratitude for the gift of what is most worth thinking, the presence of what there is (8: 151, 247; 71: 277f, 313f). Genuine thinking requires a leap into what lacks any basis, the abyss of being itself, at least as long as we look for a ground in an entity (54: 223).

In his 1934 SS lectures on language, Heidegger begins to determine the essence of thinking in terms of its nearness to poetry (*Dichtung*) and he returns repeatedly to this theme afterwards. Genuine thinking is a kind of composing (*Dichten*). "Thinking of being is the primordial manner of composing," and all such composing, both in the broad sense of art and the more narrow sense of the literary, is at bottom a thinking (5: 328f). "Thinking's poetic character is still concealed," given the hegemony of thinking in the form of computing and representing objects, i.e. what is only by virtue of being subject to subjectivity. For such thinking bent on dominating, the poetic character of thinking appears as "the utopia of half-poetic understanding." "But the poetry that thinks is in truth the topology of historical being," naming the place where the latter essentially unfolds (13: 84). Yet while genuine thinking is itself poetic, thinking and poetry "dwell on the most separate mountains" (8: 139f, 163; 11: 26; 12: 174–9; 13: 85; 16: 519f; 53: 113; 71: 305–33).

Thrownness (*Geworfenheit*)

None of us is the ground of her own existence. Instead we are thrown into the world and this thrownness is something that cannot be undone. We are thrown into the position of having to take responsibility for ourselves, to ground our respective being-in-the-world, yet we are not responsible for being in this position. "This sort of not-being [*Nichtigkeit*] in no way signifies not-being-on-hand, not obtaining, but instead means a not that constitutes this *being* of Dasein, its thrownness" (SZ 284).

Moods disclose to Dasein "that it is," and "this 'that it is' [is] the *thrownness* of this entity into its Da [its disclosedness] such that, as being-in-the-world, it is the Da." Dasein exists as this disclosedness (the clearing) by always finding itself, explicitly or not, in its thrown condition. Dasein's moods and its respective disposedness typically disclose this thrownness, not by looking it square in the eye, but by turning towards or away from it (SZ 135f, 265, 270, 284, 340). In other words, "for the most part the mood closes off the thrownness," as Dasein takes flight into the alleged freedom of a self who identifies with the crowd (*das Man-selbst*). Dasein's understanding is also thrown, accounting for the fact that it has always already run astray and misconstrued itself and must find itself again in its possibilities (SZ 144). Moreover, as long as Dasein exists, its facticity remains "in the throw" and "tossed around and into the inauthenticity" of the They (SZ 179, 284). Inauthentic possibilities—mere wishfulness, obsessions, and compulsions (*Hang und Drang*)—are also grounded in thrownness (SZ 195f). "In thrownness, Dasein is swept up, that is to say, as thrown into the world it loses itself in the 'world,' in the factical dependence upon what needs to be taken care of" (SZ 348, 406).

Nonetheless, thrownness itself is neither inauthentic nor authentic. It is simply "the type of being of an entity that respectively *is* its possibilities, in and out of which it understands itself (it projects itself upon them)" (SZ 181, 270). Dasein's thrownness reveals that it is "mine and that it is this in a specific world and alongside a specific circle of specific innerworldly entities" (SZ 221). It determines the fact that Dasein already was and constantly is "thrown into existence. As existing, it has to be how it is and can be" (SZ 275, 277).

Dasein's throwness is tied to "the *facticity of being handed over*" to itself to be. So, too, "as thrown, Dasein can project itself only upon specific factical possibilities" (SZ 299, 328). Its facticity is "phenomenally" visible in its throwness, where "facticity" (*Faktizität*) signifies not a finished matter of fact (*Tatsache*) but rather the way that, as long as Dasein is, it remains caught up in the throw and the specific world into which it is thrown (SZ 179, 276, 297). "Thrown" and "factical" are alike paired with "existing" to convey how Dasein is always in the process of projecting some factical possibilities, i.e. some of the possibilities into which it is thrown (SZ 181, 199, 223, 284f, 298, 364, 386, 394, 410, 435). So, too, Dasein's throwness typically fuses with its fallennness (SZ 175–80, 286, 406, 411–15, 424). Thus, throwness both enables and restricts Dasein's existence and freedom (SZ 366).

While moods disclose Dasein's throwness for the most part by attempting to evade it, angst is the exception. In angst lies "the most elementary disclosedness of the thrown Dasein," namely, "its being-in-the-world confronted by the world's nothingness," a world in which it finds itself alone with itself and not at home (SZ 276f, 339, 342ff). At the same time Dasein is thrown into its ownmost possibility, its death (SZ 144, 251, 255f, 276, 308, 329, 340–44, 348). Dasein's throwness is accordingly a condition for authenticity no less than for inauthenticity. Conscience calls Dasein back to this throwness, and, in the process, calls Dasein from its immersion in the crowd and ahead to the possibility that is most its own (SZ 287, 291, 382). In resolutely anticipating its death, Dasein takes over its throwness, and to do so is to "*be* authentically *what it already was*" (SZ 325). Taking over its throwness also entails taking over a legacy, the basis for disclosing factical possibilities of authentically existing (SZ 383ff).

Putting even greater stress on the throwness of Dasein, Heidegger later insists that Dasein's projection is the projection of the truth of historical being and that, as such, Dasein is itself thrown, "doing nothing other than ... becoming itself, namely, the preserver of the thrown projection" (65: 304, 230f). Only by projecting itself free from any forgetfulness of its throwness, from all pretension to master its history, and from all reduction of beings to what can be represented and produced, can the human being become herself and return to beings. But the projecting that makes up this return is itself thrown, never succeeding by human doing alone (65: 453ff). The enigma of Dasein's thrownness is that, while entailing that humans are not masters of beings, it entails that they are far more, namely, "shepherds of being" (9: 342).

Time (*Zeit*)

From the 1916 essay "The Concept of Time in the Science of History" to his 1962 essay "Time and Being" and beyond, time is a recurrent theme in Heidegger's thinking. The following entry (a) glosses his analysis in SZ, (b) highlights his subsequent accentuation of the coming or future of what already began, and (c) sketches his treatment in the 1962 essay.

Time in SZ. The "common" conception of time as an irreversible and continuous succession of intervals ("nows") springs from the experience of time that is characteristic of our everyday existence, i.e. a "world-time," which in turn springs from a more basic time that is the underlying sense of human existence. The difference between this primordial time and world-time is not a version of the difference between psychological time and physical time. The primordial time that makes up being-here is not fundamentally mental but existential, and, while time is successive in ordinary views of it, at its most basic level "the future is *not later* than having been, and having been is *not earlier* than the present" (SZ 350). Analysis of time is of a piece with fundamental ontology since traditional ontology not only fails to investigate the meaning of "being" but also uncritically assumes a particular temporal conception of being. That conception, moreover, reinforces the common conception of time mentioned above (SZ 11ff, 17f, 25f, 233, 423). "Being and time reciprocally determine each other" (14: 7).

Time is what makes sense of our being-here as its constitutive horizon, what in the last analysis our ongoing projection of possibilities is projected upon. The image of sense as a horizon is misleading if taken as something outside Dasein. The sense of Dasein's being is what makes sense of it as a thrown projection. Understood in this way, its sense grounds it. Accordingly, the analysis of time makes sense of the existential analysis by yielding a more basic account of the thrown projection of being-here (*genitivus appositivus*), but not as a phenomenon somehow constituted in advance of our being-here (SZ 151, 324f).

Against the backdrop of this conception of sense, Heidegger argues that a primordial temporality is the underlying, grounding sense of authentic existence. Authentic existence, the anticipatory resoluteness of being-towards-death, lets this possibility come to it; doing so is "the primordial phenomenon of the future." Moreover, anticipating death is also coming back to one's defining possibility, retrieving one's thrownness. In the process, Dasein's anticipation-and-retrieval makes present its situation in the fullness of the moment, allowing for the naked encounter "by what it seizes upon in taking action." "Coming back to itself futurally, resoluteness brings itself into the situation by making present .... This phenomenon has the unity of a future which makes present in the process of having been; we designate it 'temporality.'" Anticipatory resoluteness is only possible insofar as Dasein has this character of temporality, and, hence, "temporality reveals itself as the meaning of authentic care" (SZ 326).

Having thus established that temporality is the sense of authentically caring, Heidegger elaborates how temporality underlies the structure of care in general: being-ahead of oneself, already-being-in (a world), and being-alongside (entities encountered within-the-world). These aspects refer respectively to the basic existentials: existentiality, thrownness, and fallenness. Dasein's existentiality corresponds to its self-projecting for the sake of itself and, in the process, coming to itself. The way we are ahead of ourselves is thus grounded in the future. So, too, Dasein's thrownness is based on the character of having been, and its "being-alongside entities" is based upon a present (*Gegenwart*) that is, more fundamentally, a manner of making something present (*Gegenwärtigen*). Following this elaboration of the temporal meaning of these three aspects of care's structure, Heidegger concludes: "Temporality makes possible the unity of existence, facticity, and falling, and in this way constitutes primordially the totality of the structure of care" (SZ 328).

In the temporality that makes up being-here, the future takes the lead, i.e. the ways we are ahead of ourselves determine how we retrieve our thrownness and encounter the present situation. Nevertheless, no one temporal aspect is independent of the other. Each is "outside itself," ecstatically reaching out to each other and standing out towards a horizon of possibilities. Together, i.e. in their ecstatic-horizonal unity, they make up the ways that being-here relates to beings and possibilities, not least the possibility of its impossibility. This primordial phenomenon of the future entails that temporality in the primordial sense is finite. Temporality, as this ecstatic-horizonal unity, is the sense of existence, i.e. the being of being-here (SZ 329ff, 346, 350, 353).

The third last chapter of SZ ("Temporality and Everydayness") attempts to demonstrate how "the inauthenticity of Dasein" as well as "all essential structures of the basic constitution of Dasein" are rooted in temporality (SZ 332, 335). As a final step to justifying his interpretation of time, he devotes the last chapter of SZ to showing that the theoretical view of time (as a succession of nows) is derivative of a world-time (the time of circumspective concern) that itself springs from primordial temporality (SZ 405). When Jane says to John "Tomorrow we'll start painting," she expresses world-time (the time of her world) by dating the task and rendering it significant in relation to an event ("tomorrow") available to John. She makes use of the most natural means of reckoning time, "the day," but her point of reference is the present and what, from that instant, may be expected (SZ 416). In world-time the timing has a meaning intrinsic to the work-world, and the dating of the succession indicates a connection between, for example, the present and the future. By contrast, in the vulgar conception of time, time is an endless and all-encompassing succession of denumerable nows without any other relation to one another than their successiveness and without any intrinsic worldly meaning. Any differences or limits to time are reduced to this homogenous succession, suggested by the use of clocks that, like this conception of time, is not specific to any worldly context.

World-time is the time of concern, as Dasein times itself in terms of handy implements of concern, constituting a datable and publicly available timespan that is intrinsically meaningful within that world of concern. The vulgar understanding of time emerges from telling time by time-pieces where time presents itself as what is counted in a movement with respect to earlier and later. Both world-time and the vulgar conception of time are derivative of the primordial and authentic temporality fundamentally constitutive of who Dasein is.

After SZ Heidegger briefly entertains the possibility of grounding ontology (the study of the being of beings generally) in Temporality

(*Temporalität*) (24: 452–68). Yet a year later he explicitly refrains from addressing to what extent one could conceive "the interpretation of Dasein as temporality in a universally-ontological way," with the explanation that the question is "still completely obscure to me" (26: 271).

The coming of the beginning. Heidegger's early treatments of time in connection with Dasein and fundamental ontology give way, like ontology itself, to thinking of being historically and historical being's appropriation of Dasein. Correcting his early privileging of time over space, Heidegger introduces time-space. While the interconnectedness of the authentic future, having-been, and (present) moment carries over, the accent increasingly falls more on an originary beginning that an authentic future must first project, i.e. retrieve. "The origin (*Herkunft*) always remains the future (*Zukunft*)" is a trope that Heidegger repeats under several different formulations (12: 91; 13: 241f; 16: 561; 52: 55; 70: 65, 71, 83, 93ff). The destiny of humans, long since sent to them, is coming, but it remains covered up from the beginning, as long as they do not do what is most difficult, i.e. return to the source, a return only made possible by love of the other (53: 162ff).

Time and Being. In the essay under this title, Heidegger unpacks the statement "there is time," in keeping with the essay's account of the 'there is' as the appropriating event. Several early themes resurface in the essay: the need to distinguish the way time is "usually represented" as a measurable succession of nows from authentic time as it bears on being; there is no time without human beings; without itself being a being, time determines being and, indeed, determines it as a presence to the human being, a presence not reducible to the now or immediately present, but one including the presence of such absences as the having been and the future; the three aspects of time form a unity, "handing themselves" and the presences reached in them to one another (in SZ their "ecstatic" character). With the presence handed over in their unity, "what is cleared is time-space," "the open expanse" that makes space for the possible spread of the space familiar to us (14: 18f). Authentic time is four-dimensional; the nearness of the open is the fourth dimension that brings the other dimensions and their presences near one another by keeping them distant from one another.

Time-space (*Zeit-Raum*)

We typically date and place our decisions (e.g. "When I was in high school I decided to ..."). Because time and space are thus presupposed, taking our bearings exclusively from this experience precludes any decision about them. Reversing this approach, Heidegger thinks time-space on the basis of a decision (e.g. "Because I decided to ... I am now here"). However, it is not just any decision, certainly not our decision alone, but the decision of whether historical being takes hold of us or not, i.e. the decision "about belonging to historical being or being abandoned to what are not"—where saving beings hangs in the balance (65: 100, 384).

Time-space is the abyss, the grounding omission of ground that, as the self-concealed clearing, makes a decision possible. As this abyss, time-space grounds the "here" (*Da*) of being-here as the site of the deciding moment. So construed, time-space is not to be confused with a timespan (*Zeitraum*) or with four-dimensional space-time, the purely quantificational co-ordination of space and time in physics. Instead it springs from and belongs to the essence of truth "in-between" the first and the other beginning of Western thinking. The possibility of a transition to another beginning happens by entering into time-space as the site of the grounding of the truth of historical being. Indeed, what truth is can only be said adequately by grasping time-space (65: 323, 372, 377ff).

Whereas space and time come apart as intuitive or conceptual representations of ordering frameworks in the first beginning (where being is equated with presence), time-space is their primordial unity as the timing-and-spacing making up the nearness and farness in the aforementioned site of the moment of decision. Neither subjective nor objective, time-space is the "when-and-where" of the history of being, illuminating and concealing itself in keeping with the basic mood of reserve. Since being-here is the ground of any form of subjectivity, the unfolding of time-space from the site of the deciding moment is no "subjectivizing," but instead its overturning (65: 375f). Time-space is the abyss that both refuses any ground and yet, as such, is "an exceptional sort of opening up," mistakenly taken as a void or empty container. Its refusal of any ground is thus in a sense a ground, a necessarily hesitant, self-refusing ground (65: 379–82; see, too, 191ff, 272, 371–8, 383–8).

Time-space's self-refusal creates the emptiness of dispensing with a ground and awaiting a ground. This emptiness transports (*entrückt*) being-here towards what is coming and breaks up what has been, such that what has been, together with the coming, makes up the present abandonment of being. This abandonment does not sink away into merely not having anything. Instead it is the moment, the present directed to the decision. Yet everything would be decided, were it only a matter of being transported in the direction of being's refusal of itself. The self-refusing is hesitant; it is not only the transporting of timing but also the most primordial ecstatic movement of spacing, an enchantment (*Berückung*). "This enchantment is the encircling hold [*Umhalt*], in which the moment and, with it, the timing are held" (65: 384). Whereas time is the gathering of the above-mentioned ways of being transported, the enchanting character of space is the encircling hold, indeed, the encircling hold of that gathering. In this way Heidegger attempts— all too cryptically, to be sure—to characterize how, on the basis of the way that time and space are turned "counter" to one another, they are "primordially directed" to one another. Thus, time-space is at once transporting-and-enchanting, "the encircling hold that gathers together, the thus fitted and correspondingly attuned abyss, the unfolding of which becomes historical in the grounding of the 'here' by *being*-here (its essential paths of sheltering the truth)" (65: 386).

Trakl, Georg (1887–1914)

An Austrian poet and pharmacist, Georg Trakl struggled throughout his short life with material insecurity, addiction, and depression. His death came from overdosing in the wake of a gruesome experience as an orderly on the Eastern Front. His poetry—in *Gedichte* (1913), *Sebastian im Traum* (1915), and the journal *Der Brenner* (1914–15)—counterbalances themes of dissolution and death with a melodic, sometimes assuaging lyricism. At the center of Heidegger's readings of Trakl are two verses, one from "A Winter Evening," the other from "Springtime of the Soul," each indicative of a difference—the "threshold" of things and world, the soul "on" the earth—that can be the site of their undoing or saving.

Heidegger turns to "A Winter Evening" in order to show how language speaks in the poem, calling up things precisely in the fourfold structure of a world. Thus the poem's opening verses ("when the snow falls on the window," "the chimes of the evening bells," "the table is set and the house is well-provided") make things present while sheltering them in their absence. They are thereby called precisely in the way they abide together in the world's fourfold structure. The snowfall brings human beings under the night sky; the chimes bring them as mortals before the divine; the house and table bind mortals to the earth. "So called, the things gather together among themselves heaven and earth, mortals and divinities. The four are a primordially-unified relation to one another. Things let the fourfold of the four abide among themselves" (12: 19). So too the second stanza calls for the fourfold of the world by calling up the tree of grace graciously blossoming out of the earth. What the poem says "entrusts the world to the things and at the same time shelters the things in the splendor of the world ... Things bear the world. The world indulges the things" (12: 21). The difference between things and world in their unity is fundamental, unique, and wholehearted, bringing them to bear on one another, i.e. not after the fact but as their essential unfolding (12: 22). The third stanza (with the opening lines "the wanderer enters quietly, pain has turned the threshold to stone") announces the middle that calls world and things together, saving them in the wholeheartedness of their difference (12: 24–7).

In "Language in the Poem" Heidegger takes Trakl's verse "Something strange is the soul on earth" to indicate the soul's fundamental character, namely, to be underway on earth. Being underway entails "going under," to be sure, but in the sense, not of decaying but of "abandoning the decayed form of humanity," and thereby "perhaps being able to build and dwell poetically and thus first save the earth as earth" (12: 37f, 42). Heidegger finds a glimpse of that decayed form in Trakl's "Autumn Soul," where the poet notes that the wandering "separated us from loved ones, others." Once again, in order to be underway on earth, the soul must itself "go under," must lose itself but in the sense of departing from the decayed form of humanity and thus become other, other to the latter. The place of Trakl's poetry is precisely the place of this departure (12: 45–8). Drawing on various images in Trakl's poetry, Heidegger further determines that departure is the gathering of those who, following in the footsteps of the one who died earlier, are sheltered back into their quieter, more responsive, unborn childhood and thus into the promise of another beginning (12: 63, 66, 70). Playing finally on the "going under," the sunset of a life that marks the place of Trakl's poetry, Heidegger also identifies it as "the land of the evening," i.e. *das Abendland*—the West. For those who regard Trakl, the poet of the "Occidental Song" as the poet of decline, Heidegger counters that a placing of his poem shows him to be the poet of the land at evening, still hidden, yet to be born (12: 75–8).

Transcendence (*Transzendenz*)

Because we see any particular thing with other things and against a background, we never see it without also looking beyond it. When we grab something, we literally reach beyond it to grasp it. We use tools by aiming at a purpose beyond them. In a comparable way we relate to things by reference to something not identical to them. For example, we take them *as* such-and-such, i.e. in light of something else. Looking beyond, reaching beyond, aiming beyond are all forms of transcending, as is relating to something *as* this or that. By virtue of being-in-the-world, projecting possibilities in the situation into which we have been thrown, we are always already transcending all the things, including ourselves, to which we comport ourselves. Transcendence is thus something that we do—albeit not alone. Because being matters to us, we relate to beings in light of it, understanding them as being rather than not being. We transcend beings by projecting possibilities (constituting a clearing) that allow us to take things as being rather than not being. Transcending in this way, i.e. projecting possibilities, is timely, it is for the sake of something, and, hence, it has its origin in Dasein's primordial temporality (26: 203–80).

In SZ Heidegger emphasizes the worldly character of Dasein's temporally based transcendence. When we transcend beings, we do so by placing them within a world, the world that each of us projects as what things generally are for-the-sake-of. The world is the unity of temporal horizons of the three aspects of time in the primordial sense, what makes sense of Dasein as care, namely,

the way we are ahead of ourselves (future), already in a world
(having been), and alongside things (present). The world, thus
grounded in Dasein's temporality, transcends beings that are,
accordingly, "inner-worldly." "Having its ground in the horizonal
unity of ecstatic temporality, the world is transcendent" (SZ 365).
This account of the world's transcendence, rooted in Dasein's
temporality, is Heidegger's way of explaining how entities can
be encountered within the world and objectified (SZ 366; 26:
211–72). Intentionality is thus grounded in Dasein's transcendence
rather than vice versa; pre-theoretically and pre-practically, Dasein
has always already moved beyond other beings, not to another
entity, but to the world. Transcendence is the "ground of the
ontological difference," making possible "the foregoing understanding of being," on the basis of which Dasein relates to beings,
including itself (9: 135, 167f; 35: 90).

"Transcendence" and "transcendental" have scholastic roots
well-known to Heidegger. Scotus defined metaphysics as *scientia
transcendentium*, science of the transcendentals, namely, those
predicates that do not fall under any one of the list of predica-
menta (categories, highest genera), but are predicable of each of
them (e.g. "being" and "one" can be predicated of substance,
quantity, quality, and so on). Kant is the source of the modern but
related use of the term to signify the conditions of the possibility
of (understanding) whatever falls under some domain. Heidegger
appropriates both traditional notions into the ambiguous phrase
"transcendence of the being of Dasein"—ambiguous because
Dasein is not the sole source of its transcendence (SZ 38).
Heidegger's talk of transcendence in SZ thus borrows heavily from
the very metaphysical tradition he is putting in question. For this
very reason, by the mid–1930s the term "transcendental" does
not simply drop out of Heidegger's analyses. After elaborating
how the Platonic manner of representing being (*ideas*) as separate
from beings is "the origin of 'transcendence' in its various forms"
(ontic, ontological, fundamental-ontological, epistemological, and
metaphysical), Heidegger contends: "The notion of 'transcendence'
in *every* sense must *disappear*" (65: 216ff, 322, 355; 8: 232; 14:
35–7; 70: 56).

Translation (*Übersetzung*)

In contrast to a literal, technical–philological translation that remains wholly within the secure confines of the translator's native language, a genuine translation sets (*setzt*) us over (*über*) into another realm of experience. Thus, in every conversation and soliloquy, "a primordial translating holds sway," indeed, "in advance of any choice of words." Every translation is an interpretation, and, despite the lack of coincidence between languages, translation can bring to light contexts that lie fallow in *both* languages. Herein lies the import of a genuine translation. Beyond merely transporting us into another language with the help of our own, it is "an awakening, clarifying, unfolding of one's own language through the help of the encounter with the foreign language." Moreover, every interpretation, even within the same language, is a translation. Indeed, the translation within the same language is in fact harder, given our tendency to think we understand our own language without further ado. Among the translations which have shaped the history of Western thinking, perhaps none is more influential than the translation of the Greek *pseudos* into the Latin *falsum*, effectively transporting the former—and, with it, the sense of *aletheia*—into the alien, Roman–imperial realm of commands and laws (53: 75f, 79f; 54: 16ff, 57–71).

Truth (*Wahrheit*)

"The sun" is neither true nor false but "the sun shines" is. Only properly formed propositions or assertions are truth-bearers. They are true if the state of affairs to which they correspond obtains, false if not. These considerations give rise to the correspondence theory of truth, but they also invite some obvious questions. How do we know when the correspondence obtains? Mere declaration of the correspondence is, if not circular, the first step in an endless regression. To be sure, "the sun shines" is true if and only if the sun shines, but this consideration in turn merely underscores the necessity of confirming that the relevant state of affairs holds. Indeed, even if this consideration is taken to imply that the truth-predicate is redundant, iterative, superfluous, or simply an expression of assertive force, it would do so only on the basis of an independent presentation of that state of affairs (the sun's shining). In other words, truth as correspondence cannot be the end of the story; it presupposes the disclosure or discovery of that to which the true assertion is supposed to correspond, and such a disclosure or discovery presupposes in turn that the latter is not hidden but instead shows itself. In this way truth as correspondence piggybacks on a more primordial truth: truth as unconcealment or self-showing.

Early Greek thinkers tended to conceive truth as unconcealment more readily than subsequent Western thinkers did. Even Aristotle—often wrongly identified as a proponent of the correspondence theory of truth exclusively—understood assertions as apophantic, i.e. as ways of ostensively allowing things to be seen—and not as mere combinations of representations set adrift from their moorings in the process of unconcealing (SZ 33, 155, 218f, 226). By contrast, traditional logic, given its concerns with inference, often conceives propositions and assertions along the lines of indicative sentences that can be considered in their purely grammatical and formal relations to one another, separate from their content or reference. In other words, the sentences as things said are regarded as things on-hand within the world over against what they are about (SZ 214). However, the uncovering of entities via assertions is grounded in Dasein's disclosedness and, hence, the latter is "truth in the most primordial sense" (SZ 223, 297). To be sure, given Dasein's fallenness, this truth is typically not unalloyed; as much as Dasein is "in the truth," it is equiprimordially "in the untruth" (SZ 222). Nevertheless, "resoluteness" marks "the most primordial, because authentic truth of Dasein" (SZ 297).

Heidegger begins a decade of intensive work on truth (see 66: 107) with his essay "On the Essence of Truth," where he locates its essence in freedom, a freedom that, having attuned all comportment to beings as a whole, reveals beings by letting them be. Human comportment is attuned through and through to the manifestness of beings as a whole, not as something that appears within everyday calculations and preoccupations, but as something indeterminate, accorded by the concealment of beings as a whole. Letting particular beings be, and thus revealing them in the way that we individually and respectively comport to them, coincides with the hiddenness of beings as a whole. This hiddenness—older than any manifestness of this or that particular being, older, too, than the letting-be itself that relates to it—is the pre-eminent mystery holding sway over human existence. Dasein is ek-sistent, meaning that it stands out into the manifestness of beings, relating to them insofar as they are, but this manifestness itself and the mystery underlying it are forgotten in favor of an in-sistence on what is available and on measures of correctness. This insistent concern with beings as the immediately accessible and the ek-sistent turning away from the mystery of the hiddenness go hand-in-hand, constituing errancy (*Irre*). At the same time, errancy brings with it the possibility of experiencing and not mistaking the mystery. While the revealing of beings as such is at once the concealing of beings as a whole (being), errancy is this "at once." Both the mystery (the hiddenness of the hidden) and the errancy belong to the originary essence of truth (9: 192–8; 39: 119, 250ff).

In *Contributions to Philosophy*, Heidegger rethinks truth's essence against the backdrop of a history that moves from earliest Greek senses of *aletheia* through Platonic and Aristotelian conceptions of the latter as the yoke of correctness to modern conceptions of truth as certainty, culminating in Nietzsche's identification of truth with life. In the move from *aletheia* to Dasein, truth is finally detached from any connection to beings and conceived solely in terms of historical being. So conceived, truth unfolds and its unfolding grounds not simply as the clearing of beings but as the clearing for historical being's self-concealing (65: 327–51). As the clearing for this concealment, truth is not something on-hand, not some idea or ideal, but a sheltering of the way this self-concealing happens in the struggle of earth and world. "The execution of this struggle sets the truth into the work, into the implement, experiences it as the thing, brings it to completion in deed and sacrifice. But the safeguarding of the self-concealing must always be there. For only in this way does the history (grounded in keeping with Dasein) remain in the appropriation and thus continue to adhere to historical being" (65: 390f).

Plato's construal of an entity's visibility as its presence and thus its accessibility and manifestness to the soul is the first step to ignoring the open and yoking truth to correctness (65: 332, 335, 338ff). In accordance with the dominance enjoyed by the conception of truth as correctness, some philosophers find themselves—and thus construe human beings primarily—as subjects confronting objects (65: 185f, 334, 355, 358). Because correctness seems to be something that "remains back in the soul" as a process and act of the soul (and, indeed, does so in such a way that the soul as an ego forms the opposite to the object), the very presence of the entity that is represented, and the opening in terms of which it presents itself, in short, the event of being, are overlooked. "*Correctness* as an interpretation of the open becomes the ground of the subject-object-relation" (65: 316, 343f, 349–58). Hence, wherever truth as correctness takes the lead in determining the idea of truth, all paths to its origin are blocked.

Turn (*Kehre*)

From the mid–1930s on, Heidegger assigns a central significance to a turn in the essence of being itself, as something already begun and as something coming, though by no means inevitably. The presence and accessibility of beings, i.e. their mode of being, requires the openness or clearing that Dasein *is*. At the same time, Dasein is a clearing only by virtue of the presence of beings to it. In other words, the presence (being) of beings needs *what it is present to* (our being-here, being-the-clearing, Dasein), and Dasein literally belongs to the presence of beings. The presence of beings opens up (appropriates) Dasein to their presence, and so, too, Dasein opens itself up to their presence. This mutual appropriation—the appropriating event—is the end of the analysis, the grounding abyss. Within this mutual appropriation, both being (the presence itself of beings) and Dasein turn to and away from one another (in keeping with the ordinary significance of *Kehre*, namely, a U-turn). The presence of beings remains hidden as Dasein, forgetful of it, preoccupies itself with beings (albeit thanks to their presence). "The turn indicates precisely this essence of being itself as the appropriating event counter-swinging in itself" (65: 251f, 261, 286f).

The withdrawal of being (its turn from us) is not nothing but in fact affects us, drawing us to it. The being of beings, i.e. their presence as such, "goes under," concealing itself from the very beginning (the originary beginning) of Western thinking. The thinkers of the first beginning recognized but did not grasp the dynamic of this hidden unhiddenness (clearing), and the subsequent history of metaphysics is accordingly marked by the forgottenness of being. By contrast, the other beginning reverses this development, retrieves the originary beginning, and comes to terms with historical being's hiddenness (*Verwindung des Seyns*). The other beginning thus marks a turn in the appropriating event, where the truth of historical being is recognized and grounded as the "clearing concealment" (65: 185, 189, 258, 293, 351, 381, 407f; 70: 80; 8: 10f). Historical being is the event that appropriates the being of beings (their presence) and Dasein to one another. Inasmuch as the turn unfolds in this appropriating event, "Da-seyn 'is' the turn" (71: 181, 205, 207). The future of humanity depends upon whether this turn becomes history (65: 407f; 71: 192).

The 1949 address "The Turn" echoes this gloss from a decade earlier. The danger presented by the essence of modern technology brings with it a loss of the world and the nearness of things that coincides with an obliviousness to the appropriating event as the truth of historical being. When this danger becomes explicitly present, the *turn* to safeguarding that truth itself opens up, as do the world and things, as the appropriating event of another beginning. This turn can only be unmediated since there is nothing to mediate it. It comes about only as historical being's sudden self-illumination, turned on itself as the essence of modern technology, opening our eyes (*Er-äugnis*) to the utter neglect of things entailed by that essence. The opening up of the turn in historical being is "the turn from the denial of its essence into the appropriating event of its safeguarding" (79: 71–5).

Heidegger also employs the term "turn" in other contexts, albeit in ways related to the just reviewed theme of "the turn in the appropriating event." Shortly after SZ, while continuing to maintain that the entire grounding of ontology is the work of fundamental ontology, Heidegger observes that "this temporal analysis is at the same time the *turn* in which the ontology itself explicitly runs back into the metaphysical ontic, in which it always implicitly stands." The radicalization and universalization of ontology requires that it turn back to metontology, the metaphysics of Dasein (26: 201). In 1947 Heidegger explains that he held back the third division of the first part of SZ, the turn from "Being and Time" to "Time and Being," because his thinking at the time failed to say the turn adequately, though his essay on truth provides a certain glimpse of this turn (9: 327f). The aborted turn in the planned project of

SZ gives way to a different orientation in Heidegger's thinking, his shift from the transcendental project of fundamental ontology to the effort to think being historically, i.e. historical being as the turn in the appropriating event (9: 201; 11: 149ff).

Twofold (*Zwiefalt*)

The twofold is the presence of what is present (the being of beings). A human being comes to be human by corresponding (*entsprechen*) to the twofold and bearing witness to it. What carries the human being's relation to the twofold is language (12: 116, 128). The history of being is the destiny of this twofold: "the unfolding, unconcealing affordance of the cleared presencing, in which what is present appears" (7: 244). Because the twofold coincides with the unfolding of the clearing in which presence and what is present can be distinguished, it cannot be experienced immediately, least of all through a representation of the difference between being and beings (12: 119ff, 128f). Thoughtfully saying and corresponding to the twofold allows this process of being present and the presence itself to lie before the thinker, something that happens only on the path of thinking called for by *aletheia*. By contrast, in their everyday way of taking things up, mortals cling to what is unfolded and what, so unfolded, immediately puts demands on them: "what is present without regard for its presence" (7: 246).

Uncanny (*unheimlich*)

"Uncanny" is the standard translation of *unheimlich*, though it might also be translated "eerie, creepy, fantastic." The term's root "*Heim*: home" suggests how the word came to mean what lies outside the homey, comfort zone of the ordinary and everyday. Thus, angst, the experience of the utter irrelevance and meaningless of things, is uncanny in the sense that Dasein in a state of angst is "not at home," at least insofar as "home" is the familiar, everyday world of the they (where everything has its relevance and its place). Angst is uncanny because it fetches Dasein back from its immersion in the "world," disclosing that its existence is its alone. Dasein's flight into the public world is a flight from uncanniness that is not only a constant threat to this flight but is more primordial than it. For this uncanniness coincides with one's "ownmost" being towards death. The call of conscience is the uncanny, silent call by Dasein itself in its uncanniness to this ownmost being (SZ 188f, 252, 276ff, 286f, 295f, 342ff).

In the mid-1930s Heidegger deploys "uncanny" to translate the Greek *deinon* as part of an attempt to understand the Greek conception of human beings. The first chorus in Sophocles' *Antigone* deems many things "uncanny" but human beings "the most uncanny." Not only are human beings caught up in the overwhelming violence of things, preventing them from being "at home" (*einheimisch*), but they constantly overstep the boundary of home-base themselves (40: 116). This overstepping is, in a word, *techne*. Being a human being is thus uncanny because it consists in a violent, technical struggle with nature that discloses the overwhelming fittingness of nature (being). From taking possession of a place to mastering themselves, human beings epitomize nature's (being's) violence, as they force things to serve human ends. Human beings fall prey to this technical success, blinding them to the disclosure underlying it and making them forget being in their mastery of beings. Herein lies yet another sense of human uncanniness: by mistaking what they merely exemplify with something they possess, they are not at home with themselves, with the essence of who they are—and yet this same dynamic discloses, along with the overwhelming strangeness of nature (being), what it means for humans to be at home (40: 120, 127).

Returning to humanity's uncanniness in his 1942 lectures, Heidegger interprets the chorus song in the light of the "sole concern of Hölderlin's poetry": "the basic law of becoming at home" (53: 60, 73). Heidegger translates *deinon* as the uncanny, yet now with the primary accent on its unusualness, i.e. on not being at home. The chorus song accordingly means "that the human being is in a unique sense not at home and that becoming at home is its preeminent care" (53: 87, 103). Human beings are uncanny by virtue of coming from and remaining in the uncanniness of being. In the human being, this uncanniness takes the form of being fully in charge and at home when it comes to beings, yet at the same time helpless and homeless when it comes to being (53: 93f). Human beings are uncanny because they arrogantly presume to find a way

out of this homelessness by manipulating beings. Such presump-
tuousness results from forgetting the "hearth," the home-site of
being (53: 103f, 144). Yet Antigone is the uncanniest because, in
her actions, she commemorates hearth and being (53: 144, 150).
She answers—not to any particular being, gods or humans, and
certainly not to Creon—but to being itself. She is authentically not
at home because not being at home among beings coincides with
coming home to the hearth or, equivalently, becoming at home
with being. Herein lies the point of Sophocles' tragedy, namely, to
dare "to separate and decide between authentically and inauthentically not-being-at-home [*Unheimischsein*]" (53: 144, 146).

   Both later accounts of uncanniness reconfigure the role that
uncanniness plays in SZ, setting off the possibility of authenticity
from inauthenticity. However, the difference between these later
accounts is also striking. In the later account the interplay of force
and violence gives way to the uncanniness of becoming at home
(belonging to being) precisely through a non-violent process of
not being at home in the midst of beings alone. In later addresses,
Heidegger also invokes uncanniness and "not being at home" (*das
Unheimische*) characteristic of the technical world (16: 518, 525,
575–81; 40: 126).

Understanding (*Verstehen*)

If someone says that she understands French or chess, we take her
to mean that she is capable of speaking French or playing chess.
Speaking French or playing chess are not properties like her hair
color or height. They are instead capabilities of projecting various
possibilities in the appropriate situations. These projections, in
turn, disclose those capabilities and the situations. Only by enacting
these possibilities does anyone (including the lady herself) know
whether she can speak or play. She may relish the prospect, find it
annoying, or something in between. She can also be more or less
invested in the capability and more or less capable of it. When
she is sufficiently capable, she knows what's at stake and, as we
may put it colloquially, "what's up" or "what's going on" at any
juncture in speaking or playing. Nor should it be overlooked that
both capabilities are historical—in the twofold sense that French

and chess came about at a certain time and that our speaker/player at some point had to have been put in a position where she could learn and, having learned, where she could exercise the capability. Understanding in the aforementioned way is thus a pre-disposed, historical capability.

In a manner analogous to this ordinary (ontic) conception of understanding, Heidegger conceives understanding existentially as an always already disposed, disclosive capability. Just as the French speaker or chess player discloses her capability and situation by projecting various possibilities, so being-here discloses itself, its being-in-the-world, by projecting possibilities. Moreover, it owes both its capacity to project and the possibilities themselves to having been thrown into the world. As a basic existential, i.e. a basic way of being-here, existential understanding differs from understanding French or chess because, as long as Dasein is, its understanding is always engaged; that is to say, it is always projecting possibilities and, in the projecting, disclosing what it means to be for itself and others. Dasein's understanding thus corresponds to the fact that Dasein exists in projecting possibilities ("it *is* its possibilities as possibilities") or, in other words, that it is inveterately "ahead of itself." In this sense, too, the understanding is Dasein's way of knowing "what's going on" or "what it's about" (*woran*), in terms of its own capability of being. But by no means is it some sort of internal, cognitive experience belonging to a subject. Far from being "an immanent self-perception," this knowledge is "inherent in the being of the here [*Da*], that is essentially understanding," a dynamic, self-disclosing projection of being-in-the-world. In other words, even if it does not always comprehend its being, to be here is to understand its being as a thrown projection of possibilities. This understanding of being (*Seinsverständnis*) is the central presupposition of SZ. It also drives a wedge between Dasein's manner of being and that of things that are simply on-hand or handy. Thanks to this understanding, Dasein has an ontic-ontological priority over all other entities as the entity whose manner of being first deserves to be investigated (SZ 13, 142ff; 65: 259).

Understanding in this existential sense is not one type of knowing to be contrasted with another, for example, understanding in the humanities in contrast to explaining in the natural sciences, as Dilthey would have it. As a condition of the possibility of both those forms of knowing, existential understanding encompasses

Dasein's self-disclosure of its being-in-the-world precisely as what it, and the complex of implements it concerns itself with, are for (their meaningfulness) (SZ 13, 85f, 143). The understanding secures the ontological intelligibility (*Verständigkeit*) of entities within the world, enabling Dasein to encounter them. Indeed, while beings are independent of any disclosure of them, being *is* only in Dasein's understanding (SZ 183).

As an existential, understanding can be authentic or inauthentic. That is to say, Dasein can understand itself primarily on the basis of the world, or its understanding can spring from its own self. Yet the understanding in either case is a modification of the projection and thus a disclosure of being-in-the-world as a whole.

Existential understanding constitutes various forms of "sight" (*Sicht*). The circumspection (*Umsicht*) of our workworld concerns, the considerateness (*Rücksicht*) of our solicitude for one another, and the transparency (*Durchsichtigkeit*) of Dasein's full disclosure of itself as being-in-the-world, along with its opaqueness to itself (*Undurchsichtigkeit*) are familiar, figurative transcriptions of understanding. Grounding these forms of sight in understanding disestablishes the priority that intuiting and perceiving (together with their paradigmatic counterpart, the on-hand) enjoy in Western philosophy (SZ 147, 336; 24: 18; 31: 43f). Heidegger's use of the infinitive form of the word for understanding, i.e. *Verstehen*, as a noun (together with *Verständnis*) contrasts with the faculty of understanding (Kant's categorial *Verstand*), with the They's "everyday" or "concern-driven" understanding (*Verständigung*), and with "homespun" or "vulgar" understanding (*Verstand*) (SZ 260, 269, 281, 292–6, 309, 311f, 315, 334, 388; 10: 112; 29/30: 264).

Wholeheartedness (*Innigkeit*)

One of Hölderlin's oft-used expressions, "wholeheartedness" (also translated 'intimacy') signifies, not the interiority of a feeling in the sense of a lived experience, but the supreme force of Dasein, its capacity to be utterly open to, and engaged with, beings and the discord among them. Thus, the Greeks are "the wholehearted people" because, "armed with the spirit of the gods," they belonged with their entire soul to the world. There is wholeheartedness only where conflicting powers are opened up in a way that is comparable to their "harmony" in Heraclitus' sense of the term. Basic moods are "wholehearted feelings" that the poet denies precisely in order to preserve the mystery of their "concealing power," the primordial unity of the conflict embodied by them. "The mystery is only where wholeheartedness holds sway," and, when the poet names the mystery as such, he does so with the "understanding of its hiddenness as self-concealing" (39: 117ff, 124f, 148, 249f; see, too, 4: 36). Poetry's sole and authentic charge is to "barely reveal" the mystery as the wholeheartedness of the conflict in which the decisions are made "about gods and the earth, humans and everything made" (39: 250f; 65: 486). The "not" is wholeheartedly in being, thanks to the appropriating event (65: 264f).

Will (*Wille, Wollen*)

Heidegger speaks of the will within five settings: (a) the existential analysis of SZ, (b) glosses of transcendental and practical freedom, (c) exhortations to will the will of the people and the *Führer*, (d) reviews of the modern metaphysics of the subjectivity of the will, and (e) the context of letting-be.

(a) In SZ Heidegger glosses two distinct but related possibilities of willing, the first in order to show that willing (at least in the context of concern) is based upon caring rather than vice versa (SZ 194) and the second in order to show that, while conscience calls us even "against our will," to hear its call is to will to have a conscience (SZ 275, 295f). The will is thus divided against itself, or, to put it less dramatically, willing to have a conscience calls us from willing only in the context of everyday concerns—thus explaining how Heidegger can claim (in the space of few lines) that "whoever wills [*will*] to be called back, is summoned by the call" and yet that conscience is not to be reduced to the will (*Wille*) (SZ 271f). Notably, while the first reference to willing locates it within care that may be inauthentic or authentic, the second reference is to a willing that coincides with authentic care. The difference is between willing various matters of concern within the world and willing simply to have a conscience. The latter is not some "world-fleeing seclusion but instead brings one without any illusions into the resoluteness of 'acting'" (SZ 296f, 310). Hence, authentic willing is to have an effect on willing within the world of our concerns. These two senses of "will" can be found throughout Heidegger's writings, though sometimes the difference is difficult to discern.

(b) Following SZ, Heidegger identifies the will (*Wille*) (apparently regardless of its authenticity) with the freedom constituting transcendence, the very projection of a world (9: 163; 26: 238, 273). Yet echoing the account of resoluteness in SZ, he also gives, in the spirit of destruction, a tendentious reading of Kant's identification of the will and practical reason, such that "what is authentically law-giving for willing is the actual, pure willing itself and nothing else" (31: 275–85, 292). Exploiting Kant's assertion of the factuality of freedom, he contends that what a person wills to do when he actually wills entails what he—or, more precisely, his Dasein—should do (26: 289).

(c) The opening page of Heidegger's Rectoral Address appeals to the same entailment. Who members of the university *should* be depends upon their *willing* their essence (16: 107f, 116). Further echoing his gloss of Kant's practical philosophy, Heidegger claims that the will of the students, rooted in the resoluteness of withstanding German fate in its most extreme need, is a true will insofar as it submits to the law of their essence: "To give oneself the law is the highest freedom" (16: 112f). Throughout his political speeches and writings during this time of his public endorsement of National Socialism, Heidegger freely employs the rhetoric of willing. For example, in late January of 1934, addressing workers, he speaks of carrying out the "great will of the state" and following "the overarching willing of our *Führer*" (16: 236; see, too, 136, 171, 189, 193, 208, 291). Willing the will of the state is a means of willing a people's self-governance (38: 57). In an address on the current condition and future task of German philosophy, after noting that philosophy can create what becomes the "essential knowledge of the people," he adds that "this knowledge is *in itself* already *willing*" (16: 333).

(d) From the mid–1930s, as Heidegger's support for the National Socialist regime wanes, he increasingly casts a more critical eye on appeals to the will within the modern metaphysical tradition (7: 74ff; 69: 63; 67: 157ff; 77: 78f). Leibniz initiates this conception, as he equates being and willing, an equation that coincides with according an absoluteness to subjectivity of one sort or another (5: 243ff; 6.2: 213; 7: 112f; 77: 53). Heidegger elaborates this modern metaphysical conception at length through a consideration of its clearest spokesman in German Idealism: Schelling (42: 163ff; 49: 84–91; 6.2: 436). He also couches Hegel's idealism within the modern metaphysical conception of the will (5: 193, 203f; 6.1: 58; 6.2: 269) and later claims, albeit with little argument, that being as the will to power lies concealed in Hegel's and Schelling's accounts of will (9: 360). But Heidegger gives his most extensive account of this modern metaphysical conception of will in his lectures on its culminating expression: namely, Nietzsche's doctrine of the will to power (5: 239; 6.2: 177f). The essence of the will to power lies in the will itself or, more precisely, the will's reflexiveness, i.e. the way it wills itself in willing (7: 78; 90: 228). Whether individual or collective, willing is always a self-willing, a continuously self-securing, self-overreaching, and self-augmenting power (5: 111, 234–9, 291; 6.1: 33–9, 56ff; 6.2: 214, 242f).

Yet the will to power doctrine is not the last step in the history of the modern metaphysics of the will. The honor goes to technology. Nothing escapes its calculations and organization, as "the will to will" forces itself on everything, "doing so for the sake of the securing itself in an unconditionally continuous way. The basic form in which then the will to will organizes and calculates itself in the unhistorical character of the world of completed metaphysics may be called 'technology'" (7: 78; 5: 288). What is deadly is not the atom bomb but "the unconditioned character of mere willing in the sense of deliberate self-advancement in regard to everything" (5: 294).

(e) Once Heidegger has come to understand the will as the underlying principle of modernity, informing its thinking and its basic conception of being, he is confronted with the issue of thinking otherwise. By his own account, this thinking *and willing* otherwise are prefigured by his analysis of resoluteness as openness and of "a will that is most properly one's own" (5: 55; 9: 188; 40: 23; 55: 111f; 65: 15, 397). Yet he also describes this willing otherwise as foregoing willing, "the willing that, refusing willing, has let itself in for what is not a will," something inconceivable in the modern metaphysics of subjectivity and the will (77: 148). Since the will to overcome is precisely an extension of the will to power, it would seem that all avenues to willing non-willing are blocked

(77: 76ff; 6.2: 352). Yet there is nothing logically untoward about (non-reflexively) willing not to will (any more than choosing not to choose but to do something else), nor is there any reason to suppose that, should we succeed in willing not to will, what we are then doing remains the hidden expression of a subjective willing. After distinguishing these two senses of "not willing" (i.e. an act that is willed as opposed to something independent of willing), Heidegger makes it clear that the second sense of "not willing" coincides with thinking or at least preparing for thinking, the sort of thinking that is a "letting be." Beyond the activity and passivity of willing, thinking as "letting be" is "perhaps a higher activity" consisting in resoluteness, enduring reserve, and steadfastness in being released to the "open region" (77: 106–9, 142–5; 9: 162).

Word (*Wort*)

Words (*Worte*) are not the same as terms (*Wörter*). Terms are used: words are spoken. Words are not mere sounds. Even when we hear a foreign language, we do not hear mere sounds but words we do not understand. Listening to the mere sounds made when words are spoken is "unnatural" and not the same as hearing what is spoken, just as focusing on the colors of something is not the same as perceiving it. Words can be easily mistaken for terms that, together with their sound-structure, serve as mere casings or vessels for meanings, registered by dictionaries, relying upon the customary use of terms. Yet words open themselves in the sound-less play-space of what is spoken, speaking in it and not explicitly stepping forward in it. As Stefan George puts it, there are no things without words. That is to say, words first let things be as things (12: 214ff). Attending to the saying of words—and this is the path of thinking known as "philosophy"—is thus not to be confounded with preoccupation with terms (7: 47f; 8: 133–6; 12: 18; 38: 23).

The foregoing is a gloss of Heidegger's mature remarks on words. In his study of Scotus, he takes words merely as terms, conceived as "linguistic elements," belonging to a completely different realm from that of meaning. They are *of themselves* intrinsically empty, unrelated to one another and signifying nothing, becoming "sensory signs" thanks to "meaning-bestowing acts," as

Husserl dubbed them (1: 291ff, 299). In SZ a difference between words and terms makes its appearance. Words (*Worte*) accrue to meanings that are part of a pre-given world of intelligibility. They grow up and develop in the direction of the meanings, as opposed to first being mere "lexical items" (*Wörterdinge*) that are subsequently outfitted with meaning (SZ 161).

World (*Welt*)

"World" is one of the staples of Heidegger's philosophical vocabulary, shifting, sometimes incrementally, sometimes dramatically, with changes in his thinking.

In his early Freiburg lectures he introduces the notion of a *life-world*—including the surrounding world, the shared world, and the world of the self (*die Lebenswelt, die Umwelt, Mit- und Selbst-Welt*)—which is "lived in a situation of the self" (58: 45f, 59–64; 61: 94–8). Anticipating the concept of being-in-the-world, Heidegger stresses that we live "in, out of, for, with, and against a world"; as such, the world provides the content of the sense of living (61: 85f, 98). The world is what we encounter and, as such, it is "here" (*da*). It is what we are concerned about, the source of meaningfulness. The everyday world is the surrounding world or environment (*Umwelt*) (63: 85ff).

In SZ, Heidegger distinguishes four meanings of "world": (1) the totality of entities on-hand within the world, (2) the manner of being of entities on-hand within the world (or a certain region of such entities, e.g. the world of mathematics), (3) the place in which, being-here (*da-seiend*), we factually live and dwell (e.g. the public world, a household), and (4) the manner of being proper to being-in-the-world. Uses (1) and (3) are ontic, but refer to different sorts of entities. Whereas "world" in the first sense designates the collection of innerworldly entities, i.e. beings on-hand within-the-world, "world" in the third sense is existentiel, designating the place where *Dasein* lives. Uses (2) and (4) are ontological, but refer to different manners of being, the manner of being on-hand within a world and being-in-the-world, respectively. In order to differentiate these diverse meanings, Heidegger reserves the term "world" for (3), places the term in quotation marks when it designates (1), and substitutes the term "worldliness" for (4). Flagging a perennial mistake of traditional ontology, Heidegger contends that the world is not to be understood on the basis of nature but, like nature, can only be understood ontologically on the basis of the worldliness of being-here (*Da-sein*). So, too, the analysis of what it means to be must take its bearings from the world closest at hand to us, our *Umwelt* (SZ 64ff).

Whatever we encounter in our environs presupposes that we transcend them, taking them for this or that and, at the very least, understanding them as being. This transcendence is grounded in Dasein's temporality that is always at once ecstatic and horizonal. The ecstatic character is the movement of Dasein, the "futurity" of projecting and coming to itself, the "past" (literally, "having been") of coming back to its thrownness, and the "present" of being alongside entities. Each such ecstasis (standing forth, movement outward) has a horizon. Dasein projects possibilities for its own sake as the horizon of its future. It comes back to what it has been thrown into as the horizon of its having-been. It is alongside things for some intermediate purpose as the horizon of its present. These horizons, together with the ecstasies, form a unity. Thus, the way we are alongside things within the world (a way that enables us to accomplish this or that) springs from the way that we project ourselves, each (pre-egoistically) for his own sake, and, in the process, come back to our thrownness. Time, in this fundamental sense, is "the condition of the possibility of being-in-the-world, in which the being of innerworldly beings is grounded" (SZ 351). The world fuses in a single horizon what things are for, how Dasein comes to itself, projecting possibilities for its own sake, all the while returning to its facticity, to what has been left to it (SZ 365). What transcends particular beings is precisely the world, grounded in the temporality that is the sense of existence, our being-here. "Having its ground in the horizonal unity of ecstatic temporality, the world is transcendent" (SZ 365). The ecstatically–horizonally founded transcendence of the world explains how entities can be encountered within the world and objectified (SZ 366).

In 1929, Heidegger also understands the world in terms of the process of transcending entities that constitutes being-in-the-world. Not itself an entity or the sum of entities, the world is that for the sake of which being-in-the-world exists. It refers to human beings in their relations to beings as a whole. Since taking something to be is typically construed as convertible with taking it to be an entity, Heidegger cautions against claiming that the world *is*. Instead he introduces the neologism, a verbalization of the noun, "the world worlds" to characterize this simple unfolding that prevails over beings (9: 164; 5: 30f; 7: 181; 38: 168).

In Heidegger's "transcendental" period, he approaches the phenomenon of the world in three ways. The first approach (initiated in his first lectures and adopted in SZ, as reviewed above) begins with our everyday encounter of it. The second approach reviews the history of the word and the conceptions, particularly the cosmological and existential conceptions, contained therein—ancient (*kosmos*), early Christian and scholastic (both *ens creatum* and *amatores mundi*), and Kantian conceptions (both "unconditioned totality" and "the game of life")—(9: 142–56; 27: 240–323). The third approach (in the 1929/30 lectures) consists in comparing how humans have and form a world with the world-poor condition of animals (29/30: 261–4).

The dynamic of Heidegger's world-analysis shifts dramatically with the introduction of the concept of earth in the 1930s. He continues to distinguish the world from a mere assemblage of things on-hand or their imagined structure. Instead it is an openness in which all things have their places, proximities, and times. The artwork sets up the world, keeping it open, but it does so by also placing the world back firmly on earth as something hidden and impenetrable. The openness of the world accordingly conflicts with the earth's hiddenness, and the artwork instigates this strife (5: 30–6).

In the late 1930s and early 1940s Heidegger continues to think the world in its abiding, mutually sustaining confrontation with the earth, as the strife between them intersects with the confrontation of divinities and humans (65: 280, 310; 66: 188; 70: 157). The strife of world and earth corresponds to truth as the sheltering, hidden clearing and, hence, too, to the duality of historical being and beings (65: 71f, 349, 354, 389ff).

Just as the world plays a central role in determining respectively the "sense" and the "truth" of being in the first two major phases of Heidegger's thinking, so it also figures prominently in the third phase, thinking the "place" of being. In the 1949 lecture "The Thing" Heidegger characterizes the world as the inexplicable and unfathomable play of the simple unfolding of the foursome (divinities, mortals, earth, and sky). The single dimension of this play is the nearing of the nearness, the nearness of the world and things. "Only humans as mortals attain, in dwelling, the world as world. Only what rings out from the world becomes sometimes a thing" (7: 181–4). In the context of the fourfold, humans do not build a world as such, but rather the world includes them and emerges from how they dwell with things.

Heidegger's published writings, lectures, and posthumous works

The primary source for Heidegger's writings is the *Gesamtausgabe* (GA), published by Klostermann in Frankfurt am Main since 1975. The following list contains titles and dates of publication in numerical order of the GA for all volumes published before 2012; titles of planned volumes are also listed. Numbers in parentheses within the summaries refer to pages of the respective volume summarized. Where the text is the basis of a course, the semester of the course is given (WS: winter semester; SS: summer semester). Friedrich-Wilhelm von Herrmann is the editor of volumes 1–5, 7, 9, 11–12, 14, 16–17, 24, 29/30, 45, 64–6, 71–2, 82. Other editors are listed in parentheses, followed by the date of publication. The Klostermann website does not list any editors for planned volumes 73, 91–102. English translations are given below.

Published writings (1910–76)

1 *Frühe Schriften* (1978)

This volume supplements the original 1972 version with two 1912 essays: "The Problem of Reality in Modern Philosophy" and "Recent Research in Logic" (glossing writings of Husserl, Meinong, Lask, Geyser, and Frege). It also contains Heidegger's 1913 doctoral dissertation "The Doctrine of Judgment in Psychologism: A Critical-Positive Contribution to Logic," his 1915 habilitation

"Duns Scotus' Doctrine of Categories and Meaning," and his 1916 essay "The Concept of Time in the Science of History." On display is Heidegger's early interest in the grounding of logic, from Neo-Kantian and Husserlian perspectives, i.e. irreducible to psychology and pre-occupied with the problem of categories.

2 *Sein und Zeit* (1977)

First published in 1927, SZ attempts to raise the long-overlooked question of the sense of being (fundamental ontology) through a hermeneutical-phenomenological analysis of the particular being whose being matters to it: *Dasein*. SZ makes the case that time, suitably interpreted, is the sense of our being (the being of Dasein). SZ was to have two parts: (1) an interpretation of Dasein on the basis of temporality and an explication of time as the horizon for the question of being, and (2) a destruction of the history of ontology guided by the problem of temporality. The published version contains only the first part's first two sections ("The Preparatory Analysis of Dasein" and "Dasein and Temporality"). A philosophical landmark of the early twentieth century, SZ was nonetheless widely misinterpreted in Heidegger's eyes (not least as an existentialist tract), leading him to burn drafts of the remaining sections.

First section: After differentiating an existential analysis of being-here (*Dasein*) from studies of human beings, Heidegger analyzes being-in-the-world as the basic constitution of being-here. Beginning with the traditionally neglected everydayness of Dasein's world, the analysis reveals both the ontological distinctiveness (handiness) of implements (in contrast to what is merely on-hand) and Dasein's involvement with implements as a whole, making up the meaningfulness of its world. After contrasting this worldhood and Dasein's spatiality with the Cartesian conception of the world as *res extensa*, the analysis turns to who Dasein is in its everydayness, namely, the They. The penultimate chapter of the first section plumbs the existential structures of "being-in" the world: disposedness, understanding, discourse, and fallenness. The first section's final chapter demonstrates how angst in the face of being-in-the-world (i.e. in the face of the uncanniness of being thrown into being-here at all and its meaninglessness relative to everything handy within-the-world) reveals the structure of being-here as a whole. This structure is summed up in a single concept: care ("being ahead of oneself, already in the world, as being alongside entities encountered within-the-world"). The first section ends with accounts of how traditional notions of reality and truth are embedded in the quite different sense of being that is proper to being-here and "its disclosedness as the most primordial phenomenon of truth" (220f).

Second section: Because it is oriented to Dasein's everydayness and accordingly does not examine authentic existence, the existential analysis given in the first section is incomplete. To make up for this shortcoming, the second section analyses Dasein in relation to its death as its defining possibility, conscience as attesting to its authentic capability, and the death-anticipating resoluteness that, responding to its existential conscience, makes up existing authentically. Taking his cues from this account of authentic existence, Heidegger argues finally that the horizon providing the ultimate sense of Dasein's being as care, not only authentically but also inauthentically, is time. Time in this connection is primarily futural, projecting possibilities that enable one to come to oneself (the primordial past, consisting in retrieving or forgetting who one is) and thus make present (the primordial present, the authenticity of the moment that reveals the situation or the inauthenticity of simply now this, now that). The final three chapters of SZ are devoted to demonstrating how temporality, so conceived, underlies Dasein's everydayness, historicity, and its way of taking time (reckoning with and taking account of time: *Innerzeitigkeit*). The discussion of the temporality of Daseins' everydayness retraces the analyses of the first section. Grounding historicity, i.e. its happening (*Geschehen*), in authentic and thus primarily futural temporality contrasts with the ordinary understanding of history as a study of past events. Historical study (*Historie*) and its truth are "to be expounded on the basis of the authentic disclosedness ('truth') of historical [*geschichtlicher*] existence" (396). The final chapter explains how world-time and the common conception of time as a series of "nows" derive from Dasein's temporality.

Despite its success in explicating how time, suitably interpreted, provides the sense of Dasein's being, the project of SZ remains unfinished and provisional. On this point, Heidegger is explicit.

"The existential–temporal analysis of Dasein demands, for its part, that it be repeated anew within a framework in which the concept of being is discussed in principle" (333, 436f).

3 *Kant und das Problem der Metaphysik* (1991)

First published in 1929 (fourth edition, 1973), this work interprets Kant's *Critique of Pure Reason* as laying the groundwork for the possibility of metaphysics as a natural disposition in human nature. In the first section Heidegger explains why this project takes the form of a "critique of pure reason," and in the final (fourth) section he locates the genuine result of this critique in the question of human finitude (flagged by Kant's own summative question: "What is the human being?") as the question that grounds metaphysics. Demonstrating this result is the aim of the interpretation and, having achieved it, Heidegger uses this conclusion as a stepping-stone to the idea of a fundamental ontology of the sort elaborated in SZ (218, 232–42). In this way Heidegger brings Kant's critical philosophy within the orbit of his own metaphysics of Dasein.

The textual basis for the interpretation makes up the work's second and third sections. In the second section Heidegger analyzes key passages in the Transcendental Analytic, designed to demonstrate the possibility of cognition or experience of objects (A 158/B 197)—what Heidegger dubs "transcendence" (71) and "finite knowing" (119). Relying primarily on the A deduction and a novel reading of the schematisms, Heidegger argues that, on Kant's own terms, what makes experience of objects possible can be nothing else than the transcendental imagination, informed by a basic sort of temporality.

In the third section, moving away from a literal interpretation, Heidegger contends that Kant "recoiled" from the implications of countenancing the transcendental imagination as the unknown root of knowledge's two stems (sensibility and understanding) (160). Exploiting Kant's syntheses of apprehension, reproduction, and recognition in the first part of the A deduction and his doctrine of self-affection, Heidegger argues for the inner temporal character of the transcendental imagination, (176–203). Fully cognizant of the "violence" of his interpretation in this regard, Heidegger later attempts to "take back" the "over-interpretation" (XIV). The volume also contains Heidegger's famous "Davos Disputation" with Ernst Cassirer.

4 *Erläuterungen zu Hölderlins Dichtung* (1996)

The first two entries—a 1943 address on the elegy "Homecoming/ To the Kindred Ones" and a 1936 address on "Hölderlin and the Essence of Poetry"—were first published together in 1944. The enlarged, second edition in 1951 (the second major collection of essays published after the war) added a 1939 address on the poem "As When On a Holiday ..." and a 1943 essay on the poem, "Commemoration." The further, enlarged, fourth edition of 1971 adds the 1959 lecture "Hölderlin's Earth and Heaven" and the 1968 lecture "The Poem." GA 4 contains the 1971 edition along with some appendices; the entries often present condensed versions of earlier, subsequently published lectures (see GA 39, 52, 53). Illustrating the deep relatedness of poetry and thinking, these essays demonstrate how Hölderlin's poetry establishes being in words, naming the holy and grounding a new beginning, through mourning the flight of the gods and experiencing the necessity of the remote and other in order to come close to what is one's own.

5 *Holzwege* (2003)

First published in 1950, *Holzwege* is the first major collection of Heidegger's essays published after the war. The volume begins with the final version of lectures given in 1935/36 on the "Origin of the Work of Art," the 1938 lecture on the scientific picture of the modern world (*genitivus appositivus*) in "Age of the World-Picture," the 1942 essay on "Hegel's Concept of Experience," the examination of nihilism in the context of Nietzsche's thought in the 1943 lecture "Nietzsche's Word: God is Dead," and two essays from 1946: an interpretation of Rilke's poetry in "Why Poets" and Heidegger's most extensive treatment of the first of the three initiators of Western thinking in "Anaximander's Saying."

6.1 *Nietzsche I* (Brigitte Schillbach, 1996)

6.2 *Nietzsche II* (Brigitte Schillbach, 1997)

In 1961 (Pfullingen: Neske) Heidegger published these revised versions of his lectures on Nietzsche. The first volume contains the WS 1936/37 lectures on "The Will to Power as Art," the SS 1937 lectures on "The Eternal Recurrence of the Same," and the SS 1939 lectures on "The Will to Power as Knowledge" (for the unvarnished versions of these original lectures, see GA 43, 44, and 47). The second volume contains the second trimester of 1940 lectures on "European Nihilism" and the WS 1941/42 lectures on "Nietzsche's Metaphysics" (for the unvarnished versions, see GA 48 and 50). The second volume also contains the 1939 essay "The Eternal Recurrence of the Same and the Will to Power," three essays from 1941—"Metaphysics as the History of Being," "Sketches for a History of Being as Metaphysics," and "Recollection of Metaphysics"—and one essay from 1944/46, "Nihilism as Determined by the History of Being."

7 *Vorträge und Aufsätze* (2000)

This collection of lectures and essays—the third major collection to appear after the war—was first published by Neske in 1954 in three parts:

I (a) "The Question Concerning Technology," (b) "Science and Mindfulness," (c) "Overturning Metaphysics," and (d) "Who is Nietzsche's Zarathustra?";

II (a) "What is Called Thinking?" (b) "Building Dwelling Thinking," (c) "The Thing" (also GA 79: 3–21), and (d) "... poetically man dwells ..."; and

III (a) "Logos (Heraklit, Fragment 50)," (b) "Moira (Parmenides, Fragment VIII, 34–41)," and (c) "Aletheia (Heraklit, Fragment 16)."

Parts I and II are mostly texts of lectures from 1950–53 (including some radio lectures), subsequently published in journals and yearbooks, with the exception of "Overturning Metaphysics," which provides sketches, from 1936 to 1946, of the process of "getting over" metaphysics by "winding" it back (*verwinden*) to its beginning. In Part I Heidegger elaborates his conception of modern technology and science, and their roots in the metaphysical tradition's consummation, initiated by "Hegel's metaphysics of absolute knowing as the will of the spirit," given penultimate formulation by "Nietzsche's metaphysics of the will to power," and culminating in the essence of modern technology as the willful and calculating ordering of everything into a standing reserve (17ff, 68, 72ff). In Part II we learn that genuine thinking is a kind of poetic dwelling, exemplified by thinking the thing as the site of the fourfold. II (b) was written at the invitation of the mayor of Darmstadt, a city in ruins following the war, as part of a colloquium on "Man and Space." The Heraclitus essays were first published during the war as contributions to Festschriften; the Parmenides essay is an undelivered part of the lectures published by Niemeyer in 1954.

8 *Was heißt Denken?* (Paola-Ludovika Coriando, 2002)

First published by Niemeyer in 1954, these lectures (part one: WS 1951/52 and part two: SS 1952) are Heidegger's first lectures at Freiburg after the war. The purpose of the first part is to learn to think by attending to what most needs to be thought, namely, the fact that we do not yet think. The claim that we do not think "yet" echoes Nietzsche's remark that "the desert grows," since Nietzsche recognized the need for moving past the prevailing representational thinking of the "last man" to the free-thinking of the "superman," liberated from the spirit of vengefulness. Though Nietzsche's thinking remains caught in the fog of a will without end, he teaches us that what needs to be thought is the relation between being and the human being.

Taking center stage in the second part of the lectures is what we are called on to think so that, as the ones thinking, we are who we are. Following review of the primordial nearness of thinking to memory (*Gedächtnis*), devoutly commemorating (*Andenken*), and thanking (*Danken*), the lectures turn to thinking before it developed into the *logos* of logic. Parmenides' saying: "it is necessary to say and think that beings are" (*das Seiende ist*) reveals what calls for thinking: the being of beings or, more precisely, their duality (*Zwiefalt*), the way that things present come to be present in an unconcealment that, by contrast, itself remains concealed.

9 *Wegmarken* (2004)

First published in 1967 (expanded edition, 1978), this volume is the fifth major collection of essays Heidegger publishes after the war. Spanning slightly more than five decades, the collection contains four entries completed in the 1920s:

(1) 1919–21 notes to Jaspers' *Psychology of Worldviews*;

(2) the lecture "Phenomenology and Theology," identifying theology as an ontic science, rooted in faith, in contrast but parallel to phenomenology's ontological concerns;

(3) an excerpt from the last Marburg lecture, examining the clue (the ego) to how Leibniz determines the being of beings as the unifying urge (*Drang als Einigung*);

(4) "What is Metaphysics?"—the 1929 inaugural address probing the question of "nothing" as "the genuinely metaphysical question of the being of beings," where the nothing, revealed in angst, is no particular being (*Seiendes*) and yet belongs to being (*Sein*) (113, 120);

(5) Heidegger's 1929 contribution to a Festschrift for Edmund Husserl, "The Essence of Ground," in which Dasein's freedom as transcendence is identified as the ground of ground (165).

The next group of entries, all indicative of the shift in Heidegger's thinking away from the project of fundamental ontology, stem from the 1930s and 1940s:

(6) "On the Essence of Truth" (a lecture first given in 1930 but only published in 1943) was subsequently regarded by Heidegger as transitional, "carrying out in its decisive steps (leading from truth as correctness to ek-sistent freedom and from the latter to truth as concealment and errancy) a transformation of questioning that is part of the overturning of metaphysics" (199);

(7) "Plato's Doctrine of Truth" (stemming from a WS 1930/31 lecture, but not published until 1943) interprets Plato's treatment of *aletheia* in the Cave Allegory as the beginning of Western metaphysics and humanism (233f);

(8) "On the Essence and Concept of *physis* in Aristotle's *Physics*, B, 1" (written in 1939, first published in 1958) demonstrates Aristotle's closeness to his predecessors in "the fundamental book of Western philosophy" (240);

(9) the "Letter on Humanism" (first published with "Plato's Doctrine of Truth" in 1947) addresses the question of humanism in the light of Sartre's existentialism, the history of "humanism," and Heidegger's own displacement of the traditional notion of a rational animal and "master of beings" with the conception of Dasein as "the place of the truth of being in the midst of beings" and as "the shepherd of being," (332, 342);

(10) and (11) the 1943 "Afterword" and the 1949 "Introduction" to "What is Metaphysics?" in which Heidegger contends that the latter question "springs from a thinking that has already entered into the overturning of metaphysics (301, 364).

The final group of entries, published between 1955 and 1961, include:

(12) "On the Question of Being" (1955), a "meditation on the essence of nihilism," initiated by reflections on the essay "On the Line" by Heidegger's long-time friend Ernst Jünger. In order to make visual the point that the question of the essence of being dissipates as long as the language of metaphysics dominates (405), Heidegger introduces the contrivance of crossing out the word "being": "The crossing out first defends against the almost ineradicable habit of representing 'being' as something standing for itself and then occasionally coming up to human beings opposite them." But the cross itself also "points to the four regions of the fourfold and their being gathered in the locale of the crossing-through" (410f).

(13) "Hegel and the Greeks" (1958) where Heidegger shows that, while unsurpassed in certain respects, Hegel's way of experiencing history philosophically in terms of the essence of being as absolute subjectivity is, thanks to these terms of the experience, unable to think the *aletheia* that underlies this history from the outset (441–4).

(14) "Kant's Thesis on Being" (1961) where Heidegger revisits the thesis treated in his 1927 lectures (GA 24): "being is not a predicate."

10 *Der Satz vom Grund* (Petra Jaeger, 1997)

In this text, first published in 1957, Heidegger elaborates Leibniz's principle of sufficient reason (psr) initially as a principle of entities, entailing the modern equation of what is with whatever can be represented with a sufficient reason to a subject. Although the principle has "interposed itself" between the human being and its world (37), it is left unexplained (ungrounded) by science and philosophy alike. Without being able to justify itself or explain the essence of a ground, the psr (so conceived) gives modern humanity an illusory sense of empowerment, at the cost of thinking being itself: its contingency, uniqueness, historicity, and groundlessness. Grounding the psr is no entity, but being itself, though the grounding here is unlike any grounding of one entity by another. For only by itself withdrawing, can being present itself exclusively as the appearance of the objectiveness of objects, i.e. (particularly in the Kantian appropriation of the psr), "in the realm of the subjectivity of reason" (118, 130f). In order to appreciate the full import of the *Satz vom Grund*, it is necessary *to make the leap* from reading the psr as a principle of entities into reading it as a way of saying being and, thereby, *to listen* to it as a musical set, namely, as the accord between being and ground (where "leap" and "set" are additional senses of *Satz*). For in saying that no entity is without a reason, we allude to the fact that being, itself no entity, is without reason. Grounding every entity, being is itself ungrounded, an abyss (*Abgrund*), a point already flagged in Angelus Silesius' verse "the rose is without a why."

11 *Identität und Differenz* (2006)

This volume's first entry is the 1955 address "What is that—philosophy?" Given the question's Greek origin, Heidegger makes it into a conversation with the Greeks, tracing the dominant conception of philosophy to Aristotle's metaphysics while also suggesting a positive sense of philosophy as attuned correspondence to the being of beings. The second entry contains two addresses first published together in 1957 as *Identity and Difference*: "The Principle of Identity" and "The Onto-Theo-Logical Constitution of Metaphysics." In the former Heidegger links his conception of the identity of being and thinking in the *Ereignis* with a reading of Parmenides, in stark contrast to German idealism's interpretation of identity as a self-mediating unity; in the latter he contrasts his conception of difference with Hegel's absolute concept as well as the standards and characters of their conversations with the history of thinking. The volume also contains the published version of the 1949 Bremen lecture "The Turn" and the 1957 Freiburg address "Basic Principles of Thinking," both in versions slightly revised for their initial publications a few years later as well as letters to William Richardson (1962) and Takehiko Kojima (1973).

12 *Unterwegs zur Sprache* (1985)

First published by Neske in 1959, this work is the fourth major collection of essays published by Heidegger after the war. Not an object about which we can speak, language *as experienced* withdraws from us; indeed, our experience of it is mainly indirect, as when we are at a loss for words. We have to be underway to language (hence, the collection's title) because language, while never possessed by us, is not outside us and, like us, it is underway, unfinished, and historical. The experience of language is one of thinking, taking place in a region shared with poetry, a common theme of these essays. Since poetry is the primordial language, the first two entries "Language" and "Language in the Poem" interpret Georg Trakl's poetry, while the fourth and fifth entries ("The Essence of Language" and "The Word") take up Stefan George's poetic experience of language, expressed in the poem "The Word"—with its cryptic concluding verse "where words break off no thing may be." Along with its reading of Trakl, the opening entry claims that language speaks and, in doing so, calls things into their own by calling them into their difference with the fourfold of the world. The third entry is a "Dialogue on Language" with Professor Tezuka of Tokyo, revisiting Heidegger's early hermeneutics and connecting it with the twofold. The final entry, "The Way to Language," attempts to come closer to language, not as a "work of the human spirit" (Humboldt), but rather precisely *as* language, via consideration of the *saying* that, residing in *Ereignis*, is essential to language.

13 *Aus der Erfahrung des Denkens*
(Hermann Heidegger, second edition, 2002)

This sprawling collection contains many short pieces, from a 1910 paean to Abraham a Santa Clara to a greeting, composed a few days before Heidegger's death. The collection also contains "Creative Landscape: Why Do We Stay in the Province?" (1933), written after refusing a second invitation to Berlin; the 1944/45 "Conversation on Letting-be," first published in 1959 with "Letting

Be" (*Gelassenheit*); "The Thinker as Poet" (*Aus der Erfahrung des Denkens*, 1947) and "The Pathway" (*Der Feldweg*, 1949). Other notable entries include correspondence with Emil Staiger on a Mörike verse, writings on Hebel, an address on "Language and Homeland," the essay "Art and Space," and appreciative remarks on Igor Strawinsky and, especially, René Char.

14 *Zur Sache des Denkens* (2006)

This volume's first part, published by Niemeyer in 1969, contains the 1962 address "Time and Being" and "protocols" (transcripts of the proceedings) of a seminar on the address, the 1964 address "The End of Philosophy and the Task of Thinking," and "My Way into Phenomenology," a 1963 contribution to a collection honoring Hermann Niemeyer. The second part contains seven short parts of texts, ranging from Heidegger's announcement of SZ and a letter to Husserl in 1927 to notes to a 1969 oral presentation before a small circle, following a reading of "My Way into Phenomenology."

"Time and Being" revisits the theme from the third, unpublished part of SZ under that title, albeit from the post-SZ standpoint where the center of gravity for thinking time and being is the "appropriating event" (*Ereignis*). Two distinctive characteristics of the latter are flagged, its withdrawal and the way it brings human beings into their own, i.e. human beings who take up (*vernehmen*) being and remain steadfast in authentic time (14: 28). The "end of philosophy" is the consummation of metaphysics, as its inquiry into the being of beings issues into the complete reign of sciences whose approach is fundamentally technological. Whereas this end of thinking from its first beginning in the West is the culmination of the thinking that entertains only what is afforded by the clearing, the task of thinking is precisely to think the clearing itself (88, 90).

15 *Seminare* (Curd Ochwadt, 2005)

This volume contains "protocols" of the WS 1966/67 Heraclitus seminar, held with Eugen Fink and separately published in 1970; the protocols of four seminars (three at Le Thor, the last at Zähringen), translated from *Questions IV* (Paris, 1976) and separately published as *Vier Seminare* (1977); and a brief appendix containing a 1951 invited discussion (*Aussprache*) on the theme "... poetically man dwells ..." In the Heraclitus seminar Heidegger and Fink are the main interlocutors, frequently differing (Fink proceeds from fire to the logos, Heidegger in the opposite direction, as Heidegger sees it), yet with the single aim, not of making any thematic contribution to Heraclitus-research, but of "determining the matter for thinking in conversation with Heraclitus" and doing so in a non-anachronistic way (124, 141, 181f).

The first Le Thor seminar (1966) discusses Heraclitus on logos and the cosmos, the final two (1968, 1969) look critically to Hegel and Kant respectively for access to being (albeit with excursions into the danger of the ontological difference, world-views, Marx's thinking, technology, and the nothing), while the Zähringen seminar (1973) looks similarly to Husserl's doctrine of categorial intuition, and the relation between consciousness and Dasein. In the final Le Thor seminar Heidegger identifies the "profoundest sense of being as *letting* [*lassen*]," glossing the German "there is" (*es gibt*) as a way of saying that "being" stands for and, hence, *should give way to* "giving" or "letting" beings be (363f). Of the seminars' many clarifying retrospectives, perhaps the most notable is the "topology of being," a differentiation of the three main steps on the path of Heidegger's thinking. In SZ the question of "the sense of being" dominates, where the sense is to be understood from the standpoint of the realm of projection that the understanding of being unfolds. However, because the question of being's sense lends itself too readily to understanding the projection (as Sartre does) as a human accomplishment, a structure of subjectivity, it is replaced by "the truth of being." In order to avoid any (mis-)construal of truth as correctness, the truth of being needs to be placed, giving rise to the theme of the "place of being" (334f, 344).

16 *Reden und andere Zeugnisse eines Lebensweges 1910–1976* (Hermann Heidegger, 2000)

This volume is a collection of 290 entries, most no more than a page or two in length, including addresses, poems, announcements, letters, and reviews. The collection is divided into seven chrono-logically differentiated parts, and an appendix.

   I. Student and Dozent (1910–22) includes an informative vita prepared for an application for a position in Göttingen; see *Becoming Heidegger*, 106ff;

   II. Ordinary professor in Marburg and Freiburg (1923–33) includes letters explaining his refusal to accept a position in Berlin, a letter to Hannah Arendt regarding his alleged "anti-Semitism," and a telling letter (March 30, 1933) to Elisabeth Blochman relating the impact of recent events on him;

  III. Rector of Freiburg University (1933–4) includes numerous short entries (many clearly establishing Heidegger's enthusiastic support for National Socialism), the Rectoral Address "The Self-Assertion of the German University" (107–17), a recommendation for Paul Kristeller, and letters concerning yet another, rejected offer of a position in Berlin;

  IV. Professor in the Third Reich (1934–45) includes two lengthy entries: "The German University" (elaborated from perspective of "the national socialistic revolution," 285–307) and "The Contemporary Situation and the Future Task of German Philosophy" (316–34);

   V. Cleansing and Teaching Ban (1945–50) includes "facts and thoughts," some defensive, on his rectorate as well as on the repercussions of his resignation (372–94); his "application for reinstatement," outlining his reasons for joining the National Socialist Party and his relation to it after 1933 (397–404); "What is being itself?" (423f); and a letter to Marcuse, noting his "political error" and reasons for not apologizing (430f);

  VI. Pensioner (1950–1) includes entries acknowledging his "political error" (452f, 459) and a sense of "shame for what transpired against Jews" (469) yet also repeatedly denying accusations of anti-Semitism, mistreatment of Husserl, or membership in the SA or SS;

 VII. Emeritus (1951–76) contains the 1955 address "Gelassenheit" (517–29; translated "Discourse on Thinking"), pieces on

Hebel's poetry and on art, a letter to Hans-Peter Hempel on the situation of his rectorate and resignation, the 1965 address "On the Question of the Determination of the Matter of Thinking" (620–33), and, finally, two much-discussed interviews: the 1966 *Spiegel* magazine interview (652–83) and the 1969 interview with Richard Wisser (702–10).

The appendix contains newspaper reports and publications of frequently cited yet unsubstantiated remarks (three entries from 1930, three from 1933, and one from 1958).

Lectures (1919–44)

Marburg lectures (1923–8)

17 *Einführung in die phänomenologische Forschung* (WS 1923/24) (second edition, 2006)

How does Aristotle's theme, the world and being in the world, give way to consciousness as the theme of Husserl's phenomenology? Reviewing Husserl's criticisms of naturalism and historicism, Heidegger contends that care about securing known knowledge— a flight from being in the world itself—accounts for centering phenomenological investigation on consciousness. Heidegger traces the dominance of this care to Descartes. Though Descartes' philosophy marks a "turning point" toward the current "dominance of theoretical knowing as the genuine measure of all knowledge," Descartes is "thoroughly medieval." Heidegger accordingly devotes an entire chapter to the foundations of Descartes' determinations of the *res cogitans* in scholastic ontology (Aquinas). In the third and concluding part, Heidegger outlines the "fundamental differences" between Descartes and Husserl as a prelude to indicating their connection. The focus on consciousness out of a care about securing known knowledge blocks Husserl, as it does Descartes, from possibilities of access to the being of the *res cogitans*, the being (Dasein) of who is conscious. Charging Husserl with "Angst in the face of Dasein," Heidegger concludes with a plea for positive interpretations of *agathon* and Dasein's ways of fleeing itself.

18 *Grundbegriffe der aristotelischen Philosophie* (SS 1924) (Mark Michalski, 2002)

These lectures demonstrate how closely Heidegger's efforts to express Aristotle's thinking in German merge into the conceptual apparatus of existential ontology. Heidegger interprets Aristotle's basic concepts by returning to concrete human existence, its being-in-the-world and ability to speak with its world. He plumbs Aristotle's *Rhetoric, Nicomachean Ethics*, and—to a lesser extent—his *Politics, Metaphysics*, and *De anima* for accounts of these and other themes (e.g. the good, belief, *ethos, psyche, pathos*, fear, and *hexis*). The concluding part focuses on a theme "of fundamental significance for the entire ontology" (328), Aristotle's investigation of motion (*kinesis*) in terms of *entelecheia, energeia, steresis, dunamis, poiesis*, and *pathesis*.

19 *Platon: Sophistes* (WS 1924/25) (Ingeborg Schüßler, 1992)

Assuming that Aristotle understood Plato and that the fundamental question for Greek philosophy is the question of the truth regarding being, Heideggger begins these lectures with glosses of Aristotle's accounts of how we arrive at the truth: the *Nicomachean Ethics'* account of the intellectual virtues and the *Metaphysics'* account of the genesis of *sophia*. This "introductory part" (approximately a third of the lectures) concludes with an argument for the primacy of *sophia* over *phronesis*—which amounts to a criticism of Plato since he regards the science of the political (in effect, the domain of *phronesis*) as the highest (135f). Though both are *nous* (ways of disclosing without *logos*), *sophia* abides by what is complete and supreme, thereby enjoying a self-sufficiency, free from the bond to others, that praxis-oriented *phronesis* lacks (163f, 167, 171, 176f). In a transitional section, Heidegger notes that "*the basic sense of the platonic dialectic*" consists in moving beyond the idle chatter of sophistry to the matters themselves. As such, however, it is directed at something beyond it, namely, a genuine, more primordial discernment (*Anschauung, noein*), though Plato himself does not reach this level (197f; see, however, 522–33). Thus, while

Plato distinguishes dialectics from sophistry, Aristotle distinguishes philosophy from dialectics and sophistry (216).

Having set the "thematic field" of the *Sophist*, Heidegger works through the dialogue, at times line by line. In the first section, he elaborates the underlying unity of the various definitions of the sophist. In this context, largely based upon the *Phaedrus*, Heidegger also discusses how Plato's relation to rhetoric, while undeveloped, sets the stage for Aristotle's *Rhetoric* (337ff).

Yet the main issue, grasping the sophist—the master of the *techne* of error, illusion, and deception—requires coming to terms with non-being and herein lies Plato's major achievement, his "destruction" of the Parmenidean tradition (352, 394–404, 412ff, 434; see 574: "The Sophist is the facticity of *me on* [non-being] itself"). For Plato appreciates that the "not" refers, not to sheer nothingness, but to otherness (*heteron*) (476). Otherness thus provides the key to the differential unity (*kiononia*) of the many as well as the five *megista gene* themselves, though Plato himself stops short of developing the relational character (*pros ti*) that his differential unity presupposes (542–57, 566f).

20 *Prolegomena zur Geschichte des Zeitbegriffs* (SS 1925) (Petra Jaeger, third edition, 1994)

The preparatory part of these lectures reviews the three decisive discoveries of Husserl's phenomenology (intentionality, categorial intuition, primordial sense of a priori), before advancing central criticisms of Husserl's phenomenology (failure to question the sense of being in general that it supposes and the sense of being of the human in particular). The first section of the main part gives a preliminary description of the field in which the phenomenon of time becomes visible, a description that coincides with elaborating the question of being through an explication of Dasein, i.e. "who we are, the ones asking" (201). The explication gives previews of several themes of SZ, e.g. everydayness, being-in-the-world, the existentials, uncanniness, and angst. The last section moves from a phenomenological interpretation of death and conscience to the conclusion: "Being, in which Dasein can be authentically in its entirety as being-ahead-of-itself, is *time*" (442).

21 *Logik: Die Frage nach der Wahrheit* (WS 1925/26)
(Walter Biemel, second edition, 1995)

Review of the roots of Husserl's critique of psychologism leads to the question of the connection between the truth of propositions and that of intuition. Looking to Aristotle's texts for answers, Heidegger introduces the "as-structure" at hermeneutical and apophantical levels, as he explores the conditions of falsity in terms of Aristotle's analysis of *logos apophantikos*. The analysis supposes at root the presence of beings, thus relying upon an unexamined connection between being and time. Prefiguring themes of SZ, part two looks for the conditions of the possibility of falsity in temporality, albeit the temporality of care as "the basic mode of being of Dasein" (220). The rest of the volume turns to major interpretations of time (Aristotle, Hegel, Bergson) as a prelude to a searching interpretation of Kant's conception of time. Returning to the theme of the first half of the lectures, Heidegger concludes with the observation that assertions and, with them, logic ("the most imperfect of philosophical disciplines") are founded upon "the temporality of Dasein itself" (415).

22 *Die Grundbegriffe der antiken Philosophie* (SS 1926) (Franz-Karl Blust, 2004)

These lectures examine the "basic concepts that have not only ... decisively determined all subsequent philosophy but have made Western science possible at all" (1). After distinguishing philosophy as a critical science of being from positive sciences of entities, Heidegger gives a general introduction to ancient philosophy in Part One, following Aristotle's anachronistic leads in *Metaphysics*, I (32). Part Two discusses pre-Platonic philosophy, Plato's "age-less" philosophy (142), and Aristotle's philosophy. Often less than complete sentences and, even then, more expository than interpretive, the lecture notes provide basic information about the ancient philosophers' views, reliable editions and useful commentaries, and translations of Greek terms. The final section sketches Aristotle's accounts of *ousia* and analogy, categories, being as true, *dunamis* and *energeia*, and *psyche*—aiming at "an *ontology of life*" (184).

23 *Geschichte der Philosophie von Thomas von Aquin bis Kant* (WS 1926/27) (Helmut Vetter, 2006)

Though mainly expositional, these lectures contain occasional criticisms (77, 106, 166, 204f) and place the roots of modern philosophy squarely in "medieval Thomistic ontology" (1ff, 6f, 101). The introduction glosses the new cosmological problems that arise with modern mathematics and mathematical physics. It also contrasts both prescientific with scientific existence and positive science with philosophy, conceived as a critical science of being, a transcendental philosophy, and a phenomenological ontology. The lectures themselves are divided into five, successively shorter sections: (1) Aquinas' philosophical treatments of truth, God, eternity, and human nature; (2) Descartes' *Meditations*, (3) Spinoza's *Ethics*, (4) Leibniz's paths to his monadology and theodicy, and (5) the work of Christian Wolff and Christian August Crusius, marking the transition to Kant.

24 *Die Grundprobleme der Phänomenologie* (SS 1927) (second edition, 1989)

This volume reviews four theses, beginning with Kant's thesis that being is no real predicate, a thesis that, despite recognizing the difference between reality and existence, fails to explain their connection. Medieval ontology proffers such an explanation with the second thesis, i.e. the claim that the distinction between what-something-is (*essentia*) and its being-on-hand (*Vorhandensein*) constitutes what it means to be. Glossing Aquinas' real distinction, Scotus' modal distinction, and above all Suarez's distinction of reason, Heidegger contends that Dasein's producing behavior towards entities is the tacit horizon of understanding for *essentia* and *existentia* (148–67). Because the second thesis is unable to say who (rather than what) Dasein is, it leads to the third thesis that nature and spirit make up the basic ways of being. Heidegger examines this thesis of modern ontology in terms of Kant's differentiation of the ego as person from objects in nature, faulting the account for relying upon the ontology of things on-hand *within* the world to characterize human existence as being-in-the-world. That modern difference points to the need for a unitary conception of being, the lead-in to the fourth thesis, viz. that every entity may be addressed in terms of the copula. Reviewing views of Aristotle, Hobbes, J. S. Mill, and Lotze, Heidegger charges that they miss the truth of existence (Dasein's disclosure of things) that actual use of the copula supposes (310).

This conclusion introduces an attempt to show that temporality provides the sense of being in general. After reviewing Aristotle's analysis of time and its limitations, Heidegger returns to the notion of the primordial time constituting Dasein's existence, arguing that it grounds the ontological difference and, with it "two basic types of science": "objectification of beings as positive science; objectification of being as ... transcendental science, ontology, philosophy" (465f).

25 *Phänomenologische Interpretation von Kants Kritik der reinen Vernunft* (WS 1927/28) (Ingtraud Görland, 1977)

These lectures give a close reading of the first quarter of Kant's *Critique of Pure Reason*, namely, the Prefaces, Introduction, Transcendental Aesthetic, the Idea of Transcendental Logic, and the Analytic of Concepts. In contrast to Heidegger's book on Kant (GA 3), these lectures devote little space to the schematisms. Heidegger also spends far more time in the lectures developing phenomenological interpretations of Kant's doctrine of intuitions and of concepts (investing intuitions with a complexity typically assigned only to their synthesis with concepts). Confronting Neo-Kantian epistemological interpretations of Kant's first Critique, Heidegger develops his "ontological interpretation" as the point of its "Copernican turn," while also charging Kant with vacillating between ontological demands and merely securing the methodological presuppositions of ontic science (10, 51–6, 61). These lectures also contain an extensive reading of "the productive synthesis of the imagination" as the common root of sentience and understanding (417f), the origin of the categories (270–92), the presupposition of the unity of apperception (410f, 421), and, hence, the source of the categories' objective validity or, equivalently, the foundation of the transcendental deduction in both versions (368, 403–23).

26 *Metaphysische Anfangsgründe der Logik im Ausgang von Leibniz* (SS 1928)
(Klaus Held, second edition, 1990)

The first part of these lectures attempts to grasp the metaphysical grounds of logic by breaking down Leibniz's doctrine of judgment to its metaphysical foundations. Heidegger discusses Leibniz's account of the structure of judgment, ideas of truth, knowledge, and monads, with a view to showing that logic and its rules, far from being "free-floating," have essentially metaphysical foundations. The second part of the lectures examines the principle of sufficient reason as a metaphysical principle, i.e. nothing is without a ground because ground is inherent to the being of beings. Yet ground here is not mere *ratio*. The truth of assertions is founded in a more primordial sense of truth, the uncovering of things as part of Dasein's dealings with them, which in turn is grounded upon Dasein's transcendence or, equivalently, its freedom, its being-in-the-world and the temporality constituting it. Not confined to nature or beings, Dasein is always already freely passing beyond them to being, as it exists ecstatically, i.e. futurally for the sake of its world and, thus, for itself. This freedom is the origin of ground. The volume also contains a list of SZ's guiding principles (including the reason for the sexual neutrality of Dasein). In an appendix Heidegger introduces the notion of a "metontology" that, along with fundamental ontology, forms metaphysics.

Freiburg Lectures (1928–44)

27 *Einleitung in die Philosophie* (WS 1928/29) (Otto Saame and Ina Saame-Speidel, second edition, 2001)

Squarely identifying being human with philosophizing, these lectures introduce philosophizing by contrasting it with science and the promulgation of a world-view. Transforming the openness of being-here, science rests upon an implicit projection of what

entities are, e.g. as "material things, called 'physical nature,'"
a projection that transcends entities and thus enables scientific knowledge of them (189, 206f). Philosophy is, by contrast,
"explicit transcending," retrieving what we (and science) already
understand (216f). Thus, philosophy underlies science, and their
difference is the difference between ontological and ontic truths
(209f).

Philosophy does not, in a corresponding way, underlie a world-
view. After reviewing conceptions of world-views (Dilthey, Jaspers,
Scheler) and world (ancient, Christian, Kant), Heidegger returns
to the notion of transcendence as freedom, characterizing it as
the undefined (*halt-los*)—and unsheltered—being-in-the-world that
refers to factical possibilities of defining itself, i.e. world-views.
Heidegger singles out two closely related world-views, the mythical
world-view where Dasein defines itself by taking shelter (*Bergung*)
in a higher power and the world-view of the "self-defining stance"
(*Haltung*) where Dasein adopts a stance of action and, eventually,
science. While both world-views can degenerate, philosophizing (in
the sense of "explicit transcending") is "the forming of the world-
view as a self-defining stance," though it is neither the task nor the
aim of philosophy to establish and promulgate a world-view (376,
381, 396f).

28 *Der deutsche Idealismus (Fichte, Schelling, Hegel) und die philosophische Problemlage der Gegenwart* (SS 1929) (Claudius Strube, second edition, 2011)

After arguing that the basic tendencies of current philosophy
(anthropology and metaphysics) are united in the metaphysics
of finite Dasein, Heidegger turns to the metaphysical efforts of
German idealists who attempt to master that finitude and make
it disappear rather than come to terms with it (46f). The lectures
contain Heidegger's only sustained interpretation of Fichte, specifically, his Doctrine of Science and the absolute identity and activity
of the I (52–182). This interpretation is followed by brief remarks
on Schelling's philosophy of nature and a discussion of Hegel's
attempt to develop the idea of the absolute in all seriousness,
detached from the one-sidedness of the idea of an absolute I or

nature, but where both are elevated to the totality of determinacy (198f, 208f, 216).

29/30 *Die Grundbegriffe der Metaphysik. Welt—Endlichkeit—Einsamkeit* (WS 1929/30)
(third edition, 2004)

Inasmuch as metaphysics, despite its troubled history, concerns something ultimate that is irreducible to science, art, or religion, the possibility and necessity of its questions have to emerge from a grounding mood. To this end, Heidegger devotes the first part of the lectures to awakening a grounding mood in our contemporary Dasein: boredom. In profound boredom the insignificance of beings as a whole, i.e. the world's emptiness, announces itself, but also thereby its unexplored possibilities. The second part of the lectures is devoted to the question "What is the world?" Taking his bearings from the sense in which a human being appears both to be part of a world and to have a world, Heidegger attempts to understand what the world is by comparing stones (material objects) as worldless, animals as world-poor, and humans as world-forming. What links the lectures' two parts is the fact that animals do not have a world, do not relate to beings *as* beings, and, hence, cannot be profoundly bored. The lectures conclude with an analysis of what is denied animals but inherent to being human, i.e. world-forming, the world as the openness of beings, and the as-structure as a feature of that openness, underling assertions and their truth.

31 *Vom Wesen der menschlichen Freiheit* (SS 1930)
(Hartmut Tietjen, second edition, 1994)

In these lectures on Kant's conception of freedom, Heidegger aims to demonstrate that the question of what beings are is based upon the question of human freedom—rather than vice versa. After recounting how Kant grounds the notion of positive practical freedom, namely, autonomy of the will, in the spontaneity of transcendental freedom (KrV B 561f) and how he construes this spontaneity as a cause of a sort completely different from the causality of nature, Heidegger points out that the question of causality entails the question of movement as a basic determination of beings, something that Kant "utterly fails" to question (31). Rather than locate the question of freedom, along with human beings, in metaphysical answers to the leading question (what are beings?), Heidegger embeds the question of what there is in the fundamental question of the essence of freedom (not as a property of human beings, but as the ground of Dasein). He then turns to Kant's "two paths to freedom." The first path is chartered in the "Analogies of Experience" and the transcendental idea of an unconditioned causality that emerges from the resolution of the third Antinomy. Following the second path—one of Heidegger's few forays into Kant's practical philosophy—Heidegger glosses practical freedom (pure will) as the condition of the possibility of the moral law (categorical imperative). Despite this unorthodox gloss, he considers both paths dead-ends insofar as Kant gets things backwards by attempting to ground freedom in causality (191f, 213, 246, 265, 299f).

32 *Hegels Phänomenologie des Geistes* (WS 1930/31)
(Ingtraud Görland, third edition, 1997)

These lectures on the opening chapters of Hegel's *Phenomenology of Spirit* contain Heidegger's first sustained treatment of the work. The lectures are transitional, as can be gathered from the fact that, after characterizing the phenomenology of spirit as "the fundamental ontology of the absolute ontology and, that means, the onto-logy in general," Heidegger immediately adds that it is "the endstage of any possible justification of ontology" (203f). Contending that the system of science in the *Phenomenology of Spirit* is the heart and soul of Hegel's philosophy, Heidegger contrasts this "radical completion" of the Greek conception of philosophy as science with his own claim that philosophy is not a science—a clear departure from his portrayal of philosophy as the science of being a few years earlier. While cognizant that, like Hegel, he distances himself from Kant's transcendental philosophy (114, 169f), Heidegger highlights their differences. In contrast to Hegel's conception of being as infinite, a conception accessible to absolute knowing only at the cost of time, Heidegger conceives time as "the primordial essence of being" (17f, 92f, 209ff). So, too Heidegger contrasts his time-oriented questioning as "ontochrony" from

Hegel's ontology (144, 211f). At fault in part is the inadequacy of Hegel's inherited (even if dialectical) grasp of the finite (55f, 101–14).

In addition to characterizing Hegel's philosophy as 'onto-theo-logy' to expose its Aristotelian roots, Heidegger introduces the expanded term 'onto-theo-ego-logy' to capture its distinctively modern character (140–4, 183). Yet in the course of realizing metaphysics' claim to utter universality and explicability, Hegel follows tradition by not posing the *fundamental* question of what is meant by saying that these various entities exist. Instead, in the constant and complete presence of the development of things, an old albeit refurbished answer is presupposed.

33 *Aristoteles, Metaphysik, Theta, 1–3, Von Wesen und Wirklichkeit der Kraft* (SS 1931)
(Heinrich Hüni, third edition, 2006)

According to Aristotle we speak of being in multiple ways, namely, being contingent, being of a particular sort (category), being true, and being potential or actual (*dunamis* and *energeia*). The context of the task of these lectures—to interpret the investigation of *dunamis* and *energeia* in *Metaphysics*, Theta, 1–3—is the obscurity of the non-generic (hence, non-Platonic), analogical unity of being, ranging over these multiple ways of speaking of being. Heidegger challenges the medieval assumption (still alive in Brentano and Jaeger) that the meaning of *ousia* as substance (the first category) is the basis for the analogical ways of speaking about being, not only across the remaining categories, but also across the four ways mentioned above. At the same time the analogy of being is not a solution, "not even an actual working out of the question," but instead the name for a hopeless impasse (46). Against the backdrop of this impasse, the lectures examine Aristotle's investigation of *dunamis kata kinesin* (force in terms of movement) and its forms, especially capability (*Vermögen*) as force with *logos*. In this context, with a passing reference to the analysis of tools in SZ, Heidegger provides a discussion of production and work as the source of the grounding conceptions of Greek philosophy (130–48).

34 *Vom Wesen der Wahrheit. Zu Platons Höhlengleichnis und Theätet* (WS 1931/32) (Hermann Mörchen, 1997)

The first part of these lectures looks for clues to the essence of truth (*aletheia*) in Plato's allegory of the cave in the *Republic*, Book VII. Heidegger examines the allegory's four stages (the situation in the cave, liberation within the cave, liberation outside the cave, and the liberated prisoner's return to the cave) and the idea of the good in relation to unhiddenness, on the way to concluding that the allegory reveals a neglect of the hiddenness in the experience of *aletheia*, "forfeiting the power of its fundamental meaning." In the second part of the lectures, Heidegger turns to Plato's accounts of knowledge as perception and true opinion in the *Theaetetus*, with the aim of establishing that for Plato the *pseudos*—i.e. an untruth distinct from hiddenness (*lethe*)—is the incorrectness of *logos*, understood as a proposition. As a result, Heidegger charges, Plato interprets truth as a correct proposition, effectively suppressing its primordial essence as unhiddenness and the fact that hiddenness is essential to "the inner possibility of truth."

35 *Der Anfang der abendländischen Philosophie (Anaximander und Parmenides)* (SS 1932) (Peter Trawny, 2011)

These lectures return to Western thinking's beginning, not as it has been handed down, but as something hidden yet closer to us than anything else. The search for the beginning coincides with "*the end of metaphysics* on the basis of questioning, in a primordial way, the 'sense' (truth) of historical being" (1, 40ff, 237). The lectures are divided into three parts: (1) a close reading of the Anaximander fragment as articulating the essential power of being and its difference from beings (22, 32, 47), (2) an intermediate consideration addressing our unrelatedness to our beginning—a self-deception that only Nietzsche could ascertain (45f)—and recommencing the originary beginning by re-asking the question of being "as the ground of the possibility of our existence," i.e. our freedom (100), and (3) an interpretation of Parmenides' proem, including glosses of the "three paths" announced by the "goddess of unhiddenness," the unspoken fourth path (129), the "negative" and "positive" aspects of being, especially being as one (*hen*) (146f), and being as presence as such and unhiddenness (182).

36/37 *Sein und Wahrheit* (SS 1933, WS 1933/34)
(Hartmut Tietjen, 2001)

Coinciding with Heidegger's tenure as rector, these lectures demonstrate just how readily Heidegger aligns the fundamental question of his philosophy with the "national socialist revolution." Seriously asking philosophy's fundamental question coincides with "coming to know the spiritual–political mission of the German people" (4ff). "We stand and fall with the *will to know and spirit*" (263). Philosophers are the guardians of the state, with the "task of watching that those ruling [*Herrschaft*] and the state's ruling order are thoroughly under the sway of philosophy, not some sort of system but … the deepest and widest knowledge of the human being" (194; see, too, 208–13). While short on details, such remarks reveal that he considers his philosophy to be in the service of National Socialism but precisely as the source of knowledge and leadership indispensable to it.

In the first part of these lectures, as a means of finding the way into the fundamental question, Heidegger proposes a confrontation with Hegel's philosophy (14). The confrontation is rather spare, perhaps due to his duties as rector. Following a gloss of the modern transformation of metaphysics (jointly determined by Descartes' mathematical method, Christianity, and Baumgarten), the lectures conclude with expository notes and the question of the extent to which Hegel's metaphysics is the culmination of Western metaphysics (elsewhere Heidegger tells us that it is the beginning of the culmination).

The winter semester lectures set the stage for the final battle between the originary and later conceptions of truth (*aletheia*) in Plato by reviewing the Heraclitean *polemos* as the essence of beings and glossing the essence of language. The remainder of the lectures reprises Heidegger's interpretations of Plato's Cave Allegory and the *Theaetetus* from two years earlier (GA 34).

38 *Logik als die Frage nach dem Wesen der Sprache* (SS 1934) (Günther Seubold, 1998)

The overriding premise of these lectures is the necessity of understanding logic on the basis of language and not vice versa. After rejecting standard arguments for the value of traditional logic, Heidegger states his intention of undermining (*erschüttern*) it from the ground up. For traditional logic—and any "philosophy of language" oriented to it—tends to regard language as a particular domain of objects, as a mere means of expression, or as secondary to thinking. Heidegger takes the question of language, unhinged from these prejudices, as the "leading question" of logic, one that entails questions of the essence of human beings (including the "decision" who "we" are as a "people") and of history. In the second and final part, Heidegger argues that "primordial time" is the basis for all these questions. Elaborating the experience of primordial time as the experience of our "vocation" (*Bestimmung*), Heidegger discusses how a people's vocation explodes the concept of subject.

39 *Hölderlins Hymnen "Germanien" und "Der Rhein"* (WS 1934/35) (Susanne Ziegler, 1999)

In the first part of these lectures, the first on Hölderlin's poetry, Heidegger attempts to grasp the poem "Germanien" thoughtfully (*denkerisch*), not by assuming some philosophical criterion but by entering into the poetry's "power." That power derives from a basic mood, the holy mourning at the flight of the old gods. Hölderlin founds this mood "in the historical existence of our people," an existence yet to come. Far from hardening into despair, the mood allows the German people to endure "the dire straits of its godlessness," to find itself belonging in a renewed way to the "homeland waters" (*"the power of the earth"*), and to prepare itself for the possible arrival of new gods (80, 88, 93, 223).

The second part focuses on the Rhine as a demigod and the poet's need to think-and-project the demi-gods' essence. Thinking what is more-than-human and less-than-divine opens up the realm of historical being in which gods and humans reveal themselves for what they are, relative to one another (167, 173f, 185, 237). The basic mood that overcomes the poet here is the creative, passionate capacity to suffer the demi-god's fate with it (*mit-leiden*) and, in the process, to found and reveal historical being's wholehearted conflicted-ness as that fate. The Rhine as demigod is the enigma that exemplifies this wholehearted conflict—drawing constantly upon an origin from which it springs away. Springing away, it is divinely constrained by a need (*Not*) to change its course from south to north but also learns the creative discipline (*Zucht*) of coming into its own and forming the land for human dwelling—hence, its fate is anything but "fatalistic" (265). All these oppositions constitute a primordial unity, the "wholeheartedness that is the mystery of historical being" (249f). "The truest wholeheartedness" in this sense is—shades of Heraclitus—the mysterious strife between gods and demigods where the former's blessedness is a surfeit that needs another to feel and thus establishes a difference in an other, the demigod who, finding its inequality unbearable, is inimical to the gods (271ff).

Given Heidegger's later claims that anyone hearing these lectures would recognize them as a confrontation with National Socialism, it deserves noting that he identifies the "fatherland" as the historical being of a people, and the poet, thinkers, and founders of the state as the "creative powers of historical Dasein." After casti-gating as blasphemy current identifications of Christ as the *Führer*, Heidegger observes: "In his being, the true and, in each case, only leader [*Führer*] points, to be sure, to the realm of the demigods [i.e. the poets]." Note, too, the disparaging remark about appeals to the "dominion of the people and blood and soil" (120ff, 144ff, 210, 254).

40 *Einführung in die Metaphysik* (SS 1935)
(Petra Jaeger, 1983)

The title of these lectures, first published in 1953, is ambiguous. They pose the "leading question" of metaphysics "Why are there entities at all and not rather nothing?" in order to bring into view the "primary question" (*Vor-frage*) of what being is, the forgotten but constant, hidden spur to metaphysics. The leading question (elsewhere dubbed "the transitional question") entails a more basic inquiry into the ground of entities as such, a ground that cannot be another entity and that grounds them as possibly not-being. The inquiry into this ground is the inquiry into being itself. In this way, metaphysical questioning gives way to the primary question. The question is admittedly baffling (since being is nothing that we can literally get our hands on, see, or hear; from a strictly logical or onto-logical perspective, it is the most general and, hence, emptiest of concepts), and for many, Nietzsche included, the question is simply wrong-headed. That the question of the sense of being appears empty and wrong-headed, however, says less about the question than about the tradition and, indeed, the fate of the West and the earth (the mass mobilization of human beings, the unimpeded devastation and economic exploitation of the earth, technology's complete conquest of it, and the suspiciousness of everything creative). For the question of being "means nothing less than *taking-back* [*wieder-holen*] the beginning of our historical–spiritual Dasein in order to transform it into another beginning" (42). The question itself is thoroughly historical, concerning "the happening of human Dasein" in its relations to entities as a whole, at once reconnecting it with its beginning and opening up unasked possibilities. "In this questioning our Dasein is summoned to its history in the full sense of the word and called to it and to decision in it" (48).

While one might infer from the grammar and etymology of 'being' that the term is empty, this conclusion flies in the face of our ability to identify beings as such and distinguish between being and not-being. In fact, being is incomparable, both more determinate and more unique than anything else at all, and it gives wind of itself "in a rich manifold of meanings" (83f, 95f). Against the backdrop of these considerations, Heidegger contends that metaphysics focuses on entities to make up for the apparent emptiness of "being" rather than questioning why it appears so (91f). That questioning must be historical since a historically determinate sense of being prevails across its manifold meanings, i.e. the Greek interpretation of being in terms of presence and permanence.

This conclusion sets the stage for investigation of the historically dominant contrasts of being (conceived as enduring presence) with becoming, appearance, thinking, and ought—all powers to be reckoned with and not nothing (see, too, 35: 67–73). Being's differentiation from them demonstrates not only its determinate yet fraught sense since antiquity but also the need to raise anew the question of the sense of being (209ff). Given the "dominance" of the contrast between being and thinking, Heidegger devotes most of his attention to it and to requisite interpretations of *physis*, Heraclitus and Parmenides, human being, *techne*, *logos*, and logic. In the last section Heidegger chastises those looking in the muddy waters of "values" and "organic unities" for a philosophy of National Socialism. Such efforts, he notes, have not the slightest to do "with the inner truth and greatness of this movement (namely, with the confrontation of planetary determined technology and modern humanity)" (208).

41 *Die Frage nach dem Ding* (WS 1935/36) (Petra Jaeger, 1984)

First published in 1962, this volume contains Heidegger's final lecture course devoted principally to Kant's *Critique of Pure Reason*. In contrast to such studies in the 1920s, the primary passage is not the Schematism chapter, but the "System of All Principles of Pure Understanding" ("the inner, carrying middle of the entire work") since it reveals how Kant determines the essence of a thing as—at once—an "object of experience," "a natural thing," and an "object of mathematical physics" (119f, 130f, 187). As in his other treatments of Kant, Heidegger argues for the priority of intuition (over understanding) against Neo-Kantian interpretations, while also applauding their contribution (see criticism, too, of GA 3) (60, 127). In addition to introducing the general question of thinghood, Heidegger elaborates the distinctively mathematical character of modern natural science in contrast to ancient and medieval study of nature, with glosses on work of Galileo, Descartes, and Newton.

42 *Schelling. Vom Wesen der menschlichen Freiheit (1809)* (SS 1936) (Ingrid Schüßler, 1988)

First published in 1971, these lectures on Schelling's *The Essence of Human Freedom* take their bearings from his pursuit of a "system of freedom," despite the fact that freedom presumably excludes the grounding required by a system (36f). After calling into question Nietzsche- and Kierkegaard-inspired dismissals of system-building, Heidegger reviews ancient and medieval meanings of "system" (not organized knowledge but "the inner fit of what is knowable itself") before turning to the history of system-formation, closely tied to the emergence of modern science, and the will behind it (58). German idealism takes the decisive step beyond Kant by positing an intellectual intuition of the absolute, not as an object standing over against knowing, but as part of the history of the absolute being becoming itself (77, 82f). Inasmuch as the absolute is God, the ontology of German idealism (their account of being) is also a theology. Like any authentic philosophy, theirs is "ontotheology" (96, 113ff). The crucial question of human freedom is not its contrast with nature but its place in the singular necessity of God as the ground of beings, in other words, the question of pantheism (104–8).

Schelling contends that pantheism and freedom, properly understood, require each other (123, 143–53). Underlying this contention is an idealist understanding of being as willing itself, an extension of the concept of freedom but at the cost of specifically human freedom. Cognizant of this limitation, Schelling moves beyond idealism by attempting to understand "the real and living" concept of freedom as "a capacity of good and evil," which in turn demands a more fundamental consideration of the system's ground (164–70). Schelling crucially distinguishes between something's ground and its existence, what constitutes it and how it manifests itself. Insofar as God is determined by the mutually entailing ground and existence, God is the "primordial ground or rather *un-ground*" (213). Ground itself is a longing and striving for itself. At the same time God exists, i.e. manifests himself, in his opposite, human beings. What makes it possible for God to exist is also what makes human freedom possible, i.e. the possibility of inverting ground and existence, severing their unity, and asserting one's own will (the longing that has become selfish) over the universal will. But this possibility is grounded in the ground in—but also independent of—God (243–8, 259).

43 *Nietzsche: Der Wille zur Macht als Kunst* (WS 1936/37) (Bernd Heimbüchel, 1985)

Original texts of lectures re-worked, sometimes significantly, and published 1961 in *Nietzsche I–II* (GA 6).

44 Nietzsches metaphysische Grundstellung im abendländischen Denken: Die ewige Wederkehr des Gleichen (SS 1937) (Marion Heinz, 1986)

Original texts of lectures re-worked, sometimes significantly, and published 1961 in *Nietzsche I–II* (GA 6).

45 Grundfragen der Philosophie. Ausgewählte "Probleme" der "Logik" (WS 1937/38) (second edition, 1992)

This volume's preparatory part contrasts truth as a "problem of logic," i.e. a matter of the correctness of an assertion (common to idealism and realism), with "inquiry into it as a fundamental question of philosophy," i.e. an investigation of the fourfold (*vierfach*) openness that makes correctness possible. The volume's main part raises the fundamental question of the essence of truth. After demonstrating how the question of the truth is, at bottom, a question of its essence, i.e. a matter of bringing it from hiddenness into the light, Heidegger addresses the question on the basis of the first beginning, i.e. the Greek experience of truth as the unquestioned unhiddenness of beings. That first beginning, rooted in the basic mood of wonder, together with the lack of neediness ensuing from its fixation on beings and truth as correctness, sets the stage for another beginning. That other beginning inquires into the unhiddenness itself and attempts to comprehend the first beginning in a more primordial way. The transition to this other beginning calls for a different basic mood, necessitated by the very lack of neediness generated by the first beginning.

46 Zur Auslegung von Nietzsches II. Unzeitgemäßer Betrachtung (WS 1938/39) (Hans-Joachim Friedrich, 2003)

Heidegger revisits the three types of history described in Nietzsche's "The Uses and Abuses of History for Life" (SZ 396). While noting the unity of the multiple meanings of "life" for Nietzsche, Heidegger claims that he neither justifies nor investigates his supposition that being is living—and, indeed, living as a ceaseless enhancement and expansion of power—and that a human being is, at bottom, an animal subject, indeed, a predatory animal (*Raubtier*) (214–19, 232f).

47 Nietzsches Lehre vom Willen zur Macht als Erkenntnis (SS 1939) (Eberhard Hanser, 1989)

Original texts of lectures re-worked, sometimes significantly, and published 1961 in *Nietzsche I–II* (GA 6).

48 Nietzsche: Der europäische Nihilismus (Zweites Trimester 1940) (Petra Jaeger, 1986)

Original texts of lectures re-worked, sometimes significantly, and published 1961 in *Nietzsche I–II* (GA 6).

49 Die Metaphysik des deutschen Idealismus. Zur erneuten Auslegung von Schelling: Philosophische Untersuchungen über das Wesen der menschlichen Freiheit und die damit zusammenhängenden Gegenstände (1809) (Erstes Trimester 1941 Vorlesung und SS 1941 Seminar) (Günther Seubold, second edition, 2006)

This volume revisits, in a less friendly way, Schelling's *Freedom-Treatise* (GA 42). Contrasting Schelling's concept of existence with Jaspers' and Kierkegaard's human-centered conceptions provides an occasion for differentiating "existence" in SZ from the latter. However, Heidegger also locates the roots of Schelling's distinction between ground and existence in "the supreme and ultimate instance" of being as willing. As "the *summit* of the metaphysics of German idealism," the treatise contains "the essential core of all Western metaphysics," the conception of being as constant presence in the form of the will—and a prelude to nihilism (1f, 118–22). Schelling's articulation of the latter as the "will to love" lies between Hegel's "will of knowing" and Nietzsche's "will to power" (102).

50 *Nietzsches Metaphysik / Einleitung in die Philosophie—Denken und Dichten* (WS 1941/42 und WS 1944/45) (Petra Jaeger, 1990)

The first of these lectures was not given but re-worked and published 1961 in *Nietzsche I–II*. The second set of lectures, broken off as Heidegger was enlisted in the *Volkssturm* (national militia) towards the end of the war, introduce philosophy through consideration of (a) Nietzsche's basic experience of the godlessness and worldlessness of modern humanity, (b) the basic mood at work in this experience, namely, the homelessness of modern humanity, and (c) his basic thought, the will-to-power, on the basis of which the homeless leave behind a new homeland.

51 *Grundbegriffe* (SS 1941) (Petra Jaeger, 1991)

The aim of these lectures is to prepare for a critical engagement with the beginning of our history—Anaximander's saying—based upon a resolve, necessitated by our history, to get to the bottom of everything, to know the ground of beings as a whole. To this end (and since Anaximander's saying is about the being of beings, something the present age, in its pursuit of beings, considers superfluous), the first part reviews "leading words" for being, in contrast to beings. Being is the emptiest and yet fecund, the most universal and yet unique, the most intelligible and yet hidden, the most hackneyed and yet primordial, what we most rely upon and yet an abyss, the most said and yet silent, the most forgotten and yet ever reminding us of itself, the most constraining and yet liberating. The pairs of contrasting words point to a twofoldness in being. The site of this twofoldness signifies the still hidden place, laid out by being itself, where we are staying, "to which the essence of our history owes its origin" (83). The second part of the lectures interprets Anaximander's saying in an attempt to recall the first beginning as a way of saying being and "thinking ahead into the more originary beginning [*anfänglicheren Anfang*]" (92).

52 *Hölderlins Hymne "Andenken"* (WS 1941/42) (Curd Ochwadt, 1992)

The instruction to greet (in the hymn's opening stanza) is a way of letting what is greeted be (in contrast to describing it), suggesting that authentic thinking is a devout commemorating (*Andenken*). Those greeting and the greeted come together in holidays and fêtes, commemorating what is uncommon, not as long over but as a promise of what has already been. What is fêted is the holy, history as the fate of divinities and humans, and as the reconciliatory transition from Greece to Germany. (This context includes significant discussions of time and dreams.) What is most difficult—freedom as the search for and capacity to use what is one's own—demands critical engagement with what is alien or foreign. With regard to the engagement with the Greeks, Heidegger sometimes refers to the "West" (68, 79), "Germany and the West" (78), or "Germans" and "humankind" (144), but he chiefly speaks of "Germanien" and the Germans (128, 133). What is most difficult to find, i.e. what is "most one's own, the highest" is the fatherland, a fatherland equated, not with "the political" but with what stems from "the holy" (134f, 141). In this context Heidegger opposes the tendency, stemming from Nietzsche, to undercut mental terms such as "soul" and "spirit." The lectures conclude with glosses of the poet's request for a conversation with absent friends, the requisite sea and river journey to the foreign ("under the hidden law of coming-home into one's own"), and the commemorative thinking on where they are and have always already been headed.

53 *Hölderlins Hymne "Der Ister"* (SS 1942)
(Walter Biemel, 1984, 2nd issue: 1993)

With the aim of drawing attention to Hölderlin's river-hymns, Heidegger focuses chiefly, albeit not exclusively, on his poem "The Ister" (the Danube). In the first part of these lectures, as a means of drawing attention to how Hölderlin reveals the streams' hiddenness *as such*, Heidegger sets aside metaphysical interpretations of art, space, and time. The sole concern of Hölderlin's poetry is "becoming at home in one's own," a process that entails both failing to be at home and passing through the foreign. The "law" of this critical engagement between what is one's own and what is foreign is "the fundamental truth of history," exemplified by Hölderlin's interpretations of Pindar and Sophocles. The second part of the lectures glosses the Greek interpretation of human beings, sung by the chorus of Sophocles' *Antigone*. Heidegger reads the song as the poet's account of how Antigone takes up, in the most uncanny way, the uncanniness of not being-at-home and how, only by doing so, she is nearer to authentically being-at-home, nearer to the "hearth," the "holy," and "being"—all of which name the same. The third part of the lectures returns to Hölderlin's river-poems as saying the same as Sophocles' chorus, namely, history's law that one begins by not being-at-home and only comes to be-at-home by accommodating (*entgegenkommen*) the foreign. Recalling that a river is a locality and a wandering at once, Heidegger writes: "The poetry of the locality of those at home [*Heimischen*] is the wandering's arrival from the foreign" (178).

54 *Parmenides* (WS 1942/43) (Manfred S. Frings, second edition, 1992)

This volume addresses the directives of *aletheia* (unhiddenness), the goddess in Parmenides' poem. The introduction glosses the first two directives, the presupposed hiddenness and its cancellation or removal, indicative of a conflict (*polemos*) in the essence of truth. The volume's first part addresses this conflict as the third directive, more precisely, how the truth stands in oppositional relations of unhiddenness and hiddenness. In addition to elaborating the many modes of hiddenness (falsity is only one mode), Heidegger examines the Latin–Christian transformation of the opposition (encouraged by Platonic and Aristotelian thinking), such that falsity is the privation of truth in contrast to the original Greek understanding of truth (un-hiddenness) as the privation of the hidden. Heidegger also discusses the opposition of truth and hiddenness in the context of Greek accounts of the essence of humans and gods, including the concluding myth of the *polis* in Plato's *Republic*. The second and final part of the volume is devoted to the fourth directive, namely, the openness that first makes unhiddenness possible, i.e. its "ground and essential beginning"—about which the Greeks are silent (213).

55 *Heraklit: 1. Der Anfang des abendländischen Denkens / 2. Logik. Heraklits Lehre vom Logos* (Sommersemester 1944) (SS 1943 and SS 1944) (Manfred S. Frings, third edition, 1994)

The 1943 lectures scour Heraclitus' fragments for the meaning of *physis*, "the fundamental word" of the thinkers of the first beginning, in an attempt to show that *aletheia* as "dis-closing" (*Ent-bergung*) is its "essential ground" and the "essential beginning" and, thus, "the fundamental feature of being itself" (87, 175). The 1944 lectures move from glosses on logic and the Greek understanding of *logos* as assertion to an attempt to hear the pre-metaphysical sense of *logos*. The originary significance of *logos*, like that of *physis* in the previous lectures, coincides with the originary meaning of *aletheia* (371).

Early Freiburg lectures (1919–23)

56/57 Zur Bestimmung der Philosophie: 1. Die Idee der Philosophie und das Weltanschauungsproblem / 2. Phänomenologie und transzendentale Wertphilosophie / 3. Anhang: Über das Wesen der Universität und des akademischen Studiums (Kriegsnotsemester 1919, SS 1919)
(Bernd Heimbüchel, second edition, 1999)

"Ultimate origins are only to be conceived from themselves and in themselves. One has to relentlessly keep in mind the circle set in the idea of the primal science itself" (16, 95). The aim of the first of these 1919 lectures is to make the case for phenomenology as a pre-theoretical primal science, capable of disclosing the sphere of experience, without ignoring that circle. Making this case requires a response to Paul Natorp's objections to phenomenology and to his re-constructive method of determining what is immediate in experience (76). "Where then do I get the criterion for the re-construction from?" Heidegger asks, adding that Natorp's "basic pan-logistic orientation keeps him from any free access to the sphere of experience" (107f). By contrast, phenomenology presents the possibility of experiencing and expressing the experience pre-theoretically and pre-objectively, "the *hermeneutical intuition*" of it in its worldly meaning (117).

The summer semester lectures contain "a phenomenological critique of the transcendental philosophy of value," where "truth is considered a value and theoretical knowing a practical comportment standing under a norm" (127, 155). Heidegger takes aim mainly at the Neo-Kantian or, better, the "Neo-Fichtean" critical philosophy of culture and history, developed by Wilhelm Windelband and his student (Heidegger's teacher) Heinrich Rickert (142–7). After sketching Windelband's philosophy, Heidegger notes phenomenology's influence on Rickert as a prelude to a resounding critique of his philosophy. Noteworthy, given Heidegger's mature views of negation, are his critical discussions of the Neo-Kantians' treatment of it (155–8, 200–3).

58 *Grundprobleme der Phänomenologie* (WS 1919/20) (Hans-Helmuth Gander, 1992)

After setting out the idea of phenomenology as a science of the origin of life in itself and dispatching contemporary distortions of phenomenology, the first section attempts to establish life as phenomenology's domain. Heidegger sketches the problem of the givenness of this domain and, in a provisional way, delimits the concept of life by introducing the "factical life" that announces itself in the form of the surrounding world (*Umwelt*), shared world (*Mitwelt*), and—above all—the world of the self (*Selbstwelt*). The second section addresses basic and traditional difficulties besetting phenomenology as a science of factical life.

59 *Phänomenologie der Anschauung und des Ausdrucks: Theorie der philosophischen Begriffsbildung* (SS 1920) (Claudius Strube, 1993)

These lectures attempt a phenomenological destruction of two problems issuing from life as the most basic phenomenon: the problem of the a priori and the problem of lived experience. Because "factical experience belongs in a completely primordial sense to the problematic of philosophy," philosophy's method must take the form of a destruction of transmitted senses, in which the meaningfulness of that experience has faded (*verblasst*). After examining six meanings of "history," Heidegger argues that the problem of the a priori (primarily in Rickert, Simmel, and Scheler) is incoherent inasmuch as the sort of history in its sights, namely, the "objective past" is precisely "a theoretically idealizing and abstract determination," one "that has left behind the concrete existence and the access to it" (64f, 72, 74). "The conclusion of the destruction of the a-priori problem is that transcendental philosophy goes down its secure path by forgetting the *unum necessarium* [the one thing necessary]: actual existence."

Natorp's and Dilthey's sensitivity to the problem of lived-experience raises hopes that the world of the self would move into the center of concerns. Yet, despite the greater promise of Dilthey's philosophy, neither philosopher gives actual existence its due, because "philosophy's primordial motive" (to attain what is primordial) was forgotten, as philosophy slipped hopelessly into a "theoretical attitude" (169ff). By contrast, "philosophy has the task of upholding the facticity of life and fortifying the facticity of existence" (174).

60 *Phänomenologie des religiösen Lebens: 1. Einleitung in die Phänomenologie der Religion* (WS 1920/21) / *2. Augustinus und der Neuplatonismus* (SS 1921) / *3. Die philosophischen Grundlagen der mittelalterlichen Mystik* (undelivered course 1918/19) (1. M. Jung and T. Regehly; 2. Claudius Strube; 3. Claudius Strube; 1995)

Heidegger's phenomenology of religion and his reforming of phenomenology into an examination of factical life-experience are on display in this volume. A compilation of student's notes (regrettably no manuscript remains), the 1920/21 lectures address the necessity and problem of "attaining the enactment of the historical situation" through interpretations of St. Paul's epistles to the Galatians and the Thessalonians (85). The second part, based upon Heidegger's handwritten text, is a commentary on *Confessions*, Book Ten, saying little about Augustine's Neo-Platonism but unpacking several themes later at work in Heidegger's existential analysis. The notes to the undelivered course on medieval mysticism make reference to Eckhart, Schleiermacher, Rudolf Otto's *The Holy*, and St. Bernard's *Sermons on the Canticle of Canticles*.

61 *Phänomenologische Interpretationen zu Aristoteles. Einführung in die phänomenologische Forschung* (WS 1921/22) (Walter Bröcker and Käte Bröcker-Oltmanns, second edition, 1994)

Instead of presenting an interpretation of Aristotle's thought, this volume sets the stage for the interpretation by giving "a formally indicative definition of philosophy" as a cognitive, reflexive comportment to beings. Heidegger elucidates this comportment via senses of content, relation, and enactment as well as the question of the university as the concrete situation of philosophizing. Turning to the theme of "factical life," he defines philosophy as "a basic manner of living itself, so that in each case it actually retrieves life, taking it back from the fall away [from itself]" (80). It also entails "having time," the kairological manner in which life announces itself (137ff). Employing the notion of a "lifeworld"—encompassing the surrounding world, the shared world, and the self's world—Heidegger identifies living with "caring" in a world, a context of meaningfulness (90–8). After recording the pitfalls (the carelessness) that spring from life as care itself, Heidegger claims that "philosophy is nothing other than the radical execution of the historical character of the facticity of life," such that the differentiation of system and history is alien and irrelevant (111). The lectures conclude with a review of four formally-indicative characters of "ruinance" (*Ruinanz*), that seductive movement within factical life to fall on its face, its tendency towards a "collapse" (*Sturz*).

62 *Phänomenologische Interpretation ausgewählter Abhandlungen des Aristoteles zu Ontologie und Logik* (SS 1922) (Günther Neumann, 2005)

With a view to determining the situation and the everyday terms of factical life in which Aristotle set out to specify "authentic understanding [*sophia*]" (53ff), Heidegger translates and interprets *Metaphysics*, Alpha, 1–2. After glossing authentic understanding as a "movement of living," a matter of circumspection and dealing with the world and what is handy (92f, 115f), Heidegger turns to Aristotle's *Physics* to understand his ontology. He justifies the turn by observing that Aristotle's interpretation of movement (*kinesis*) underlies his ontological categories and makes it possible to understand the context of the aforementioned phenomena of life (authentic understanding, circumspection, etc.) (119). In the third and final chapter, Heidegger translates *Physics*, Alpha, 1–4. Since these parts of Aristotle's *Physics* criticize the Eleatics, Heidegger also translates and interprets Parmenides' didactic poem before returning to the implications of Aristotle's criticism of it. The volume also contains "Phenomenological Interpretations of Aristotle (Indication of the Hermeneutic Situation)." According to this text (instrumental to Heidegger's hiring in Marburg the following year), "the problematic of philosophy is the *being* of factical life," and philosophy is "the ontology of facticity," a matter of interpretation, and, hence, "the *phenomenological hermeneutics of facticity*" (364).

63 *Ontologie—Hermeneutik der Faktizität* (SS 1923) (Käte Bröcker-Oltmanns, 1988)

This volume, preoccupied with methodological questions, introduces hermeneutics as the self-interpretation of facticity, before turning to issues of the interpretation of the present and Dasein both in historical consciousness and in philosophy. The second part glosses "the phenomenological path" to this hermeneutics, including a formal indication of what the investigation begins with ("Dasein [factical life] is being in a world"), followed by consideration of the everyday world and meaningfulness as the character of the encounter of the world. In addition to the themes mentioned, the volume anticipates several other, subsequently central themes, such as existentials, idle talk, curiosity, timeliness (kairological), care, concern, environment, being-in-the-world.

Unpublished essays, lectures, thoughts

64 *Der Begriff der Zeit* (2004)

"The Concept of Time" is the title of the essay and the lecture (both from 1924) making up this volume. With numerous anticipations of SZ, the essay is, in its editor's view, the "original form" of the latter. Coming on the heels of the publication of the Yorck–Dilthey correspondence, most of its opening section on the latter is reproduced verbatim in § 77 of SZ. The essay's remaining three parts are devoted to interpreting (a) the fundamental structures of Dasein in which time becomes apparent, (b) Dasein's temporality, both that of death-anticipating, resolute authenticity and that of inauthenticity; and (c) temporality and historicity. In the course of demonstrating that historicity is fundamental to Dasein's constitution, this section flags the need for a phenomenological destruction of ontology, "to enable deciding about the respective origin and adequacy of the categories handed down" (103). In the wonderfully compendious lecture, Heidegger reviews the inauthenticity of the plaint "I have no time," driving home the point that, far from being in time, Dasein is time itself (118f, 123; see, too, SZ 268n).

65 *Beiträge zur Philosophie (Vom Ereignis)* (1989)

These *Contributions to Philosophy*, from 1936–8, form a six-part sketch or fugue of the basic outline of the transition from metaphysics to thinking being historically. Since this "fugue" is sandwiched between a preview and a concluding section on historical being, the published text has eight sections. The preview (I) introduces the notion of the "appropriating event" at length as the basis of the *Contributions*. The fugue starts with (II) the *resonance* of "historical being in the distress of the abandonment of being," marked by machination, lived experience, the gigantic, nihilism, and "the growing consolidation of the machinational-technical essence of all sciences" (155). The attempt to think being historically is to make (III) the *pass* between "the first and the other beginning," requiring a "confrontation with the first beginning and its history" (196) (from the interpretation of beings as *physis* through Plato's doctrine of *idea* to German idealism and Nietzsche's metaphysics), and (IV) a *leap* into the other beginning, i.e. the projection of the essence of historical being as the appropriating event (230, 254ff). The next movement in thinking being historically is (V) its *grounding* in being-here, truth, time-space, and truth's sheltering in beings. The entire exercise is a preparation for (VI) *the future ones* whose steadfast way of knowing is superior because it is true (396) and (VII) *the last God*, whose passing-by and need of the appropriating event coincide with empowering human beings, honoring the divinity and sheltering beings in the process. The work's concluding section (VIII) is "an attempt to grasp the whole once more" (512).

These movements are intertwined. "Only in the thoughtful execution of the resonance, the pass, and the leap is Da-sein to be spoken of in a grounding way" (310). So, too, Heidegger plays on the connection in German between the words for "mood" (*Stimmung*) and "harmony" (*Zusammenstimmung, Einklang*). "Resonance and pass, leap and grounding have their leading mood respectively, that harmonize primordially from the basic mood," and "the primordial harmony of the leading moods is only fully attuned by the basic mood" (395f). Like a Bach fugue, *Contributions* is intricate, complex, and haunting, though its difficulty is heightened by its attempt to articulate something radically originary (*anfänglich*).

66 *Besinnung* (1938/39) (1997)

Composed in 1938-9 as the first of four attempts to think the turn identified in GA 65, this volume comprises 28 parts (to which the Roman numerals below refer), ranging over every major theme in Heidegger's corpus before 1938. Following a sampling (I) of verse and translations (Periander, Aeschylus, and Pindar), "The Leap Ahead into the Uniqueness of Being" (II) provides a preliminary glimpse of the appropriating event, prepared to "leave behind" all thinking that remains beholden to "machination" and "metaphysics": "the culmination of modernity" and "the groundless dominance of 'to be' (*Sein*) determined by representational thinking" (24f). In (III) Heidegger characterizes philosophy as mindfulness (*Besinnung*) of "what, as essential thinking, it has to think," namely, bringing historical being to words through a "critical engagement with its history (as metaphysics)" (49f, 57f, 74f). Parts IV–VI address the struggle of articulating being and truth, the uniqueness of which escapes metaphysics. While there is no recourse to entities in the clearing, it is not the void. Insofar as we listen to it, we are already appropriated by the "refusal" that unfolds in it, a refusal that presents us with our questionableness and the gods with the neediness of being (129). In a section entitled "Truth and Use," Heidegger poses a series of critical questions, disparaging Hitler's claim that there is no stance that could not be justified by its usefulness to the collective, a claim that represents "the final renunciation" of everything that he (Heidegger) is trying to accomplish (122f). Parts VII–XII address the relation of historical being to humans, anthropomorphism, history, and technology. Parts XIII–XVII treat historical being's unrelatedness to power and impotence, its relation to being and beings, forgetting and thinking being, and its history. Part XVIII is devoted to "Gods," while the remaining parts (XIX–XXVIII) address themes at the intersection of metaphysics and thinking being-historically (e.g. errancy, Schelling's importance, and the transitional question: why there is something rather than nothing?). The Appendix ("A Look Back at the Way") provides an illuminating, two-part retrospective on the course of his thinking to that point.

67 *Metaphysik und Nihilismus: 1. Die Überwindung der Metaphysik (1938/39) / 2. Das Wesen des Nihilismus (1946–1948)* (Hans-Joachim Friedrich, 1999)

68 *Hegel: 1. Die Negativität (1938/39) / 2. Erläuterung der "Einleitung" zu Hegels "Phänomenologie des Geistes" (1942)* (Ingrid Schüßler, Second Edition, 2009)

69 *Die Geschichte des Seyns: 1. Die Geschichte des Seyns (1938/40) / 2. Koinón. Aus der Geschichte des Seyns (1939)* (Peter Trawny, 1998)

70 *Über den Anfang* (Paola-Ludovika Coriando, 2005)

71 *Das Ereignis* (2009)

72 *Die Stege des Anfangs* (1944)

73 *Zum Ereignis-Denken*

74 *Zum Wesen der Sprache und Zur Frage nach der Kunst* (Thomas Regehly, 2010)

75 *Zu Hölderlin—Griechenlandreisen* (Curd Ochwadt, 2000)

76 *Leitgedanken zur Entstehung der Metaphysik, der neuzeitlichen Wissenschaft und der modernen Technik* (Claudius Strube, 2009)

77 *Feldweg-Gespräche (1944/45)* (Ingrid Schüßler, Second, Revised Edition, 2007)

78 *Der Spruch des Anaximander* (Ingeborg Schüßler, 2010)

79 *Bremer und Freiburger Vorträge* (Petra Jaeger, Second, Revised Edition, 2005)

80 *Vorträge*

81 *Gedachtes* (Paola-Ludovika Coriando, 2007)

Notes, drafts, selected letters, reflections

82 *Zu eigenen Veröffentlichungen*

93 *Ausgewählte Briefe II* (Alfred Denker)

94 *Überlegungen II–VI*

95 *Überlegungen VII–XI*

96 *Überlegungen XII–XV*

97 *Anmerkungen II–V*

98 *Anmerkungen VI–IX*

**99 *Vier Hefte I—Der Feldweg/ Vier Hefte II—Durch
Ereignis zu Ding und Welt***

100 *Vigilae I, II*

101 *Winke I, II*

102 *Vorläufiges I–IV*

English translations, with editors, followed in parentheses by translator, publisher, and date[2]

1   *Becoming Heidegger: On the Trail of His Earliest Occasional Writings, 1910–1927* (Theodore Kisiel and Thomas Sheehan [eds]; multiple translators; NUP, 2007; contains translations of the three early essays in GA 1)

Supplements: From the Earliest Essays to Being and Time and Beyond (John van Buren [ed.]; multiple translators; SUNY, 2002; contains translations of two early essays in GA 1)

2   *Being and Time* (John Macquarrie and Edward Robinson, Harper, 1962; and revised edition, Dennis Schmidt; Joan Stambaugh [tr.]; SUNY, 2010)

3   *Kant and the Problem of Metaphysics* (Richard Taft, Indiana, 1997)

4   *Elucidations of Hölderlin's Poetry* (Keith Hoeller, Humanity, 2000)

5   *Off the Beaten Track* (Julian Young and Kenneth Haynes, Cambridge, 2002)

6   *Nietzsche* (David F. Krell, Harper: Vol. One, David F. Krell [tr.], 1979; Vol. Two, David F. Krell [tr.], 1984; Vol. Three, Joan Stambaugh, David F. Krell, and Frank A. Capuzzi [trs], 1987; Vol. Four, Frank A. Capuzzi [tr.], 1982)
    The End of Philosophy (Joan Stambaugh, Chicago, 2003; contains three chapters from GA 6.2)

7   *The Question Concerning Technology* (William Lovitt, Harper, 1977; contains translations of first, second, and fourth essay of GA 7);
    The End of Philosophy (Joan Stambaugh, Chicago, 2003; contains a translation of the third essay);
    Poetry, Language, Thought (Albert Hofstadter, Harper, 1971; contains translations of the sixth, seventh, and eighth essay);
    Early Greek Thinking (David Krell and Frank Capuzzi, (ed.), Harper, 1984; contains translations of the final three essays)

8   *What Is Called Thinking?* (Fred D. Wieck and J. Glenn Gray, Harper, 1968)

9   *Pathmarks* (William McNeill, multiple translators, Cambridge, 1998)

10 *Principle of Reason* (Reginald Lilly, Indiana, 1991)

11 *Identity and Difference* (Kurt F. Leidecker, Philosophical, 1960)
    Identity and Difference (Joan Stambaugh, Harper, 1969)
    What is Philosophy? (Jean T. Wilde and William Kluback, NCUP, 1958, 2003)

12   *On the Way to Language* (Peter D. Herz and Joan Stambaugh, Harper, 1971, 1982)
14   *On Time and Being* (Joan Stambaugh, Chicago, 1972, 2002)
15   *Heraclitus Seminar* (Charles H. Seibert, Northwestern, 1993); **Four Seminars** (Andrew Mitchell and François Raffoul, Indiana, 2003)
16   *Discourse on Thinking* (John M. Anderson and Hans Freund, Harper, 1966)
17   *Introduction to Phenomenological Research* (Dan Dahlstrom, Indiana, 2005)
18   *Basic Concepts of Aristotelian Philosophy* (Robert D. Metcalf and Mark B. Tanzer, Indiana, 2009)
19   *Plato's Sophist* (Richard Rojcewicz and Andre Schuwer, Indiana, 1997)
20   *Prolegomena to the History of the Concept of Time* (Ted Kisiel, Indiana, 1985)
21   *Logic: The Question of Truth* (Thomas Sheehan, Indiana, 2010)
22   *Basic Concepts of Ancient Philosophy* (Richard Rojcewicz, Indiana, 2007)
24   *Basic Problems of Phenomenology* (Albert Hofstadter, Indiana, 1988)
25   *Phenomenological Interpretations of Kant's Critique of Pure Reason* (Parvis Emad and Kenneth Maly, Indiana, 1997)
26   *Metaphysical Foundations of Logic* (Michael Heim, Indiana, 1984)
29/30   *The Fundamental Concepts of Metaphysics* (William McNeill and Nicholas Walker, Indiana, 1995)
31   *The Essence of Human Freedom* (Ted Sadler, Continuum, 2002)
32   *Hegel's Phenomenology of Spirit* (Parvis Emad and Kenneth Maly, Indiana, 1988)
33   *Aristotle's Metaphysics: Theta 1–3. On the Essence and Actuality of Force* (Walter Brogan and Peter Warnek, Indiana, 1995)
34   *The Essence of Truth* (Ted Sadler, Continuum, 2004)
36/37   *Being and Truth* (Gregory Fried and Richard Polt, Indiana, 2010)

64   *The Concept of Time* (Ingo Farin with Alex Skinner, Continuum, 2011)
65   *Contributions to Philosophy (From Enowning)* (Parvis Emad and Kenneth Maly, Indiana, 1999; Richard Rojcewicz and Daniela Vallega-Neu, Indiana, 2012)
66   *Mindfulness* (Parvis Emad and Thomas Kalary, Continuum, 2006)
71   (Richard Rojcewicz, Indiana, Forthcoming)
77   *Country Path Conversations* (Bret W. Davis, Indiana, 2010)
79   *Bremen and Freiburg Lectures: Insight Into That Which Is and Basic Principles of Thinking* (Andrew J. Mitchell, Indiana, 2012)
85   *On the Essence of Language* (Wanda Torres Gregory and Yvonne Unna, SUNY, 2004)
89   *Zollikon Seminars* (Medard Boss; Franz K. Mayr and Richard R. Askay [trs]; NUP, 2001)

NOTES

1 See the work of Charles Bambach, Julian Young, Holger Zaborowski, and Michael Zimmerman.

2 Places and full names of publishers cited: "Cambridge" = Cambridge: Cambridge University Press; "Chicago" = Chicago: University of Chicago Press; "Continuum" = New York: Continuum; "Humanity" = Amherst, New York: Humanity Books; "Indiana" = Bloomington & Indianapolis: Indiana University Press; "Harper" = New York: Harper & Row; "NCUP" = New Haven: College and University Press; "Northwestern" = Evanston, Illinois: Northwestern University Press; "Ohio" = Athens, Ohio: Ohio University Press, "Regnery" = Chicago: Regnery; "Philosophical" = New York: Philosophical Library; "SUNY" = Albany, New York: State University of New York Press; "Yale" = New Haven & London: Yale University Press.

3 The list of English translations for GA 43, 44, 47, and 48 is misleading. Though they correspond respectively to the lectures from 1936 to 1940 that are reproduced in those volumes, they are not based upon the respective volumes of the Complete Edition, volumes that appeared long after the translations had been made. Instead these English translations are based upon the 1961 editions, i.e., GA 6.1 and 6.2, that often differ significantly from the subsequently published lectures themselves (i.e., GA 43, 44, 47, and 48). Despite this incongruence, these translations remain the best, present access to Heidegger's Nietzsche lectures for those relying solely on English translations.

GLOSSARY

Abgrund	abyss
Abschied	departure
Abwesen	absence
Alltäglichkeit	everydayness
Als-Struktur	as-structure
Andenken	commemoration
Anfang	beginning, inception
Angst	anxiety
Anklang	resonance, echo
Anwesen	presence
Ausdruck	expression
Auslegung	interpretation
Aussage	assertion
Bauen	building
Bedeutsamkeit	meaningfulness
Bedeutung	meaning
Befindlichkeit	disposition
Befreiung	liberation
Benommen	captivated
Bergung	sheltering
Besinnung	mindfulness
Besorgen	concern, concern for, taking care of
Bestand	standing reserve
Bewandtnis	relevance, involvement
Bewusstsein	consciousness
Biologie	biology
Biologismus	biologism
Boden	basis, soil
Bodenständigkeit	autochthony
Dasein	being-here
Denken	thinking
Destruktion	destruction
Differenz	difference

Ding	thing
Eigentlichkeit	authenticity
Einfühlung	sympathy
Einsamkeit	solitude
Ekstasis	ecstasis
Entscheidung	decision
Entschlossenheit	resoluteness
Entsprechen	correspond
Epoche	epoch
Erde	earth
Ereignis	appropriating event
Erkennen	cognition
Erschlossenheit	disclosedness
Ethik	ethics
Existenz	existence
Existenzial	existential
Existenziell	existentiel
Faktizität	facticity
Fest	fête
Formale Anzeige	formal indication
Fragen	questioning
Freiheit	freedom
Fug	fitting
Fuge	fit
Fügung	fittingness
Furcht	fear
Fürsorge	solicitude
Ganzheit	totality
Gefahr	danger
Gegenständigkeit	objectivity
Geheimnis	mystery
Gelassenheit	letting be, releasement
Gerede	idle talk, palaver, gossip
Geschehen	happening, historizing
Geschichte	history
Geschichtlichkeit	historicity
Geschick	destiny
Gespräch	conversation
Gestell	positionality
Geviert	fourfold, foursome
Gewissen	conscience
Geworfenheit	thrownness
Glaube	belief

Gleichursprünglichkeit	equiprimordiality
Gott, der letzte	the last God
Göttlichen	divinities
Grund	ground, reason
Grundbegriffe	basic concepts
Grundfrage	fundamental question, basic question
Gründung, die	the grounding
Heilige, das	the holy
Heimkunft	homecoming
Herd	hearth
Hermeneutik	hermeneutics
Herstellen	produce, production
Himmel	sky
Historie	historical study, science of history, chronological or historical record
Historizität	historicality
Humanismus	humanism
Idealismus	idealism
Identität	identity
In-der-Welt-sein	being-in-the-world
Innerweltlich	innerworldly, within-the-world
Innigkeit	wholeheartedness
Insistenz	insistence
Inständigkeit	steadfastness
Intentionalität	intentionality
Interpretation	interpretation
Inzwischen	in-between
Irre	errancy
Jemeinigkeit	mineness
Kehre	turn
Konservativ	conservative
Kunst	art
Langeweile	boredom
Leiblichkeit	bodiliness
Leitfrage	leading question
Lichtung	clearing
Logik	logic
Logistik	symbolic logic
Machenschaft	machination
Man, das	They, the One
Mensch	human being
Metaphysik	metaphysics

Metontologie	metontology
Mitsein	being-with
Modalität	modality
Möglichkeit	possibility
Nähe	nearness
Natur	nature
Negation	negation
Neugier	curiosity
Neuzeit	modernity
Nichtigkeit	nullity
Nichts	nothing, nothingness
Nihilismus	nihilism
Not	distress
Objektivität	objectivity
Offene	open
Offenheit	openness
Ontisch	ontic
Ontologie	ontology
Onto-theo-logie	onto-theo-logy
Phänomenologie	phenomenology
Philosophie	philosophy
Psychologismus	psychologism
Rationalität	rationality
Räumlichkeit	spatiality
Realismus	realism
Realität	reality
Rede	discourse, talk
Rektoratsrede	Rectoral Address
Revolutionär	revolutionary
Riesige, das	the gigantic
Rücksicht	considerateness
Sage	saying, saga
Sammlung	gathering
Schicksal	fate
Schönheit	beauty
Schritt zurück	step back
Schuld	guilt
Schweigen	silence
Sein	being
Seinkönnen	capability of being
Selbst	self
Seyn	historical being
Sich-verbergung	self-concealment

Sinn	sense
Situation	situation
Sorge	care
Spiel	play
Sprache	language
Sprung	leap
Ständigkeit	constancy
Sterblichen	mortals
Stimmung	mood
Streit	conflict, strife
Subjectität, Subjektität	subjectification
Subjektivität	subjectivity
Technik	technology
Theologie	theology
Tiere	animals
Tod	death
Topologie	topology
Tradition	tradition
Transzendenz	transcendence
Trieb	drive
Übereinstimmung	correspondence
Übergang	transition
Überlieferung	tradition
Übersetzung	translation
Überwindung	overturning
Umgebung	surroundings
Umsicht	circumspection
Umwelt	environment, surrounding world, surroundings
Unheimlich	uncanny
Untergang	going under, descent
Unterschied	difference
Unverborgenheit	unconcealment, unhiddenness
Ursprünglichkeit	primordiality
Verantwortung	responsibility
Verbergung	concealment, hiddenness
Verborgenheit	concealment, hiddenness
Verfallen	fallenness
Vernunft	reason
Verstehen	understanding
Vertrautheit	familiarity
Verweisung	reference

Verwinden	getting over, coming to terms with, winding back
Volk	people
Vorhandenheit	on-handness, present-at-handness, objective presence
Vorhandensein	being-on-hand
Vorstellen	represent, place before
Vorstruktur	forestructure
Wahl	choice
Wahrer	preserver
Wahrheit	truth
Welt	world
Weltanschauung	worldview
Weltbild	world-picture
Werk	work
Wesen	essence
Wiederholung	repetition, retrieval
Wille	will
Wissen	knowing
Wissenschaft	science
Wohnen	dwelling
Wollen	will
Wort	word
Zeichen	sign
Zeit	time
Zeitraum	timespan
Zeit-Raum	time-space
Zuhandenheit	handiness, readiness-to-hand
Zuhandensein	being-handy
Zukünftigen, die	the future ones
Zuspiel	pass, playing forth
Zwiefalt	twofold

INDEX

errancy (*Irre*) 64–5, 150, 225,
   248, 285
   with *aletheia* 12
essence (*Wesen*) 65–7
ethics (*Ethik*) 67–9
everydayness (*Alltäglichkeit*) 29,
   37, 48, 50, 62, 69, 72–3, 83,
   138, 154, 161, 196, 200,
   207–8, 214, 216, 228, 233,
   237, 239, 242–3, 257, 281–2
existence (*Existenz*) 3, 15, 22–3,
   27–30, 35–6, 42, 47, 53,
   57, 61, 63, 65, 68–73, 80,
   85, 97, 104, 108, 111,
   130–1, 133–4, 139, 158,
   161, 185–6, 197–8, 208,
   212–16, 225, 238, 243
existential (*existenzial*) 33, 37, 42,
   47, 60, 69–71, 77, 84–5,
   94, 106, 108, 214–15, 231,
   239, 242–3
   and death 52
   and discourse 61
   and disposedness 63
   and subjectivity 204
existentiel (*existenziell*) 55, 68,
   70–1, 77, 123, 159–60,
   172, 185, 237
expression (*Ausdruck*) 99,
   115–16, 130, 166, 268
   of the will 235–6

facticity (*Faktizität*) 37–8, 42,
   71–3, 92–94, 238, 280–2
   in angst 16
   with throwness 212–13
fallenness (*Verfallen*) 16, 42, 62,
   69–73, 112, 215, 242
familiarity (*Vertrautheit*) 112, 127
fate (*Schicksal*) 73, 100, 133, 234,
   269, 270, 276
fear (*Furcht*) 15–16, 63, 133–4,
   256

fête (*Fest*) 73, 276
fit (*Fuge*) 13, 73–4, 154, 271–2
forestructure (*Vorstruktur*) 25–6,
   93
formal indication (*formale
   Anzeige*) 74–5, 282
fourfold, foursome (*Geviert*) 7,
   35, 42, 63–4, 75–6, 116,
   138, 209, 220, 240, 247,
   249, 251, 273
freedom (*Freiheit*) 10, 14, 28, 41,
   53, 67, 71, 76–81, 85, 144,
   181, 185, 195, 202, 224,
   248, 261–4, 271–2, 274,
   276
   and openness 150
   and throwness 212–13
   and will 233–4
future ones, the (*Zukünftigen, die*)
   55, 81–2, 283

gathering (*Sammlung*) 55, 75–6,
   84, 86, 92, 116, 124–5,
   149, 154, 219
George, Stefan 82–3, 236, 251
getting over, coming to terms
   with, winding back
   (*Verwinden*) 13, 31, 96,
   152, 227, 247
gigantic (*das Riesige*) 68, 83–4,
   283
going under (*Untergang*) 10, 31,
   82, 95, 153, 220–1
ground (*Grund*) 18, 23, 30, 47,
   59, 66, 84–6, 95, 138–9,
   147–51, 176–7, 179–80,
   195–6, 212, 214–19, 248,
   250, 261, 269–72, 274–5,
   277–8
   and abyss 9–10
   and the clearing 46
   and errancy 65
   and freedom 77–8